Roelf L. Haan

Special drawing rights and development

enfert Kroese

SPECIAL DRAWING RIGHTS AND DEVELOPMENT

PUBLICATION OF THE NETHERLANDS INSTITUTE
OF BANKERS AND STOCKBROKERS NO. 8

Special drawing rights and development

An inquiry into the monetary aspects of a link between special drawing rights and development finance

ROELF L. HAAN

H. E. STENFERT KROESE N.V. / LEIDEN 1971

SOLE DISTRIBUTOR FOR ASIA
NIHON SHOSEKI LTD./OSAKA

LIBARY OF CONGRESS CATALOG CARD NUMBER 79-153470
ISBN 90.207.0258.0

© 1971 H. E. STENFERT KROESE N.V./LEIDEN/THE NETHERLANDS

... the point is that the benefit from creating costless money rather than costly money must accrue to someone, and who should be the beneficiary is necessarily an arbitrary decision.

The following consideration may be of help in evaluating the proposals partial to the poor countries. Under the gold standard, industrial countries earned increases in their gold reserves through export to South Africa; workers in mines and refining plants (and, of course, also managers and stockholders) received the equivalent of what the industrial countries exported in exchange for the gold. Under a system of allocating fiduciary international money to developing countries, industrial countries would earn these new reserve assets through exports to any of the developing countries that spend the allocated money; workers in development projects, such as in the construction of highways, schools, or hospitals, would receive goods and services equivalent to the industrial countries' exports. The effects on the industrial countries would be the same in both cases; the effects on the developing countries would differ in that the development projects may sooner or later help to increase the productivity of their people.

FRITZ MACHLUP,
Remaking the international monetary system
The Rio agreement and beyond, page 60.

Contents

Preface

This study is not intended to cover every aspect of the link between deliberate reserve creation and international development financing. It deals mainly with the monetary aspects of the problems involved on which it offers some personal views as a contribution to the current discussions. Development may be called the primary challenge in international economics, but it is considered here only as a means of providing the Special Drawing Account with what Professor Triffin has called its 'missing link', namely, a desirable mechanism for injecting special drawing rigths into the international monetary circuit. The emphasis of the study, therefore, is not so much on 'development' as on 'special drawing rights'.

In addition to the parts of the book directly related to the 'link', the reader will find a few chapters containing descriptive material on the special drawing rights system, together with some general observations on international monetary economics. Some digressions on methodology that seem to me relevant have been included at chapter II and chapter VIII. Those who are less interested in 'theories on theories' may omit these chapters without losing the thread of the argument as a whole.

The present method of SDR creation is commented on, and proposals for alternative methods are discussed, in chapter IV (especially section 2), V, VI, VII and IX.

I am greatly indebted to Professor F. de Roos of the Free University of Amsterdam, under whose guidance this study was originally prepared as an academic thesis. Of those who further gave me valuable advice and much appreciated assistance, I wish in particular to mention Mr. John Kay, who was good enough to read through my draft in English. All the remaining mistakes, and notably those inserted in the last stages of preparation for the press, are mine. I am aware that some of the terms retained in chapter II are highly technical and not current language.

I want to thank also the Nederlands Instituut voor het Bank- en Effectenbedrijf and the Staal Stichting 1966 which supported this publication financially.

All the views I have expressed are entirely personal; they do not necessarily correspond with those of the agency by which I am employed.

February 17, 1971   R. L. Haan

I. Introduction

I. MONETARY ECONOMICS

The term 'monetary economics' can be used in different ways. As A.C.L. Day has put it: 'The interpretation of the phrase 'monetary economics' is a broad one: the subject is taken to include the whole of what is often called the theory of macro-economics, as well as a discussion of monetary events and institutions' [1]. He considers a precise definition as almost impossible. 'Monetary economics simply lays emphasis on certain aspects of the broader subject' (the study of economics as a whole) 'which are particularly closely related to the existence of money' [2]. However, this does not seem to detract from the usefulness of making some distinction. It is possible to speak of monetary economics in a narrow sense and monetary economics in a broader sense [3].

1 A. C. L. Day, *Outline of monetary economics*, Oxford, 1957, p.v.
2 *Ibid.*, p. 11.
3 C. J. S. Korteweg and F. A. C. Keesing (*Het moderne geldwezen*, 8th ed., Amsterdam, 1961) make a similar distinction between monetary policy in a narrow sense and monetary policy in a broad sense: 'The former derives its norms only from the money system itself, and its purpose is to enable the monetary system to function as effectively as possible from a technical point of view. The latter aims at objectives which lie beyond the monetary system, and, in so doing, handles money as an instrument'. ('De eerstgenoemde ontleent haar normen uitsluitend aan het geldwezen en tracht te bewerkstelligen dat het geldwezen van technisch standpunt zo doelmatig mogelijk functioneert. De laatstgenoemde tracht doelstellingen te verwezenlijken, die buiten het geldwezen zijn gelegen, en hanteert in dat verband het geld als een instrument', p. 112).

Monetary theory in the narrow sense deals with the primary functions of money, the way in which it comes into being, the different kinds of money and their technical characteristics, and the 'monetary institutions'. Monetary economics in the broader sense is not concerned with the management of money by individual persons or private institutions but the very functioning of the money system as it fits into the economic system as a whole, from a macro-economic point of view. It relates to the functions of money with respect to the price, income and employment situation, and the balance of payments position of a given country. Indeed, it can be said that in general it makes little sense to separate monetary economic theory as defined here from other approaches in macro-economic theory. Monetary phenomena (arising from the way the monetary system works) have a bearing on the whole economic process and 'non-monetary' methods (lying beyond the scope of the monetary system itself) can be used for the 'monetary' purpose of maintaining internal and external price stability.

Therefore, terminological difficulties arise if the label 'monetary' policy is reserved exclusively for the policy aimed at stabilizing the value of the monetary unit; it seems more practical to call all policy carried out by means of monetary instruments, whatever the ultimate objectives may be, 'monetary policy'. The former sense then, is obviously included as far as monetary instruments are involved [4]. Wether it has a 'monetary' aim or not, manipulation of the money system as such is in practice always considered a matter of 'monetary policy'. The only viable distinction seems to be the one we have just made: monetary policy in the narrow sense, which has to do with the organization of the money system; monetary policy in the broader sense, which looks at the monetary system not as a goal but as a means tobe used for a general objective beyond the system itself and relating to the whole economic process, whether it be price stability, a balance of payments equilibrium, full employment, a certain rate of economic growth or some other objective.

4 Thus, in principle, monetary policy can be used for any economic objective. Far more restrictive is M. W. Holtrop: 'Approaching the problem from a practical instead of a theoretical point of view, I am inclined to say that the primary objective of monetary policy can best be formulated as that of maintaining, under conditions of reasonably full employment, the internal and external value of the monetary unit or, in other words, stability of the price level and stability of the exchange rate'. (M. W. Holtrop, 'Monetary policy in an open economy: its objectives, instruments, limitations and dilemmas', *Internationale monetaire vraagstukken,* introduced by F. de Roos, Amsterdam, Brussels,1967, p. 92). Of course, monetary policy, in general, is only able to accomplish this when the *in*stability is brought about by the monetary situation itself. Otherwise monetary policy alone is unlikely to be able to do the job.

II. THE PROBLEM OF INTERNATIONAL LIQUIDITY

The main subject of discussion in recent years in the field of *international monetary economics*, not only in academic circles but also on the official [5] level, has been the problem of overall international liquidity. The outcome has been a major amendment (effective July 28, 1969) of the hitherto unchanged Articles of Agreement of the International Monetary Fund [6], for the purpose of creating special drawing rights as a 'supplement to existing reserve assets' [7].

The new scheme for deliberate creation of international liquidity is of great historical importance; no one has considered it, however, as the final solution of international monetary problems; a lot of 'unfinished business' [8] still remains. Doubts have arisen about the applicability of the scheme even from the outset; indeed, some observers have remarked

5 See the following official documents: *The adequacy of monetary reserves,* a report prepared by the International Monetary Fund for the Economic and Social Council of the United Nations, publ. in *Staff Papers,* Vol. III (1953) pp. 181-227; *International reserves and liquidity,* a study by the Staff of the International Monetary Fund, 1958; *Annual Reports,* International Monetary Fund, 1963, pp. 31-52; 1964, pp. 25-39; 1965, pp. 9-19; 1966, pp. 9-20; 1967, pp. 9-10; 1969, pp. 14-32; *Ministerial Statement of the Group of Ten and Annex prepared by Deputies* ('Examination of the outlook for the functioning of the international monetary system and its probable future needs for liquidity'), 1964; *Report of the study group on the creation of reserve assets, report to the Deputies of the Group of Ten,* 1965; Group of Ten, *Communiqué of Ministers and Governors* and *Report of Deputies* on 'improvements needed in the international monetary system including arrangements for the future creation of reserve assets, as and when needed', 1966.
6 See International Monetary Fund, *Annual Report,* 1968, ch. 2 and Appendix I, pp. 158-170, which gives the full text of the amendment. The 'Outline', which was agreed upon at the 1967 Annual Meeting of the Fund and can be read as a summary of the full text of the amendment, has been printed on pp. 171-174; it has been reproduced in F. Machlup, *Remaking the international monetary system,* Baltimore, 1968, pp. 123-127, together with the text of those new Articles which relate to the special drawing rights system. Further information about the functioning of the SDR system is embodied in: International Monetary Fund, *By-Laws, Rules and Regulations,* twenty-ninth issue, November 30, 1970, and International Monetary Fund, *Selected decisions of the Executive Directors and selected documents,* fourth issue, April 1, 1970. See further: International Monetary Fund, *Annual Report,* 1970, pp. 28-31. (See also footnote 20 to chapter III).
7 Cf. the first of the newly written Articles, Section 1: 'To meet the need, as and when it arises, for a supplement to existing reserve assets, the Fund is authorized to allocate special drawing rights to members that are participants in the Special Drawing Account' (Art. XXI).
8 Title of the last chapter of the book written by F. Machlup, mentioned under 6 above, dealing with the new SDR facility. In the meantime (1970) another important report has already appeared: *The role of exchange rates in the adjustment of international payments,* a report by the Executive Directors of the IMF to the Board of Governors. (Washington, 1970).

that it was necessary to go against its very objectives in order to put it into operation. 'Now that the United States has imposed mandatory restrictions on capital movements and proposes to impose restriction on purchases of foreign services, the blessing of a scheme to create liquidity seem less promising', wrote Professor Machlup [9]. 'The main justification – perhaps the only one that really counts – of the creation of international reserves is the avoidance of restrictions. If it takes restrictions to activate a plan for the creation of reserves [10], the whole idea is defiled'.

The discussions and studies carried out during the preparations for the SDR scheme were focussed mainly on the problem of the level of overall international liquidity. The very purpose of the facility is to prevent the occurrence of a shortage of world reserves. The approach adopted was a rather academic one, as the crucial question of the definition of the 'need for reserves' or the 'adequacy of reserves' was left to be dealt with after the completion of the scheme. At the drafting stage, this caused no difficulty because the scheme for reserve creation was only meant to be a 'contingency plan'. The question when to 'activate' the mechanism, and to what extent, was a matter to be decided upon collectively, once the facility had been established [11].

Other liquidity problems, such as those concerning the composition of international monetary reserves (the 'quality' instead of the quantity of international liquidity) were only obliquely touched upon. Fundamental problems such as the functioning of the international balance of payments adjustment process [12], the role of gold, the par value system, or the

9 *Remaking the international monetary system,* p. 122. Here the author seems to be referring to the proposals by the U.S. Government, made on January 1, 1968, not only to tighten substantially its restrictions on capital payments abroad but also to impose a tax on American travel abroad. This would amount to an indirect restriction on current payments. The restrictions on the transfer of capital, although not in conflict with the U.S. convertibility obligations under Article VIII of the Fund Agreement, indicated that a spontaneous overall U.S. balance of payments equilibrium was not yet in sight.

10 The reader should recall Article XXIV, Section 1 (b) of the Fund Agreement: 'The first decision to allocate special drawing rights shall take into account, as special considerations, a collective judgment that there is a global need to supplement reserves, *and the attainment of a better balance of payments equilibrium, as well as the likelihood of a better working of the adjustment process in the future'.* (Italics are mine). This rather informal language is of the greatest importance. Obviously, 'better' means: better than at the time, i.e. April 1968.

11 See *Fund Agreement,* Article XXIV, especially Section 4.

12 The Ministers and Governors of the Group of Ten actually left the problem of the adjustment process for study to Working Party 3 of the Economic Policy Committee of the Organization for Economic Cooperation and Development, which published a report entitled *The balance of payments adjustment process* in August

specific problems of the balance of payments of the underdeveloped world, were not studied in the course of the deliberations and negotiations, and were not intended to be, as far the most important parties were concerned. The aim was to deal with a clearly circumscribed problem: how to secure a secular growth of world reserves. Although of course the ultimate objective was to prevent distortions in the 'real' sphere of the world economy, no *direct* link was made between the problem of reserve creation and other matters of general concern relating to the global economic process; the SDR system became a monetary affair in the narrow sense defined in section 1 above. The present study will investigate possibilities concerning a better integration of SDRs in the international economic cooperation.

As for the primary purpose of the reserve creation plan, i.e. to provide a mechanism for securing an adequate level of total foreign reserves in the hands of the world's national monetary authorities, it is desirable to handle the new instrument cautiously.

It has often been stressed, and rightly so, that the 'liquidity' problem is not to be viewed in isolation from the 'stability' and 'confidence' problems [13]. Creation of liquidity cannot release countries from behaving according to the rules of the game of the adjustment process. If, indeed, 'there is too much liquidity, the adjustment mechanism may function too slowly, and a delay in taking measures necessary to restore balance will in the end be harmful at home as well as abroad' [14]. From this it follows that a facility for the deliberate creation of monetary reserves, if it were improperly managed, could constitute a danger for the stability and smooth functioning of the international monetary system. With or without a scheme for the deliberate creation of reserves, the main condition for the lasting proper functioning of the present system – based as it is on different national currencies which are largely *de facto* convertible into each other and are generally maintained at stable exchange rates –

1966. The Working Party deals with the international coordination of balance of payments policies on a continuing basis.

13 'Instability' in the international monetary system can be due to the system itself, for instance, the existence of too much 'bad' liquidity – short-term credits between central banks –, unbalanced composition of reserves (giving easy play to the law of Gresham), *etc.* 'Instability' may also have its origin in faulty *behavior under* the system, i.e. failure to restore equilibrium over time in international payments; this is the 'adjustment' problem. On adjustment, liquidity and confidence, see *International monetary arangements: the problem of choise,* report on the deliberations of an international study group of 32 economists, Princeton, 1964, pp. 25-37.

14 Annex prepared by Deputies attached to the *Ministerial Statement of the Group of Ten,* 1964, paragraph 5.

lies in the continuous preservation of balance of payments equilibrium over time among the countries concerned.

III. LIQUIDITY NEEDS OF DEVELOPED COUNTRIES

In general, it can be said that only relatively high income countries which have reached the 'maturity' stage of growth [15] – i.e., where the economy has been integrated into a single market economy – are fundamentally in a position to keep their convertible currencies strong and stable without having recourse to direct exchange controls. When faced with a decrease in their stock of ammunition for defending the exchange rate parity – their monetary reserves – these countries can employ the indirect policy instruments needed to correct a balance of payments deficit. The burden of restrictive measures to curb excessive spending is fairly equally distributed over the whole economy. Economic growth, of course, will be negatively influenced in the short run, but the damage to the long term development process will not necessarily be substantial. Furthermore, with reasonably high incomes and still steadily improving technology, these countries can afford a short setback in their growth rate.

If an industrialized country finds itself in a situation of 'fundamental disequilibrium' [16] and decides to correct it by changing the par value of its currency, the market mechanism can be relied upon to carry out the required shift to exports and to import substitution in order to restore the country's trade balance.

While an overall shortage of monetary reserves as such is undoubtedly possible in view of the restricted supply of monetary gold, one great difficulty in any scheme for the deliberate creation of reserves is related to the fact that the collective decision on this matter will be entirely dependent on the outcome of a political decision-making process. In itself this is unavoidable, and indeed a major improvement, compared to the past; problems will arise, however, because of the specific form chosen

---

15 See W. W. Rostow, *The stages of economic growth,* Cambridge, 1960, p. 59, where the concept of 'economic maturity' is defined as 'the period when a society has effectively applied the range of (then) modern technology to the bulk of its resources'. This is the technical prerequisite for maturity in the economic sense.

16 Art. IV, Section 5 (a) of the *Fund Agreement* reads: 'A member shall not propose a change in the par value of its currency except to correct a fundamental disequilibrium', and Section 5 (f): 'The Fund shall concur in a proposed change (. . .) if it is satisfied that the change is necessary to correct a fundamental disequilibrium (. . .)'.

for the decision-making procedure in its relation to the fact that newly created SDRs accrue directly to the participants in the scheme (proportionately to their IMF quotas). Some industrial countries may claim that there is a need for newly created liquidity and others, possibly finding themselves in surplus positions, may not. All these countries, however, are basically in a position to use indirect measures, to adjust their balance of payments disequilibria over time, and thus prevent themselves from experiencing a real liquidity shortage. This *freedom of choice* on the domestic scene makes it possible to use balance of payments policy as a political instrument for national interests rather than for the sake of international monetary cooperation [17]. This means that there is a danger of political bias in the process of collective decision-making in connection with the creation of reserves, persistent deficit countries being likely to promote creation and stable countries being likely to oppose it. It is very doubtful whether this 'politicalization' of international monetary economics should be encomaged; it gives politicians an important and *direct* role in matters concerning the functioning the world monetary system, while domestically the relative independence of the central bank from daily political influences is rightly considered to be of great value.

The probability that national politics (which can be defined as the pursuit of goals of national interest) will play a significant role in the decision-making process in the system of special drawing rights is directly related to the fact that allocations of SDRs are made in proportion to the IMF quotas of the participants in the scheme. There are countries and groups of countries with relatively high quotas and there are countries with comparatively low ones; the former have a much greater direct interest in the creation of a given total amount of special drawing rights than the latter group – the more so if they are going to be debtors under the scheme. It is not an ideal situation in which to take collective decisions when there are conflicting interests among decision-makers who are not

17 The wording of the telegram President Johnson sent to his French colleague on the occasion of his decision on November 23, 1968 not to devalue the franc but to adjust the national economy through a series of far reaching internal measures is illustrative in this respect. The telegram read: 'I have read today of the decision you have taken. I know that the American people wish me to tell you of the common hope that your course of action will be succesful and that we are ready to cooperate in any way we can to achieve *your* objective consistent with *our national purposes*. With warm personal regard, Lyndon B. Johnson' (*Washington Post,* November 25, 1968; my italics). See in this connection Mr. Roosa's comment on the dominant role of the dollar: 'It is a role which naturally accompanies our leading economic and *political* position' (my italics). (*Business Review Supplement,* Federal Reserve Bank of Philadelphia, September 1962, p. 9, quoted by R. Triffin, *The world money maze,* 1966, p. 290).

equally powerful. Political pressure based on the isolated desires of *individual* nations may play the part that should be performed by sound economic reasoning.

Different attitudes are possible *within* the group of developed countries and also as between the industrial and the developing countries. As the former have the biggest quotas and the majority of the votes in the IMF, there is a tendency for the amount of SDR creation to be established primarily in accordance with the liquidity desires of the developed countries.

Up to now the adequacy of the quota structure in the IMF did not present a problem, as it served only as a basis for granting conditional credit. If, however, it becomes the basis for across the board distribution of 'owned' reserves, which can be spent unconditionally, then the question will arise whether this is a proper criterion for allocation of claims on productive resources. What guarantee is there that the quota structure is best calculated to serve the needs of the international monetary system and the world economy in this respect? The arbitrariness of this method in my mind also raises doubts from a normative legal point of view.

IV. LIQUIDITY NEEDS OF DEVELOPING COUNTRIES

There is a large group of countries – in fact by far the majority – which lacks the degree of economic freedom referred to in the preceding section. These countries are bound by the rigidities and distortions of their underdeveloped state. As their economic growth for the main part depends on importing capital goods and other productive resources from abroad, they have a need for foreign exchange far beyond their ability to repay by export earnings, and can thus be regarded as countries facing *structural* balance of payments difficulties. These difficulties are not due to the play of internal politics, nor can they be solved by political means. Often, they can only be eliminated by dealing severe blows to the strategy of development. In the early stages of growth such a setback is more serious than a similar decrease in the growth rate of a developed country would be, quite apart from any consideration of the low absolute level of income, and the fact that a similar percentage rate itself implies different absolute amounts at different levels of wealth.

If it is accepted that sustained economic growth is desirable and in the underdeveloped areas of the world is indeed the *primary objective* of economic policy, those areas are bound to face a structural payments problem. Essentially, the problem is a *liquidity* problem in the literal sense of the word, as these countries generally possess large natural and human resources which are only awaiting the capital and organization needed to exploit them. As soon as they become integrated into the economic process they will produce more 'liquid' assets. The basic problem is the long duration of the 'pay-out period', which is too long for financing by short-term capital means. This is why primarily there is a need for long-term loans or grants rather than for monetary credits; the latter are only fit to bridge temporary balance of payments deficits.

Still, there remains a case for *structural* reform of the international *monetary* system in view of the payments problems, which are really of a structural nature, of the underdeveloped countries as a group. Sound economic reasoning might lead to the conclusion that it might be as well to devise different means of creating international liquidity, and particularly a better way of allocating special drawing rights, if the common interests of all the countries in the world are to be taken in consideration.

The liquidity needs [18] of the *industrial* countries are in general not likely to be of a structural character, unless, at some point in the future, the amount of gold available in the monetary circuit falls short of what is needed. In view of this possibility, or indeed probability, the contingency scheme for SDR creation may be considered a valuable one in spite of the various objections that can be raised to certain elements of the scheme. Apart from the possibility of a gold scarcity, however, it can be argued that there is a structural need for liquidity in the *developing* countries, even though this is of a rather different character from that which the drafters of the SDR agreement had in mind. The need is directly related to the desired growth rate in those countries. Discussion about this matter during the SDR negotations was limited to the expression of fears that the reserves, which were intended 'to be held' and not 'to be spent' after being allocated to countries, would be used by certain groups of countries on a more or less permanent basis (i.e. without being earned back later) [19].

18 It need not be stressed that one economic 'need' must always be seen in relation to other 'needs'. I referred earlier to the liquidity needs of the under-developed countries as being dependent on their desired growth rate. One has to realize that, in the case of industrial countries, any reference to a need for international liquidity is based on similar policy aims. As the growth need of these countries is obviously less urgent than the development needs of the developing countries and as the need for external monetary reserves in the industrial countries is less *directly* linked to their growth targets, this has consequences for the determination of the liquidity 'needs' of both kinds of countries.

19 See, for instance, Group of Ten, *Report of Deputies,* 1966, paragraph 40: 'We

The Deputies of the Group of Ten [20] stated: 'It is the global need for reserves with which we have been concerned. We use the word 'global' in two senses: first, to take account of the interest in this problem not only of the Group of Ten, but also of other countries; second, to direct attention not to the reserve needs of specific countries in particular deficit situations, but to the provision of adequate monetary reserves for the system as a whole' [21].

The first principle mentioned here is fully subscribed to in my own approach (although in my view the sentence quoted should rather read: 'to take account of the interest in the problem not only of the developing countries, but also of other countries'). The second principle may raise confusing theoretical problems as to the concept of the *adequacy* of reserves for the '*system*' as a whole, which will be discussed later

The primary difficulty lies in the very use of the word 'system' which actually reminds one – or ought to do so at least – more of physics than of economics. The imagery sometimes used, of the function of oil in an engine (international reserves in the international monetary system) is far from realistic. One of the false elements in the analogy is that there is in fact no single cohesive independent system but a great number of different functional relationships within what is called the 'system' as well as between the 'system' and all kinds of factors, economic (monetary and non-monetary) and non-economic, outside the 'system'. The system does not exist in isolation, but is the result of international cooperation in the whole field of economic policy [22]. Even the concept of international reserves is not a clear-cut, generally accepted one.

are agreed that deliberate reserve creation is not intended to effect permanent transfers of real resources from some countries to others'.

20 The 'Deputies of the Group of Ten' are the deputies of the Ministers of Finance and Central Bank Governors of the ten countries that concluded the 'General Arrangements to Borrow' (GAB) with the IMF, which entered into force on October 24, 1962. See on the contents of the arrangements: IMF, *Selected decisions,* 4th issue, pp. 68-86, and on the use made by the Fund of GAB borrowing: the Fund's monthly statistical survey *International Financial Statistics*. The 'Group of Ten' thus formed in 1962, has since served as an important forum for discussion of international monetary problems (cf. footnote 5 above). The members are the U.S.A., theU.K., Japan, Canada, Sweden and the five major EEC countries; Switzerland has been associated with the Group since 1964.

21 *Report of Deputies,* 1966, paragraph 30.

22 'Monetary policy, credit and fiscal policy, commercial policy, wage policy, investment policy, growth policy, employment policy, counter-cyclical policy etc. etc. are so closely related to one another that it would not be possible to formulate a rational policy concerning the international monetary system irrespective of all other areas of economic policy' (Fritz Machlup, *International monetary economics,* Londen, 1964, p. 365).

Nor is the 'system' a homogeneous entity as far as *currencies* are concerned, because there are different kinds of currencies, for example, convertible or market currencies (mainly the currencies of developed countries [23]) and non-convertible currencies. This is only one problem relating to defining the 'needs' of the system. There is a more or less cohesive monetary 'system' between the convertible currency countries. The developing world, as a group, however, is characterized by inconvertibility and by numerous bilateral payments relations.

The Deputies of the Ten failed to take into account the *typical* balance of payments problems of the major part of the world which is still in the early stages of economic development. The following chapters will deal with the borderline allegedly separating [24] monetary from development economics.

23 The countries that had accepted the convertibility obligations of Art. VIII of the Fund Agreement by April 30, 1970 are: El Salvador, Mexico, Panama, United States (1946); Guatemala (1947); Honduras (1950); Canada (1952); Dominican Republic, Haiti (1953); Belgium, France, Germany, Ireland, Italy, Luxemburg, The Netherlands, Peru, Sweden, United Kingdom, Saudi Arabia (1961); Austria (1962); Jamaica, Kuwait (1963); Japan, Nicaragua (1964); Costa Rica, Australia (1965); Guyana (1966); Denmark, Norway, Bolivia (1967); Argentina, Singapore, Malaysia (1968), totaling 34 countries.

24 The 1966 *Report of Deputies* of the Group of Ten reads in paragraph 7 (f): 'We have been aware that the problem of ensuring a proper supply of international reserves is of interest and concern to all countries of the international community. We have, therefore, from the beginning taken account of the needs of all countries. In doing so, we have treated reserve creation as a problem *distinct from* (my italics) the provision of capital for developing countries'.

II. The international monetary problem

I. THE INTERNATIONAL MONETARY SYSTEM

The expression 'international monetary system' is such a common one that it is vain to seek for it in the indices of handbooks on international monetary economics. In daily talk and writings observations on 'the international monetary system' are numerous; its 'functioning', its 'stability', its 'development', its 'management' *etc.* are the subject of many books and articles.

This language, however, often hides more than it reveals, as has already been indicated at the end of the previous chapter. The international monetary scene embraces all kinds of phenomena: which of them are meant by the word 'system'? This question is the more important as it is usual to consider the system as being subject to its own rules which determine what is 'technically' possible or desirable and what is impossible or undesirable with respect to the functioning of the system. This kind of appeal to what is required or forbidden from the 'technical' point of view asks for an investigation into the nature of what is called the international monetary system.

A possible definition of the vague concept of the international monetary system might read as follows: it is *the whole complex of relationships between countries set up to deal with the international monetary problem.*

Of course this wording does not help us much as to a systematic formulation of precise concepts. We are left with the question how to describe the meaning of the 'problem' instead of the 'system'. But this circumscription of the word 'system' has at least the advantage showing that the system is man-made and that reference to the 'requirements' of the system only *seem* to bear a neutral and impartial character and in reality are dependent on subjective human insight and choices. The system as it stands cannot set its own norms, being itself the result of human formative power which is open to judgment. The judgment of the economist has to be made from the economic viewpoint.

There are two fundamental questions from this viewpoint: 1) does the system or the part of the system under review represent the right *answer* to the problem that one wishes to solve? and 2) – even more fundamental – has the economic aspect of the problem been formulated in the right way?

One may raise the objection here that such a way of putting the matter is not necessarily in conformity with reality. One may argue that in many cases international monetary developments were the consequence of no international consultation or deliberate organization at all. Consider for instance the 'reserve-currency system': it has not come into being as a result of the formulation at a certain moment of an international problem and the attempt to find a solution for it. It has grown spontaneously (in spite of reproaches which sometimes can be heard as to the selfish national interest of the reserve currency countries supposedly lying at the basis of the system [1]).

The answer must be twofold. Firstly, as to the example just mentioned, although there was no question of deliberate *government* action to create a special status for the main trading and investment currencies, their appearance was nevertheless the consequence of real international problems for which *private* persons and enterprises did 'spontaneously' find their own solutions. The U.K. pound and the U.S. dollar only reached the position of official monetary reserve assets – thus becoming subject to government policies – once they had started being widely used in international trade and finance. Secondly, when we focus our attention on the role played by governments, it can be said, that the international monetary system is largely the answer of the nations of the world at least to what they have seen or recognized as being aspects of the international

---

1 Reproaches of this kind were often heard from the French, especially during the later years of the government of President de Gaulle. Ironically, the argument does appear to be valid for the reserve currency role of the French franc itself. The holding of monetary reserves in French francs by the so-called CFA countries and the Malagasy Republic is governed by an agreement with France which sets out the terms for the use of the 'comptes d'opération' which have been established by the French Treasury and placed at the disposal of the CFA countries.

monetary problem. It is true that isolated national interests still play a dominant role [2] and that, for instance, South Africa may claim a gold price increase to be in the interest of the international monetary system while the United States may claim the opposite, but this does not detract from the desirability and the validity of considering controversial matters from a truly international point of view. This means formulating international problems and seeking international answers. The international coordination and cooperation impressively shown, for instance, in the charter of the International Monetary Fund, as originated and as amended, has been strengthened considerably since the Second World War; it needs to be extended and most probably will be extended in the future. This is why our subject matter is such an interesting one.

The international monetary problem arises from the fact that the world forms one economic space with many different national monetary authorities and money systems. This fundamental problem can be split up into many separate problems: convertibility, exchange rates, balance of payments adjustment and financing, international liquidity, *etc.*

In the field of international liquidity, the Special Drawing Account constitutes a major historical development, as it provides for a *deliberate* managing of the level of world reserves and of the use of their new component: SDRs. Its establishment 'has rightly been called the most important event in monetary affairs since Bretton Woods' [3]. 'It is (. . .) a great improvement that international cooperation more and more takes place in permanent organizations with a specific task, instead of being confined to the loose association of *ad hoc* conferences where nothing is produced but resolutions so general in wording that they bind nobody' [4]. It is all the more urgent, however, that these organizations should not carry on an isolated life of their own, but should always keep in mind that they constitute only one institution for international cooperation, and that this cooperation extends to other fields of action than their own. In referring to the particular tasks of specific agencies, the fundamental issues must not be lost sight of: what is the best structure for a particular international organization, given the very aim and nature of international cooperation? and: what are the policy objectives of this particular type of cooperation? The economist, then, is bound to ask whether there

---

2   See, for instance, footnote 17 to the previous chapter.
3   International Monetary Fund, *Summary Proceedings,* Annual Meeting 1968, p. 126 (Statement by the Governor of the Fund for the United Kingdom, Roy Jenkins).
4   J. W. Beyen, *Money in a maelstrom,* New York, 1949, p. 6.

might not perhaps be economic inconsistencies within the whole pattern of deliberate international action and goals.

II. THE INTERNATIONAL MONETARY PROBLEM AS AN ECONOMIC PROBLEM

International monetary economics is part of the economic science. This must be clear from the method followed by it. What are the general characteristics of the economic method?

This question is answered by different methodologists in different ways. It would lead us too far away from the topic under discussion to elaborate on this point, although, theoretically it should be tackled first before entering on any economic inquiry whatsoever. Our view of the nature and significance of economic science has a bearing on the study of specific problems. Any position taken on any subject necessarily implies a cosmological world view, and a view of science as such; for the inquirer's attitude on such matters is bound to color his treatment of the contents of and of the relationship between the various branches of science, and his insight into the nature of the structures of society. These relationships, which are either implicit or explicit, have been very clearly explained in the pioneering work of the philosopher Professor Herman Dooyeweerd, most extensively in his systematic trilogy *A new critique of theoretical thought* [5]. As Dooyeweerd shows, the fundamental fields of research of the various special sciences (biology, psychology, sociology,

5 Amsterdam, Philadelphia, 1953-1957; Volume I, *The necessary presuppositions of philosophy;* Volume II, *The general theory of the modal spheres;* Volume III, *The structures of individuality of temporal reality* (Library of Congress catalog card number A 54 - 7310). A fourth volume (1958) contains an index of subjects and authors. See on *economics* particularly though not exclusively: Vol. I, p. 555; Vol. II, pp. 66-68, 122-123, 334-345, 360-362; Vol. III, pp. 386-387, 426, 452, 480-485; and especially the separate publications: 'Het wetsbegrip in de economie' (The concept of law in economics), a two-page summary in the periodical *Mededelingen van de Vereniging voor Calvinistische Wijsbegeerte*, August 1946, of a lecture given in 1946; and: 'De sociologische verhouding tussen recht en economie en het probleem van het zgn. 'economisch recht'' (The sociological relationship between law and economics and the problem of 'economic law'), to be found in: *Opstellen op het gebied van recht, staat en maatschappij*, Amsterdam, 1949, pp. 221-265. A useful introduction (in Dutch) to Dooyeweerd's thinking is L. Kalsbeek, *De wijsbegeerte der wetsidee*, Amsterdam, 1970; a number of English-written lectures delivered by Dooyeweerd in the United States and Canada in 1959 are published under the title *In the twilight of western thought*, Philadelphia, 1960 (Library of Congress catalog card number LC 60-6645). This book too may serve as a first introduction.

economics *etc.*) are defined in terms of 'the different *modal aspects* of human experience in its integral sense' [6].

Theoretical thought does not conceive things in the integral coherence of all their modal aspects, as the naive attitude of experience does. For instance, economic theory, when dealing with 'economic facts', examines only the *economic aspects* of *real* facts. The answer to the question 'what is economic theory' must be: 'the theoretical investigation of the economic aspect of reality'. 'Production, distribution and consumption display as concrete social phenomena as much modal aspects as reality itself. Economic theory grasps them under the economic aspect only' [7].

The following quotation from one of Dooyeweerd's lectures may make more clear what is understood by 'modal aspect'.

'How is the theoretical attitude of thought characterized? What is its inner structure by which it differs from the non-theoretical attitude of thinking? It displays an antithetic structure wherein the logical aspect of our thought is opposed to the non-logical aspects of our temporal experience. To comprehend this antithetical relation it is necessary to consider that our theoretical thought is bound to the temporal horizon of human experience and moves within this horizon. Within the temporal order, this experience displays a great diversity of fundamental aspects, or modalities which in the first place are aspects of time itself. These aspects do not, as such, refer to a concrete *what*, i.e., to concrete things or events, but only to the *how*, i.e., the particular and fundamental mode, or manner, in which we experience them. Therefore we speak of the modal aspects of this experience to underline that they are only the fundamental *modes* of the latter. They should not be identified with the concrete phenomena of empirical reality, which function, in principle, in all of these aspects. Which, then, are these fundamental modes of our experience? I shall enumerate them briefly.

Our temporal empirical horizon has a numerical aspect, a spatial aspect, an aspect of extensive movement, an aspect of energy in which we experience the physico-chemical relations of empirical reality, a biotic aspect, or that of organic life, an aspect of feeling and sensation, a logical aspect, i.e., the analytical manner of distinction in our temporal experience which lies at the foundation of all our

6 As much as possible I quote literally from Dooyeweerd's English publications. I recognize, however, that his terminology may be new to the reader or may deviate from daily language.
The quotation made here *(A new critique,* Vol. II, p. 55) continues: '(. . .) within these modal boundaries there is room for further specialization'. It may be noted that those concerned with the realization of a particular subjective human *purpose,* such as a specific goal of 'economic' policy, are bound to study not only the economic aspects but also the social, juridical and other implications. Failures of practical 'economic' policy may well have something to do with this cosmological point. These remarks, however, do not detract from the theoretical requirement that the economic viewpoint as such should have its own specific content.
7 Dooyeweerd, 'De sociologische verhouding tussen recht en economie', p. 256 ('Productie, verdeling en verbruik vertonen als concrete sociale verschijnselen evenveel modale aspecten als de werkelijkheid zelve. De economische theorie vat ze slechts onder economisch, de rechtswetenschap onder juridisch aspect').

concepts and logical judgments. Then there is a historical aspect in which we experience the cultural manner of development of our societal life. This is followed by the aspect of symbolical signification, lying at the foundation of all empirical linguistic phenomena. Furthermore there is the aspect of social intercourse, with its rules of courtesy, politeness, good breeding, fashion, and so forth. This experiential mode is followed by the economic, aesthetic, juridical and moral aspects, and, finally, by the aspect of faith or belief.

This whole diversity of modal aspects of our experience makes sense only within the order of time. It refers to a supra-temporal, central unity and fulness of meaning in our experiential world, which is refracted in the order of time, into a rich diversity of modi, or modalities of meaning, just as sun-light is refracted by a prism in a rich diversity of colors. A simple reflection may make this clear. In the order of time, human existence and experience display a great diversity of modal aspects, but this diversity is related to the central unity of the human selfhood, which, as such, surpasses all modal diversity of our temporal experience. In the order of time the divine law for creation displays a great diversity of modalities. But this whole modal diversity of laws is related to the central unity of the divine law, namely, the commandment to love God and our neighbor.

However, in the theoretical attitude of thought we oppose the logical aspect of our thinking and experience to the non-logical modalities in order to acquire an analytical insight into the latter. These non-logical aspects, however, offer resistance to our attempt to group them in a logical concept and this resistance gives rise to theoretical problems. Such theoretical problems are, for example, What is the modal meaning of number? of space? of organic life? of history? of economy? of law? of faith? And these problems are of a philosophical character since they refer to the fundamental modi of human experience, which lie at the foundation of all our concrete experience of diversity in things, events, and so forth.

It is true that in principle the different modal aspects delimit also the special viewpoints under which the different branches of empirical science examine the empirical world. This merely corroborates our view concerning the modal diversity of our experiential horizon and our view of theoretical thought in general. But these special sciences do not direct their attention upon the inner nature and structure of these modal aspects as such, but rather upon the variable phenomena which function in them in a special manner. The inner nature and structure of the special modal aspects which delimit their field of research is a presupposition of every special science.

It is only philosophy which can make this presupposition into a theoretical problem. For it is impossible to conceive the special meaning and inner structure of a modal aspect without having a philosophical insight into the whole temporal coherence of all the different modal aspects of our temporal horizon of experience. The reason is that every aspect can unfold its proper modal meaning only in this total coherence which expresses itself in its own inner structure. This is the reason that this modal structure displays a great diversity of components, or moments, which in turn unfold the modal meaning of the aspect concerned only in their total coherence.

In the first place, every aspect, or mode of experience, has a modal kernel which guarantees its irreducible special meaning. But this modal kernel of its meaning can only express itself in a series of so-called analogical moments referring to the modal kernels of all the other aspects of our experience which precede or succeed, respectively, the aspect concerned in the temporal order. In accordance with the different direction of their reference, they may be distinguished into retrospective and anticipatory moments. Viewed in themselves these analogical moments are multivocal since they occur also in the other experiential aspects wherein they display a different meaning. Their proper modal sense is only determined by the modal kernel of the aspect in whose structure they function. Nevertheless, they maintain their coherence with the aspects to which they refer.

Let us take, for example, the sensitive aspect of our experience. Its modal kernel is that irreducible moment of feeling which cannot be defined in a logical way. *'Was man nicht definieren kann, das sieht man als ein Fühlen an'.* But this German adage is applicable to the modal kernel of each aspect. The nuclear moment of feeling, however, unfolds its modal sense only in an unbreakable coherence with a whole series of analogical moments, referring backward to earlier arranged aspects of our experience. Feeling has its own mode of life, bound to the aspect of organic life by its sensory moment. It is emotional, and emotion is a sensitive and intensive mode of movement, referring backward to the modal kernel of the original aspect of extensive movement. It has its own mode of energy or force, with grades of intensity, its causes and effects, by which it manifests its coherence with the physico-chemical aspect. It manifests its coherence with the spatial aspect in spatial analogies, namely, the subjective sensation of spatiality and the objective sensory space of our sensory perception, whose modal meaning is quite different from that of pure mathematical space, physical space, biotic space, and so forth.

All these structural moments of the sensitive aspect are also present in more developed animal feeling. But in the human experience this aspect unfolds also structural moments of an anticipatory character in which its coherence with the subsequently arranged aspects of our temporal horizon manifests itself. Feeling for logical coherence, cultural feeling, linguistic feeling, aesthetic feeling, legal feeling, moral feeling, and so forth, are such anticipatory analogical moments in the modal structure of the sensitive aspect which deepen and open up, or disclose, its modal meaning.

Thus this modal structure reflects the whole coherence of the different aspects of our experience in a special modal sense. And the same holds good with respect to each other aspect, as I have shown in detail in the second volume of my work: *A new Critique of Theoretical Thought.* This may be called the universality of each experiential aspect within its own modal sphere' [8].

Dooyeweerd's discovery of the internal structure of the modal aspect is of fundamental importance. The concept of economic equilibrium, for instance, points to the 'retrocipatory moment' (backward reference) of *energy* within the *economic* sphere. This means that the problem of economic equilibrium never may be put in physical terms but always must be seen from the economic point of view. The same holds true for all other economic problems; economic growth, for instance, is subject to other laws than biotic life. Economic development shows only *analogies* with the biotic modal aspect. Among the other modal spheres in which the economic aspect is founded are the analytical and the social aspect, which will be touched upon later. The neglect of such elements of the structure of the economic aspect distorts one's idea of economic life and results in theories that thus may disregard the nature of economic problems as they present themselves in empirical reality.

The question of what economics is about is therefore crucial. But how

---

8 Dooyeweerd, *In the twilight of western thought,* pp. 6-11.

is the economic aspect to be identified? In this, Dooyeweerd succeeds by careful analysis of the sequence of aspects within the order of time [9]. This sequence is an irreversible one, with an unbreakable inner coherence. Each sphere appears to have its own internal structure, displaying the same pattern of modal moments (features) as the totality of modal aspects themselves. The difference is that *within* each modal aspect there is one moment (feature) which qualifies the meaning (determines the basic significance) of the whole pattern of its structural moments; this central moment Dooyeweerd has termed the 'meaning kernel' or 'nucleus' of the aspect. It provides every aspect of reality with its own irreducible significance [10]. The other moments of the aspect (law-sphere) concerned refer backward or forward to the other modal aspects of reality, without bearing the *original* meaning of the latter; they are therefore called 'analogical moments or analogies' [11]. (See the passage quoted above).

Backward references ('retrocipations') make up the primary structure of the aspect; they refer to the original law-spheres in which the aspect concerned is founded.

Forward references ('anticipations') provide the possibility of deepening the meaning of the primary structure of the aspect. When the anticipatory moments are disclosed or opened they give depth to the experience of the aspect in question that was lacking before.

It is, however, theoretically quite possible *to form a concept* of economics in a primitive society where economic functions are not yet 'deepened', in the sense that they do not yet have any forward looking to the 'higher' aspects of reality. Very schematically we may demonstrate these relationships in a figure:

9 On 'meaning' and on 'time' see *A new critique*, Vol. I, pp. 3-34, and Vol. II, pp. 3-79.

10 'It is the very nature of the modal nucleus that it cannot be defined, because every circumscription of its meaning must appeal to this central moment of the aspect structure concerned. The modal meaning kernel itself can be grasped only in an immediate intuition and never apart from its structural context of analogies' (*A new critique*, Vol. II, p. 129).

11 Dooyeweerd generally uses the term 'analogy' exclusively for retrocipations (see *inter alia: De modale structuur van het juridische oorzakelijkheidsverband*, Amsterdam, 1950, pp. 27 and 46). I do not see any objection to using it for all non-nuclear moments, both 'anticipatory' and 'retrocipatory' ones. At some places Dooyeweerd himself also calls anticipations 'analogies' or at least uses the adjective 'analogical' (see for instance *A new critique*, Vol. II, p. 66, or *De analogische grondbegrippen der vakwetenschappen en hun betrekking tot de structuur van den menselijken ervaringshorizon*, Amsterdam, 1954, p. 9; also the passage quoted above). This question, however, is only a minor terminological one.

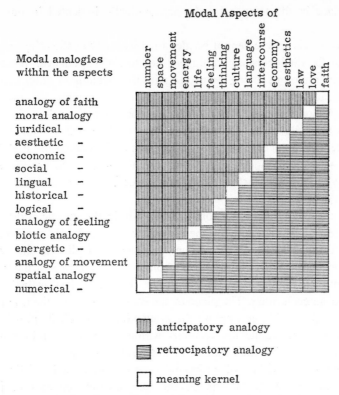

Modal Aspects of

Modal analogies within the aspects

	number	space	movement	energy	life	feeling	thinking	culture	language	intercourse	economy	aesthetics	law	love	faith

analogy of faith
moral analogy
juridical   –
aesthetic   –
economic   –
social   –
lingual   –
historical –
logical   –
analogy of feeling
biotic analogy
energetic   –
analogy of movement
spatial analogy
numerical –

▨ anticipatory analogy

▦ retrocipatory analogy

☐ meaning kernel

I have to apologize for perhaps giving the reader who is not familiar with the philosophical approach concerned a too rigid idea of it.Dooyeweerd did not intend to offer anything like a 'closed system'. As a matter of fact, there are no schematic keys, even in a verbal form – and certainly no diagrams – in his writings. The scope of the present inquiry does not allow me to comment upon his philosophy in greater detail.

The foregoing, however, was necessary in order to indicate the method to be used in order to arrive at an idea of the economic aspect of reality. Whenever the word 'economic' is used, there is a concept of 'weighing' and 'saving'. Examples are expressions like 'economy of thought', 'economy of style' and the like. These expressions point to the existence of a separate economic aspect with its own character, to be sought for at a higher place in the cosmic order because we can form an intrinsic concept of the logical aspect or the aspect of language *apart* from the economic concept. The analytical aspect evidently is not based upon the economic one. Therefore, there must be another aspect, the essence of which has something to do with 'saving', and this aspect must be sought for at a higher place in the temporal order schematically indicated in our diagram [12].

The economic sphere cannot be identified with any of the other aspects which can be distinguished within our horizon of experience. Wherever we find the notion of saving connected with the meaning of other aspects, this moment appears to be distinct from the proper meaning, the 'meaning kernel' of those aspects. When indicating the 'saving' analogy in those aspects we need a qualifying adjective, because the word 'economy' here cannot be used in its original sense. This leads to the conclusion that there must be an original modus of frugality which enables us to use the word 'economy' without a further qualifying adjective (logical, social, legal (juridical) *etc.*).

Thus, the place of the economic aspect within the cosmic order and, *consequently,* the structure of the economic sphere itself, can only be defined through an analysis of the structure of reality in its whole coherence. This involves in principle a simultaneous analysis of the modal aspects in their totality. The aspects present themselves just in their being distinct from each other. The place of the economic aspect, then, appears to lie after the social, and before the aesthetic and juridical spheres, because there are economic *'anticipations'* within the social [13], and economic *'retrocipations'* within the aesthetic [14] and juridical [15] aspects.

Dooyeweerd's 'method of antinomy' here performs an heuristic function. 'If we are in doubt whether the fundamental concepts of jurisprudence, economics, historical science, and so on, are related to specific modal aspects of human experience and empirical reality, we may try to reduce them to the fundamental concepts of other sciences whose modal fields of research have already been defined. When this attempt leads to specific insoluble antinomies, a negative proof has been given

12 '(. . .) Analytical economy (. . .) is doubtless a modal anticipation, not a retrocipation. In other words, the economic law-sphere is founded in the logical sphere and not the other way round. This appears convincingly from the fact that the meaning-moment of logical economy can only function in deepened, theoretical thought. In pre-theoretical logical thought – rigidly bound in its analysis to its sensory substratum of feeling as it is – analytical economy cannot develop because the pre-theoretical concept is not systematic'. (. . .) 'The principle of economy in its logical qualification presupposes the general logical principles implied in the retrocipatory structure of the analytical law-sphere: those of identity, contradiction and the sufficient ground. Analytical economy can only deepen their modal meaning but becomes meaningless apart from them' (*A new critique,* Vol. II, pp. 122, 123/124).
13 Cf. *A new critique,* Vol. II, p. 66/67.
14 Cf. *ibid.,* Vol. II, p. 127/128.
15 Cf. *ibid.,* Vol. II, p. 135/136.

of a theoretical violation of the modal boundaries between irreducible law-spheres'[16].

The place of the economic aspect in the modal structure of reality is of fundamental importance when considering its own structure and nature. As it is founded in the logical sphere, the economic principle is clearly given to us as a norm, which can be applied or not, as we wish [17]. Economic life in its empirical appearance has a normative structure, depending on the way the economic principle has been given a *positive content*.

Hence, an expanded answer can be given to the question raised at the beginning of this section. The economic method implies viewing events from the standpoint of 'saving'. The material content of economic science, however, depends on the problems chosen for study. The setting of such problems is determined by the historical development and the nature of the individuality structures of society (see following section) whose economic activity is to be investigated. Some remarks, therefore, must be made in the following section about the type of community which is primarily involved in the functioning of the international monetary system.

Regarding the stage of historical development, the actual organization of economic life must be taken into account in view of its bearing on the problems concerned. As to the future, it is possible that not only will there be more perfect adherence to the agreed norms of economic conduct, but also an intensification of the economic aspect of reality through a better understanding of economic principles themselves. A further deepening – in the sense mentioned above – of the economic aspect of international cooperation requires what Mr. Dell has called 'economic statesmanship' [18]; or, to put it in the words of Professor Byron L. Johnson, 'to engage creatively with history' [19]. As human reality is *dynamic,* economic theory remains sterile if it just wishes to explain economic relationships or 'facts' as if they were static or autonomous in nature. The question is not only how to explain the 'technical operation' of the international monetary system as it stands, but also and essentially: 'Does this system provide an adequate answer to the economic problem with which it is supposed to deal, and is it used properly?'

16   *Ibid.,* Vol. II, p. 48/49.
17   Cf. *ibid.,* Vol. II, p. 238.
18   Sidney Dell in: 'Linking reserve creation and development assistance', *Hearing* before the Subcommittee on International Exchange and Payments of the Joint Economic Committee, Congress of the United States, Washington, 1969, p. 9 and 60.
19   *Ibid.,* p. 84.

III. THE INTERNATIONAL MONETARY PROBLEM AS AN
INTERNATIONAL PROBLEM

The general functional viewpoint that results from the analysis of the
economic law-sphere or aspect as such is not sufficient. The economist
investigates economic relationships within or between individual communities, persons, things, *etc.* Therefore, an insight into the *structures of
individuality* of reality is equally indispensable as the general 'modal'
viewpoint on which some sketchy observations were made in the previous
section.

Dooyeweerd has briefly indicated the difference between the typical
concept of a structure of individuality and the modal concept of function,
in the following way:

'In every modal aspect we can distinguish:
1. a general functional coherence which holds in mutual correspondence the
   individual functions of things, events, or social relationships within a specific
   modal law-sphere; this coherence exists independently of the typical differences
   between these things, events or social relationships which function within the
   same modal aspect.
2. the typical structural differences manifesting themselves within a modal aspect
   and which are only to be understood in terms of the structures of individuality
   of temporal reality in its integral inter-modal coherence'. [20]

I quote also the following example concerning the juridical aspect, be
cause *mutatis mutandis* it applies to economics as well, and particularly
to the subject of the present study.

'In the juridical aspect of reality, all phenomena are joined in a juridical-functional
coherence. Viewed according to the normside of this aspect, this means, that
constitutional law and civil law, internal ecclesiastical law, internal trade law,
internal law of trade-unions and other organizations, international law, *etc.* do not
function apart from each other, but are joined in a horizontal-functional coherence,
a coherence guaranteed by the modal structure of the juridical aspect itself. When
we view only this universal functional coherence between the various sorts of law,
we abstract it from the internal structural differences which the latter display.
    This general functional view-point is highly abstract; it only teaches us to
recognize the modal functions within the juridical aspect apart from the typical
structures of individuality which are inherent in reality in its integral character. It
is absolutely impossible to approach the internal structural differences between the
typical sorts of law, solely with a general juridical concept of function. Therefore,
it must be clear that the general modal concept of law can never contain the
typical characteristics of *state*-law.'[21]

Without paying due regard to the individuality structures of society, such
as, for instance, a state or an international institution, there cannot be

20   *A new critique,* Vol. I, p. 552/553.
21   *Ibid.,* p. 553. These states of affairs are explained in detail in the second and
third volume of *A new critique.*

thrown proper light on the economic relationships within or between them. Business economics is different from family economics or state economics, though they are interrelated. It is impossible to understand the internal structural differences between the *typical* complexes of economic law with a general economic concept of function alone. The general economic viewpoint is highly abstract [22]. The distinction between 'micro-economics' and 'macro-economics', is hardly helpful in this respect. It refers to differences in quantity rather than in quality. 'But there is no single science, except pure mathematics, which is not confronted with reality in its typical structures of individuality' [23].

To revert to our particular subject, national monetary systems are regulated by national authorities. The need for governmental guidance in this field can easily be demonstrated and needs no extensive explanation. National control of the money supply and interest rates, the centralization of external monetary reserves, and so forth, are all matters of public interest. The juridical principle of *public interest (res publica),* indeed, is the chief, or what Dooyeweerd calls the 'leading' ('qualifying'), structural law of the body politic.

The state's conduct of economic life is ruled by this principle and is made possible through its compulsory powers which are ultimately based on a monopoly of military force. This is essentially the way in which the 'individuality structure' of the state is manifest [24].

---

22 Cf. *ibid.,* p. 553.
23 *Ibid.,* p. 554.
24 See *A new critique,* Vol. III, pp. 434-439, 480-485. The leading aspect of a state expresses itself in all its aspects, among which the economic one. Thus, economic policy also has to be geared to the public interest. Houthakker, speaking about the reasons a government may have for adjusting or not adjusting its balance of payments gives this speech to title: *'The public interest in the balance of payments'* (Remarks of Hendrik S. Houthakker, Member, Council of Economic Advisers, at the Fall Conference of the Financial Analysts Federation, Baltimore, Maryland, October, 1969, *press release).*
The following passage taken from *A new critique,* Vol. III, p. 481/482 is illuminating:
'The structural principle of the State necessarily expresses itself in its internal economic aspect. This really *political* economic sphere can never be understood in terms of private inter-individual economic intercourse. The internal political economy is a territorial *'Zwangswirtschaft'* (compulsory economy), in which the economic function has been structurally opened in a typical direction to the public juridical leading function of the State. The system of taxation, as a typical political manner of economic provision of income and capital, forms the basis of the whole of the State's internal economy, and unmistakably displays of a political individuality structure. In this typical economic structure the system of taxation is subject to politico-economic norms of a communal character. In the modal economic principle of a frugal administration of scarce means, in the alternative choice

Just as there is a need for harmonizing private interests within the state by means of systems of domestic public and private law, so there is equally a need for harmonizing the interests both of states and of private persons in the international field. This cooperation is characterized by – I quote again – the '*juridically qualified principle of international public interest*' [25].

The need for *international organization* is with respect to economic life particularly evident. A change in the par value of a currency, for instance, has consequences both for national and for foreign users of the currency. It is not surprising that this issue was made the key-stone of the Articles of Agreement of the International Monetary Fund [26] at the Bretton Woods Conference in 1944.

of their destination, according to a well balanced scale of needs, has been typically individualized and opened under the leading of the juridical idea of public interest.

The modal economic principles are not at all eliminated from the internal political economy: but here the question as to *what* (not *how*) is economic, is entirely dependent on the individuality structure of this typical economic sphere. The internal economic value of the material apparatus of a military and a police organization, of a network of roads, *etc.*, for the political economy of the State cannot be measured according to the market value of the required goods and services, nor according to a certain marginal utility.

In the internal economy of the State it *may* be justifiable in an economic sense to deviate from the prices in the free market and from the principles of profitability prevailing in a free economic enterprise, if such deviations are required by the politico-economic structural relations (footnote: Remember the expensive administrative services required by the juridically qualified 'public interest'. These services must not be judged according to the principles of profit earning in a free enterprise).

From the teleological viewpoint the entire economic sphere is considered to be merely a means for the attainment of non-economic purposes. But this view is in its subjectivity destructive to a correct insight into the internal structural relations in the economy; for it just excludes the question as to *what* is economic from economic theory (footnote: The *economic* needs of the State are in principle dependent on its individuality structure).' (I have amended on one or two points the translation of the original 1936 text).

25 Dooyeweerd has made some scattered remarks on this subject in *A new critique,* Vol. III, pp. 473-477, 596, 599-601, 660/661. The quotation used here has been taken from p. 601.

26 Speaking of the objections usually raised to greater exchange rate flexibility, Houthakker mentions the argument about sovereignty. 'The fixing of par values, this argument holds, is a prerogative of each country which cannot be subjected to outside control or to an automatic formula. Actually the supposed sovereign right of countries to fix their exchange rates had already been limited by the Bretton Woods Agreement. As the International Monetary Fund points out in its recent annual report' (1969, p. 32), ' "the determination of the rate of exchange for each currency is a matter of international concern" ' (Houthakker, 'The public interest in the balance of payments', p. 15/16). See also *The role of exchange rates in the adjustment of international payments,* A report by the Executive Directors, International Monetary Fund, Washington, 1970, Chapter 1, Section a, 'The exchange rate in its international aspect'.

The first purpose listed in Article I of the agreement is 'To promote international monetary cooperation through a permanent institution which provides the machinery for consultation and collaboration on international problems'. The same Article mentions a number of other specific matters to be 'promoted', among which is the maintenance 'of *orderly* exchange *arrangements*' [27].

This example illustrates a widely prevailing and deeply rooted misunderstanding of economic theory, which gave rise to the controversy between 'pure theory' [28] (or 'abstract' theory) and the 'institutional' approach. Economic theory should take into account the *real* structures of society, such as states, international institutions like the International Monetary Fund and other structural international relationships. Even

---

27 Cf. *Charter of the United Nations,* Article 13, sub 1: 'The General Assembly shall initiate studies and make recommendations for the purpose of a) promoting international cooperation in the political field and encouraging the progressive development of international law and its codification (. . .)'. Also *the Statute of the International Court of Justice,* Article 36, sub 2: 'The states parties to the present Statute may at any time declare that they recognize as compulsory *ipso facto* and without special agreement in relation to any other state accepting the same obligation the jurisdiction of the Court in all legal disputes concerning: a) the interpretation of a treaty, b) any question of international law, c) the existence of any fact which, if established, would consitute a breach of an international obligation; d) the nature or extent of the reparation to be made for the breach of an international obligation'. All this is in fact new international law. The United Nations, however, by its nature, cannot but remain a voluntary association of free nations, keeping their own competence 'in matters which are essentially within the domestic jurisdiction of any state' (Charter, Art. 2 sub 7), which competence is historically founded in their own military force. As for the latter, the assurance given in the preamble of the U.N. Charter, 'that armed force shall not be used, save in the common interest' – which is of course essential for the maintenance of international order – cannot be realized otherwise than voluntarily.
28 Whatever form it may have taken, when it came to empirical reality, 'pure' theory had to be 'applied'; its logical 'validity' did not guarantee 'applicability'. The fact that nowadays very little is written about 'applied economics' is in line with the gradual disappearance of 'pure' economics: the assumptions of 'pure' theory, 'shadowy abacus of forms and inevitable relationships' – in the words of L. Robbins, *An essay on the nature and significance of economic science,* London, 1952 (reprint), p. 39 – regarding the basic 'data' needed to be increasingly differentiated. Economic theory, of course, had in practice to turn to the study of real problems on the basis of actual ever changing, institutional arrangements. The result was the creation of more realistic and more generally applicable economic theories, accompanied by a loss of systematic methodology. The 'nature and significance of economic science' – and its unity – are still a major economic problem, now that abstract formalized models have increasingly yielded to more realistic approaches (cf. J. Wemelsfelder, 'De kansen ten aanzien van een Calvinistisch wijsgerige fundering van de economische methodologie', *Philosophia Reformata,* 1949, pp. 171-187, especially p. 183).

Eduard Heimann is his masterly *Introduction to economic theory*[29] adopts an antithesis between 'abstract theorizing' and 'historical analysis' in this way[30].

The 'great antinomy' – to use the words of Eucken[31] – between the two is not, as Eucken suggests, a product of reality, but of modes of thought. Every real economic problem has its historical setting. Economic theory by its nature as a theoretical science is bound to abstract from reality. This does not necessarily lead to conflict with other methods of theoretical thought, e.g. the historical method, provided that one avoids any technique that defines the economic field of investigation in such a way that it will *a priori* embrace other aspects of reality besides the economic one. As soon as the economist claims that he is competent to explain human social phenomena in all their aspects, he cannot but come into conflict with other branches of science which are also concerned with social reality. It is in this way that theoretical antinomies occur, and theoretical thought involves itself in self-contradiction[32]. The only way, then, to avoid giving a distorted picture of the economic field of investigation seems to be applying all the various artificial modes of thought so well described by Eucken (Eucken's *'Denkformen'*). The historians – or the former adherents of the 'historic school' of economic theory – only aggravate the 'great antinomy', if they too pretend to give a 'full' account of reality[33].

The 'great antinomy' or, in other words, the conflict between 'pure' and 'institutional' theory becomes all the more acute when neither theory

29 Main title: *History of economic doctrines*, London, New York, Toronto, 8th ed., 1959.
30 See for instance *ibid.*, p. 62.
31 Walter Eucken, *Die Grundlagen der Nationalökonomie*, 7th ed., Berlin, Göttingen, Heidelberg, 1959, pp. 21-23.
32 See *A new critique*, Vol. II, Part I, Chapter I, Section 5, 'The logical aspect of the criterion of meaning and the method of antinomy'.
33 See on the historical method: *A new critique*, Vol. II, pp. 181-365. See on the internally antinomic exclusivism of the 'transcendental-logical forms of knowledge' in the epistemology of 'cultural' or 'mental sciences' applied by Neo-Kantianism: *A new critique*, Vol. II, p. 209: 'The material (the content of experience), assumed to be grasped in these 'forms of knowledge', was in fact outlawed. The 'pure theory of law' transferred this content to sociology, psychology, and the science of history. 'Formal sociology' referred it back to the other 'cultural sciences', and 'pure economics', 'pure grammar', 'pure aesthetics' or 'ethics' could not give shelter to the 'historical material of experience' either. If Kelsen's or Stammler's 'pure theory of law' were correct, 'pure economics' and 'formal sociology' would be precluded. If 'pure or formal sociology' with its formalistic conception of the sociological categories were right, there would be no room left for 'pure theory of law' or 'pure economics'.

takes into account the structural laws of societal [34] communities and inter-personal or intercommunal relationships [35]. Whenever the principle method of economic theory becomes formalized and disregards the societal structures of individuality, serious theoretical confusions must arise [36].

Just how necessary it is to pay regard to the 'institutional' setting can be illustrated by reference to our present subject of study. How can one conceive of international monetary relations without having regard to international agreements, government authority, the legal position of

34 Dooyeweerd often uses the term 'societal' referring to human society as such, as confusion may arise with the *social aspect* of 'societal' phenomena in the *modal* sense. Distinction must be made too between general sociology which is philosophic in nature and sociology as a special science, investigating the social aspect of society, just like economics deals with the economic aspect alone.

35 Dooyeweerd gives the following definitions:

'By 'community' I understand any more or less durable societal relationship which has the character of a whole joining its members into a social unity, irrespective of the degree of intensity of the communal bond.

By inter-individual or inter-communal relationships I mean such in which in-dividual persons or communities function in coordination without being united into a solidary whole. Such relationships may show the character of mutual neutrality, of approachment, free cooperation or antagonism, competition or contest' (*A new critique*, Vol. III, p. 177).

36 Social structures differ as to their nature. So does, consequently, their economic behavior (see the quotation from Dooyeweerd on the state in footnote 24 above). Interpersonal and inter-communal relationships – i.e. relationships not between members of a community, but between persons or communities that stand in coordination with or in opposition to each other – also have typical structures, of a supra-arbitrary nature. A free market, for instance, is a set of inter-personal and inter-communal relationships that is historically founded and economically qualified (see Dooyeweerd, *inter alia: Verkenningen,* Amsterdam, 1962, p. 140).

The following remarks are important in this connection. 'What have we seen take place under the influence of the positivistic view of the task of science? In keeping with the postulate of continuity of the Humanistic science-ideal, the concept of function was absolutized in order to eradicate the modal diversity of meaning which exists between the modal aspects. At the same time the attempt was made to erase completely the typical structures of individuality which reality displays within the modalities investigated. But, especially in the so-called 'pure theory of law' ('*reine Rechtslehre*') and in 'pure economics', there often can be observed a curious confusion of the modal-functional and the typical structural view-points. Often unintentionally, under the guise of a general concept of function, a specific concept of a typical structure of individuality is introduced in order to level all other typical differences of structure within the investigated aspect of reality.

Consequently, the supposed merely general modal concept of function is in truth transposed into a typical structural concept.

Under the guise of an abstract purely functional view-point the so-called Austrian school in its 'pure economics', absolutized free market relations at the expense of the other typical structures of society, which manifest themselves within the economic aspect of reality'. (*A new critique*, Vol. I, p. 555). See also the two publications mentioned at the end of footnote 3.

South African mineworkers, the dominant influence of the United States in international relations, the pattern of world markets and many other structural features of society? The regulation of economic relationships by public law, for instance, does not bear a typical economic character, but is based on the legal 'principles of public law itself' [37]. Disregard of this kind of basic fact can only result in an amorphous picture which does not correspond with observed reality.

Therefore, Eucken needs a 'morphologic apparatus' (*'morphologischen Apparat'*) [38] *to create* a theoretical order. There is no evidence to indicate the criterion he uses in choosing the 'elements' (*'Formelemente'*) he assembles in his 'general theoretical analysis' [39]. He somehow constructs his 'ideal types' – which represent his solution to the problem of the 'great antinomy' – out of 'elements' which can supposedly be found in 'every economic order at any time and in any place' [39] as if those 'elements' were interchangeable or even comparable. Economics cannot speak of 'elements' like chemistry may do!

What is meant by this concept of 'elements'? Similar phenomena do not necessarily function in the same manner at all times and in all places. The budget deficit of an enterprise is different from the budget deficit of a government. The government of a nation in classical antiquity functioned differently from the government of a differentiated modern state, and so forth. The number of 'forms of order' (*'Ordnungsformen'*) is incalculable, Eucken says. But if every new problem brings new 'forms of order' into the picture or means reshuffling them again and again, what is left of the very concept of order? Just as it is possible to form an enormous number of different words out of two thousand letters, one can construct an incalculable number of economic orders out of a limited number 'elementary, pure forms', Eucken maintains [40]. But while admittedly an *a* is an *a* is an a *b* is a *b*, the *meaning* of a *set* of letters depends on the connection in which they are used, and even identical words may have different meanings in different sentences. Every new example shows that the analogy is false.

37 See Dooyeweerd, 'De sociologische verhouding tussen recht en economie', p. 238 where he states that 'ook een publiekrechtelijke regeling van de economische verhoudingen naar haar aard niet door een typisch economische bestemming kan zijn gekwalificeerd, maar slechts door de typische rechtsbeginselen van het publiekrecht zelve').
38 Eucken, *Grundlagen*, p. 123.
39 *Ibid.*, p. 124. '(Die Idealtypen) enthalten in ihrer Gesamtheit (. . .) *alle* Formelemente, aus denen *alle* konkreten Wirtschaftsordnungen *zu allen* Zeiten und *überall* aufgebaut sind'.
40 *Ibid.*, p. 72.

Monetary analysis, according to Eucken, operates with three different forms of 'pure monetary systems' depending upon the way in which money is created. The three forms of money are: commodity money, money which comes into being as the result of the monetization of goods, and money created by credit [41]. These concepts may be very helpful in textbooks, but they do no more than state the ways in which money can be technically created. Can monetary theory be divided into three main streams along these lines? Do money problems generally have to be formulated differently, according to the way in which the money was created? Once money has been put into circulation, its behavior does not usually depend on the circumstances in which it was generated. Once the agreement has been reached on the techniques of SDR creation, the main problem of how to regulate the holding and use of special drawing rights had still to be solved. When a solution to that problem had in turn been found, the question 'what are special drawing rights?' could only be answered by reference to all the Articles in the Fund Agreement relating to special drawing rights and to the relevant regulations subsequently decided upon by the participants in the Special Drawing Account.

Another similar comment may be made. According to the method applied by Eucken, the 'pure form' of gold should differ from the 'pure form' of SDRs, and they should be brought into being in different 'pure systems'. Yet Machlup calls the differences 'chiefly technological and sociological'. *Economically,* he mentions four similarities: 'SDRs, like gold will be official reserve assets; SDRs, like gold, will be 'non-debt money' among monetary authorities; SDRs were invented to supplement gold in the monetary reserves of the nations; SDRs may over the years assume very significant proportions, not unlike gold, in the world's total reserves' [42]. Machlup could have added that SDRs also have the same foreign exchange value as gold [43].

Criticism of Eucken's 'morphological' method can only gather weight when it is considered that, as he himself admits, 'pure forms' do not really exist. Yet he tries to make his method explain not only monetary systems themselves but also the influences of money upon the daily economic process [44].

---

41 Ibid., p. 117 ff.
42 Fritz Machlup, *Remaking the international monetary system,* p. 35/36.
43 Fund Agreement, Art. XXI, Section 2: 'The unit of value of special drawing rights shall be equivalent to 0.888671 gram of fine gold'.
44 Eucken, *Grundlagen,* p. 122.

This section may have served to show that economic theory lacks proper direction when it is based on an economic methodology that disregards the empirical setting of economic problems and the nature of the structures of society at which they become manifest. In particular, economic theory has to ask 'What is the *leading* aspect (main feature) of the typical social structure whose economy is to be studied?', and 'What are the subjective aims of the institutions involved?' The subjective establishment of particular aims has a bearing on the way in which a positive content is given to the structural principle of these communities or inter-communal relationships, i.e. on the particular shape of the institutions [46].

Just as modern nations have historically been communities founded to further the public interest, so have international associations been formed in the light of what was conceived of as the public interest as well. There can be no other explanation: the external relations of communities cannot be seen apart from their internal structure. The task of international associations is to advance the cause of international [47] relations from the point of the common interest, according to collectively chosen goals. The setting up of permanent institutions to carry out international agreements makes it possible for the multinational community to shape particular policies in conformity with agreed purposes. The actual behavior of the institutions can be judged by comparing it to the agreed purposes.

It is impossible to look into the international monetary problem either form the 'monetary' or from the 'international' viewpoint separately. Economics, including monetary economics, is always related to typical and particular 'individuality structures of society'. No light can be thrown on international monetary issues without first having an implied view of the principles of international cooperation and international policy goals.

---

45 Dutch: 'verbanden'; societal structures displaying an internal unity of cohesive relationships.
46 On the difficult question of subjective aim *versus* structural principles, see Dooyeweerd, *Verkenningen*, p. 109 and pp. 132-137.
47 'International' originally means: 'between nations', in which meaning it is used here. Unfortunately, the word is also used in a different meaning: an 'international' organization is not only something between nations, but a new institution whose members are nations, a separate legal entity for regulating certain inter-national relations. The word 'supranational' can not fully serve as a synonym; 'multinational' would be better.

IV. THE SOCIAL DIMENSION OF THE INTERNATIONAL
MONETARY PROBLEM

In the first section of this chapter we defined the expression 'international monetary system' as the set of relationships between states established to overcome the international monetary problem. This problem has many facets which affect our daily experience. They all reveal a need to create the best possible monetary conditions for the development of the world economy in the absence of a single universal currency.

Control of money is a matter of public interest, and is thus typically a task to be undertaken by the state. The creation of a single currency would require one state, because a single currency can be managed only by one organized will [48]. A monetary union in the sense of an area with only one currency and one central bank always presupposes one political will; otherwise there is only *inter*national monetary cooperation. The economic need for international cooperation is obvious.

As was shown in section 2, economic life can only develop on a foundation of social life. The experience of Robinson Crusoe can never be helpful in analysing economic theory. Robinson Crusoe, alone on his island, was only faced by problems of a technical and biological character: how to feed and to clothe himself, how to cope with seasonal problems while doing so, and so forth. However, once a fellow man, Friday, entered the scene, economic problems arose. Contrary to the teachings of the individualistic liberal economic theorists of the 19th century, Marxian economists rightly stress that 'Political economy investigates (. . .) the economic relationships between man' [49]. These economic relations are to be distinguished from the technical aspects of production, with which Robinson Crusoe was concerned. This 'aspect of production is investigated by the use of the technical and natural sciences – physics, chemistry, metallurgy, mechanics, agriculture and the others' [49]. Robinson Crusoe

---

48 'The 'will of the State' is by no means a fictitious legal abstraction, but the real organized will of a communal whole. It is true that this will is *qualified* by the juridical relation between the government and its subjects and *founded* in historical military power. But it asserts itself in all the aspects of our social experience as an organized unity of volitional direction, realized in the *organized* actions of a societal whole'. (*A new critique*, Vol. III, p. 436).
49 Akademie der Wissenschaften der USSdR, *Politische Oekonomie, Lehrbuch,* Berlin 1964, p. 16. 'Die Produktion hat eine technische und eine gesellschaftliche Seite. Die technische Seite der Produktion wird von den technischen und den Naturwissenschaften erforscht: von der Physik, der Chemie, der Metallurgie, der Maschinenkunde, der Agronomie und von anderen Wissenschaften. Die politischen Oekonomie hingegen erforscht die gesellschaftliche Seite der Produktion, die *gesell-*

certainly had control of his goods; he did have to make decisions as to whether to work or relax, to consume or save, to produce, say, potatoes or strawberries, but he was not involved in an 'economic process'. His activities did not take place within a community (cf. the Greek word *'oikos'*), nor did they involve any intercommunal or interpersonal relationships, such as markets.

Furthermore, although economic methodologists have dropped the assumption of a specific 'economic' goal as the basis of all economic action, and adopted the completely subjective and indeterminate concept of 'welfare' [50], we have to realize that this development emerged – and unavoidably so – within an individualistic scheme of thought. Certainly something more definite can be said of the true economic problem than that it is a merely formal one. However personal and indeterminate the 'economic' objectives of Robinson and Friday individually might have been, they entered structural relationships of an economic kind being open to economic investigation, such as employment or exchange competition in the struggle to exploit one single pool of productive resources. In these circumstances, a decision to save or consume was no longer a choice affecting Robinson alone, since it would also enable him to exchange more or less goods with Friday or to pay him a higher or lower wage. *The scarcity of means becomes an economic problem only in a social context* [51]. Once societies exist, individualism is bound to lead to

schaftliche Produktionverhältnisse, das heiszt, die ökonomischen Verhältnisse der Menschen. 'Die politischen Oekonomie', schrieb W. I. Lenin, 'befasst sich keineswegs mit der 'Produktion', sondern mit der gesellschaftlichen Beziehungen der Menschen in der Produktion, mit der gesellschaftlichen Struktur der Produktion' (W. I. Lenin, 'Die Entwicklung des Kapitalismus in Rusland'. In *Werke*, Bd. 3, S. 51)'.

See also footnotes 6 and 7 to this chapter. Such a definition of economic science does not mean that, in its phenotypical appearance, it cannot be concerned with investigations of a physical or technical character, especially when physical considerations have a special bearing in the economics ones. After all, economic life can only develop on the basis of physical existence.

50 See the interesting and extensive inquiry into the history of economic methodology in this respect, *Economisch motief en economisch principe*, by P. Hennipman, Amsterdam, 1945.

51 P. Hennipman, in his admirable essay 'Doeleinden en criteria der economische politiek' (Objectives and criteria of economic policy) in: *Theorie van de economische politiek*, edited by J. E. Andriessen and M. A. G. van Meerhaeghe, Leyden, 1962), on page 54 calls it 'remarkable', that in the theory of economic policy the old idea that economic action is characterized by a specific purpose persists more than in the analysis of individual behavior'. ('Het is een merkwaardig verschijnsel dat juist in de theorie der economische politiek de oude mening, dat een specifieke doelstelling kenmerkend is voor het economisch handelen, zich in veel sterkere mate handhaaft dan in de analyse van het individuele gedrag'). In view of the observations just made, however, this is quite understandable.

economic conflicts and theoretical antinomies [52]. The economic 'process' of society as a whole cannot be a matter of indifference, for the economic problem consists of finding a way to ensure cooperation and coordination between separate free individuals or communities, each endowed with free choice regarding the accumulation and disposal of wealth. Deepening [53] the economic aspect of human life in fact means continually enhancing the possibilities of free economic choice for everyone.

What holds true for interpersonal relations, does so also for international economic life. Nations also have to cooperate economically if they want to avoid economic conflicts. The creation of a body of international law is intended to give legal form to the harmonization of the interests of individual nations.

Finally, if social phenomena manifest themselves in many aspects of reality [54], how, can we call particular social problems economic ones? The economic aspect of such problems is the only part that the economist is interested in, and it seems presumptuous to label the problems themselves as economic ones.

The answer is to be found in Dooyeweerd's theory on *the structures of individuality of temporal reality,* referred to in the previous section. Individuality structures display a typical configuration of modal aspects. For instance, we have mentioned that the structure of the state is based on its monopoly of military force, and that its *raison d'être* (in Dooyweerdian terms: its leading function) is the preservation of the public interest. This *raison d'être* permeates ('qualifies') the whole structure. In this sense we can speak of juridical, economic, moral, and other individuality structures. Monetary systems are typically qualified by their economic function, i.e. *facilitating the smooth distribution of generally wanted goods in society* [55] – an aspect that will prove particularly relevant to the main

---

52 Unfortunately the English language, like other languages, has no way of differentiating between the two senses of the word 'economics', namely, 'economic practice' and 'economic theory'.

An 'economic' problem in the latter sense properly would have to be termed an 'economological' problem. 'Economics' is the science of 'economic' problems, just as 'socio*logy*' studies social problems, 'bio*logy*', biotic problems, *etc.*

53 The meaning of this term is explained in section 2.

54 See footnote 7 to this chapter.

55 The expression 'economic goods' in itself is not helpful in defining what economics is about. A table, for instance, is a physically qualified thing, i.e. it has a subjective function in the physical aspect, but it can have all kinds of objective functions in the social, economic, aesthetic, legal or moral sphere and so forth. (cf. Dooyeweerd, *A new critique,* Vol. II, Part I, Chapter V, 'The subject-object relation in the model aspects'). So a table can be an economic good as well as a legal object, *etc., etc.* (cont. p. 36)

subject to be discussed below. Monetary problems are therefore rightly called economic problems, and they should never be considered in an isolated way, apart from their general economic context (cf. chapter 1, section 1). Money as such is primarily an economic phenomenon and the actual contents of the international monetary problem can be a matter for study in the present economic inquiry.

Of course, economic arrangements can be put in legal form. The contents of an international treaty on intrinsically economic matters, however, will have to take the typical economic relationships into account, and these may prevent the formal application of the juridical principle of equality of all partner nations as set out in Article 2, sub 1 of the U.N. Charter. To give an example, the economic status of the US dollar, which is widely used by other countries as an intervention currency in foreign exchange and money markets, makes it impossible to devise a mechanism of exchange rate adjustment that is entirely symmetrical. If agreement is reached on a uniform maximum limit ('band') for exchange rate fluctuations around par, the margin for fluctuations against other currencies is half as wide for the United States as it is for other countries, due to the specific role of the dollar. The economic relationships concerned do not permit formal equality or uniform freedom for every country. The countries of the world are not interchangeable 'elements' within the structure of the world economy. Reference may be made also to the position of developing countries in the international monetary system.

What is important is that any rules of international public law shall be qualified by the legal principle of international public interest. 'A regulation of public law concerning economic relations can, of its nature, not be qualified by a typical economic destination, but only by the typical legal principles of public law itself' [56]. This does not detract from the economics of the problems concerned, but sets the perspective in which they must be considered.

Calling a table an economic good clarifies nothing unless one has an idea of what is 'economic'. Thus, it leaves a blank in the definition. As an economic good, the table functions in a typical economically qualified subject-object relationship. The same table, however, may have a social function (for instance, if it is used for drinks during a cocktail party), or a symbolic one (the table behind which a chairman and other board members sit during a meeting of an association), an aesthetic function, a moral function, *etc.*

When we speak about 'economic goods' we mean 'goods in their economic object function'. Essential to the economic problem is the fact that the possible objects of our economic valuation and organization giving rise to our 'economic opportunities' are, in principle, wanted by *all* men.

56 See footnote 37 above.

V. SCOPE OF THE FURTHER INQUIRY

International monetary economics is concerned with the difficulties arising from the existence of different national currency systems. The existence of these differences urges international cooperation. A central issue is the management of *international money*. National governments have to deal with this topic in two different ways: they have to carry out a policy concerning their own international monetary reserves (how much and what kind of it are desirable?), and they have to cooperate internationally on problems of total world liquidity (again: how much and what kind of it are desirable?). The two tasks are closely interrelated.

The management of the total world money stock so far as *quantity* and *composition* are concerned does belong primarily to the field of monetary economics in the narrow sense, as was described in the first section of chapter I. Its *distribution*, especially the distribution of international financial means based on official international money *creation*, is rather a matter of international monetary economics in the 'broad' sense.

It is the latter which will be our subject. To tackle the field of international monetary economics in the 'broad' sense would raise problems of definition: an investigation of matters that are 'closely related to the existence of money' [57] would mean dealing with almost everything connected with international economic relations. We have therefore narrowed the whole issue.

As mentioned in section 1, private individuals are not primarily engaged in finding a solution for the creation and management of international currency. If they possess balances in national currency and have to make international payments, they can get any foreign currency they need provided that *government* policy allows them to convert their national currency. This is why the international monetary problem is typically a governmental problem, and I shall therefore leave private economic behavior out of account. I shall also make no reference to private international liquidity, such as private dollar holdings. This is certainly a major exclusion but it is justified in the light of the specific points we wish to make in the course of our study.

Another exclusion can also be made. The field of international liquidity is larger than that of international reserves. We shall be concentrating on international reserves and not on liquidity in the form of short-term central bank credit, conditional drawing rights in the IMF, and so forth.

57 See footnote 2 to chapter I.

Thus, within that field we shall devote attention to the question of *official monetary reserves,* i.e. holdings of external means of payments centralized under the control of the national monetary authorities.

Our specific subject will be the way in which *special drawing rights* are created. Their initial distribution and use will be particularly discussed.

III. Some essential features of special drawing rights

I. INTERNATIONAL MONEY

International money for our purposes means central bank money; not in the sense of money issued by a central bank – although it may be that too, when national currencies are used as international money –, but of money used as a means of payment *between* central banks, in other words inter-central-bank money.

National money differs from international money and national monetary policy is different from international monetary policy, a state of affairs which seems often to be neglected, especially in writings on the global need for international reserves. Although the differences are usually put in economic terms, they fundamentally stem from the different 'individuality structures' [1] of national and international money systems. Both kinds of money however have individuality structures of a typical *economic* nature and both can be made into objects for the exercise of an organized political will. The principal difference lies precisely in the political structures with which the monetary systems are interwoven. As mentioned above, national political power is compulsory in nature, while internationally the principle of public interest can only be materialized on a voluntary basis. International money differs from national money in that it is an emanation of cooperation between nations while national

1 See on the concept of individuality structure chapter II, section 3.

money only affects the internal operation of nations, and lies within their exclusive power; i.e. the former is a matter of collective multinational responsibility, and the latter of internal national responsibility.

A number of differences are briefly and clearly set out in a most interesting recent article by Mr. J. J. Polak [2].

First, domestic money serves to make all types of payment while international reserves can only be used to settle the *net balances* of a country's international payments. It is desirable, in my view, to stress the difference without losing sight of the similarity. It may be said that international money serves also to make payments; only the payers and payees are different: not private persons or institutions, but national public authorities, representing a national community *as a whole*. These payments are made, of course, after a certain time lag and subject to the technicalities of our multilateral payments system, but, in principle, they are not different from settlements among nationals. A *country* that runs a payments deficit *makes* payments, a surplus country *receives* means of payment. In the preceding chapter I tried to lay particular emphasis on the fact that it is *states* that are the responsible bodies and also the agents that are predominantly active in what is called 'the international monetary system'.[3]

A second difference between domestic and international money that is referred to by Polak relates immediately to the very subject of the present study. *Holders* of *national* money 'count in the millions even in small countries, and monetary policy proceeds on the assumption that operation on the total money supply or on total credit will produce the desired effect on spending on a stochastic basis. By contrast, the total of *international* money is held by the monetary authorities of no more than a hundred-odd countries, with a very small number accounting for a large

2 J. J. Polak, 'Money – national and international', *Essays in honour of Thorkil Kristensen,* Paris, 1970, pp. 171-185.
3 See the remarks of Benjamin J. Cohen on page 14 of his *Adjustment costs and the distribution of new reserves* (Princeton, 1966); I quote some of them: 'Conventional analysis of payments imbalance and adjustment does not really take the state seriously. Like the positive (as contrasted with normative) pure theory of international trade, it is concerned principally with the competitive actions and reactions of large numbers of single, atomistic individuals and firms who, as it happens, can be classified into roughly homogeneous sub-groups by their nationality. The state as such has been given little importance beyond the fact that some of the participants in international trade and finance live and work there, obey its laws, and use its currency; the structural attributes of nations, such as size and level of development are treated as largely extraneous. In normative theory, to be sure, the state is taken much more seriously.'

proportion of the total' [4]. This has a bearing on the interest of countries and their role in any deliberate action to manage international liquidity, on which I touched in section 3 of chapter I. Mr. Polak noted in this connection, that the first decision to create SDRs was based on an explicit reference to the behaviour of two major 'elements' in the international monetary 'system': the United States and the United Kingdom.

Closely related to this state of affairs is, as Polak points out, the fact that on the international plane there is a problem of *distribution* while, 'with respect to the domestic money supply, one would never seriously hear the suggestion that not only the total stock, but also its distribution was a matter of major importance' [5]. I quote further: Domestically, monetary policy 'injects credit into the system and can expect, by and large, that the credit will have its influence throughout the economy. (. . .) By contrast, internationally, a blindfolded approach to the distribution of money is impossible. (. . .) The suggestions for 'Fund investment' put forward earlier in the liquidity discussions did not refer to anything like a central bank's open market operations. 'Investment' could only be investment in the liabilities of specific countries (or international institutions). Since in all normal circumstances the Fund would not be able to do anything else with the liabilities so acquired than to hold them, the proposals for Fund investment did not in economic substance differ from the method of distribution that was actually selected: the allocation of special drawing rights to countries. *The problem of allocation is thus inherent in international reserve policy'* [6].

In spite of the differences, however, both kinds of money, domestic and international [7], are money, and that is why monetary theories in many respects cover both subjects. As is common in the theory of money in general, distinctions can be made as to different functions of money.

Money serves as a *medium of exchange* and as a *measure of value*. It is not unusual to add more functions to the list. These are, however, all derived from the two principal tasks of money. The longer the list is made, the less analytical sense it makes. I agree in this respect with F. Benham [8] who does not see any value in distinguishing a separate function of serving as a 'standard for deferred payments', neither a

4 Polak, 'Money – national and international', p. 176.
5 *Ibid.,* p. 177.
6 *Ibid.,* p. 179/180 (my italics).
7 Among the other differences mentioned by Mr. Polak is the fact that the *composition* of international reserves is far more important than the composition of domestic money.
8 *Economics, A general introduction,* 5th ed., London, 1955, pp. 424-425.

separate function of serving as a 'store of value' [9]. However, he rightly observes: 'what is true (. . .)' is 'that by definition money is the most liquid of all assets' [10]. Though it is only by definition that money is the most liquid store of value, for our purposes it is useful to stress this particular aspect of money [11]. External reserve assets held by central banks as a cover against national currency circulation, are normally kept in liquid form. In most cases the central bank is not allowed to invest them in medium or long term financial assets without special authorization. This is one of the reasons why gold, with its highly liguid and universal character, under the presently prevailing availabilities of other reserve assets, is still the largest component of world reserves. It may even be said that in practice gold is primarily a store of value and mostly functions as a means of payment only in the last resort.

II. INTERNATIONAL MONETARY 'STANDARDS'

Some brief remarks may be in order on the expression 'standard' as in 'gold standard', 'gold exchange standard', 'composite commodity standard', *etc.* Which of the three functions of money just mentioned are we referring to if we say that the regime we live with, for instance, is that of the gold exchange standard? I think there is a certain amount of confusion here. The concept of standard often is mixed, containing

9   On the other hand, P. C. Bos, in his *Money in development* (Rotterdam, 1969), Chapter II, 3, lists no less than eight functions, namely means of payment, means of fixing of amount of payment, means of preparing for payment, means of diversification, specialization and growth of the economy, means of integrating economic regions, means of channeling the result of the saving effort of economic subjects into investment, means of keeping up total effective demand, means of income distribution. It would be better, in my opinion, to say that the first two of these functions are almost indispensable as a *means* for reaching the economic *objectives* implied in the last five items of the list. (On the method used by Bos, see also my article 'Monetaire methodologie, aantekeningen bij een studie over geldwaarde en geldgebruik', *Maandschrift Economie,* March 1970, pp. 318-330).
10   Benham, *Economics,* p. 425.
11   See also G. A. Kessler, *Monetair evenwicht en betalingsbalansevenwicht,* Leyden, 1958, p. 5, who, too, distinguishes two functions of money, namely its function as 'concrete' money (medium of exchange) and its function as 'abstract' money (measure of value). Concrete money functioning not in the sphere of current transactions but of capital transactions, namely as the most liquid form of property, is called 'means of treasuring' ('thesauriseringsmiddel'). Central bank money, we may observe, is held as 'means of treasuring' to cope with demands for foreign currency by residents both for payments in international *current* transactions and in international capital transactions.

elements of all the three functions of money. A gold standard, then, is considered a system in which gold plays a dominant role; and the expression 'gold exchange standard' stands for a system in which another means, convertible into gold and *vice versa,* plays a dominant role. Often the term 'standard' really means no more than the word 'system'; Triffin, for instance, speaks about the current reserve creation system as a 'negotiated credit-reserves standard' [12], thus pointing only to the function of international money as a store of value.

Properly the word 'standard' means: unit of measurement, unit of account. The choice of such a unit depends on circumstances and purposes. Lenghts are measured in meters or yards or other units according to the area in which we live. When we have the possibility of choosing between different units, we take that one that makes most practical sense, that is most useful from the specific viewpoint that matters. Thus, it is no wonder that the unit of account which is most used in international money calculations is the U.S. dollar, being the currency which of all currencies plays the most extended role in international economics. Still, this function of the dollar as a common denominator of currencies does not make us call the present international monetary system a dollar standard. This indicates that the word 'standard' has acquired a broader and vaguer meaning.

There are two reasons why opinions differ as to the extend to which a dollar standard has materialized.

First, the concept of 'standard' is not used in a clear and unequivocal sense.

Second, there can never exist only one standard, one unit of account. People differ – and among them governments – and so do their viewpoints, circumstances and objectives. The most useful unit of account for one country will not necessarily be the same as for another country. Also, the same people or the same country may use different standards of value for different purposes.

Countries that are closely linked to the U.S. economy or money system may use the U.S. dollar as their ultimate unit of account, while other countries or areas may prefer to express their monetary reserves in terms of another asset, like gold. In that case we can measure the gold value of these reserves, either directly as a certain weight of gold, or, indirectly, as a matter of convenience, in terms of U.S. dollars, assuming a fixed dollar price for gold.

---

12   R. Triffin, *The fate of the pound,* Paris, 1969, p. 18.

When seeking the best common currency denominator we meet a difficulty which does not exist in the case of other units of account (lengths, weights, *etc.*). Money assets do not always have the same fixed quantitative relationship to each other. Currency values can change with regard to each other, and we like to choose a standard of money value which is comparatively stable in relation to the things we wish to buy with our money.

To use this standard of value for measuring our money holdings, however, makes sense only, if we also have access to the particular kind of money from which the unit is taken or the right to convert our money holdings at will into this kind of money at a guaranteed exchange rate. A gold standard in this strict sense of the word (i.e. the use of gold as the most relevant unit of account) cannot exist without a gold 'standard' in the broader and vaguer sense of the word, which implies a widespread use of gold for monetary holdings. Otherwise we have to be satisfied with another unit of account denominated in terms of the money we actually hold or are able to acquire, provided that this finds general acceptance.

This example shows that the choice of the standard of value, originally and essentially a calculating technique, often has something to do with confidence and, therefore, with the function of money as a liquid store of value. This is of paramount importance for any international means of payment that is held in official national monetary reserves. It is with regard to this store function that the choice of the unit of account is most significant. Money holdings are expressed in terms of the means of payment that is regarded as having the most stable value, and these holdings must be convertible into the trusted asset at a fixed exchange rate or have a guaranteed value expressed in terms of that asset.

It is only because the U.S. dollar still has a fixed gold value that the function of gold in this respect is a more or less hidden one. As to confidence, behind many dollar statements we find gold. For instance, all computations relating to the currencies of IMF members for the purpose of applying the provisions of the Fund Agreement are on the basis of their par values (if established); these par values are 'expressed in terms of gold as a common denominator or in terms of the United States dollar of the weight and fineness in effect on July 1, 1944' [13]. Thus, whether the

---

13 *Fund Agreement*, Art. IV, Section 1. Section 8 provides that the gold value of the Fund's assets shall be maintained, unless a uniform proportionate change in the par values of the currencies of all members takes place and the Fund decides not to maintain the gold value of the Fund's assets by an eighty-five percent

dollar stands for itself, or for the unit of account used in measuring the reserve positions in the General Account [14] of the Fund, or whether it is used for the purpose of conducting the operations of the Special Drawing Account [15], it represents a fixed gold value.

In these circumstances, the use of the expression 'standard' is clearly often rather confusing. Indeed it is quite inappropriate as a description of the functioning of the international monetary system (which means the way that nations cooperate in the monetary field). To use it in that way would be an anachronism dating from the time when one single kind of international money (gold) performed almost exclusively the functions of means of payment and store of value: in those times obviously gold was also the *standard* of value and the use of the expression 'gold standard' could easily be extended to apply also to the whole international monetary regime, which was a gold regime.

Nowadays, gold has still an important place on the international monetary scene, especially as a standard of value; yet we cannot speak of gold 'standard' in a general sense any more. Which standard we apply in our calculations depends on the specific purpose of the calculations. When international money functions as a means of international payment, we mostly use the dollar standard; when it functions as a liquid store of value, gold is still widely used, notably in General Account and the Special Drawing Account of the International Monetary Fund, the main international monetary institutions.

Saying that a single *general* money standard can not exist because of the difference between the purposes for which standards are used means that it is *a fortiori* impossible to establish a general standard to measure the value of money in terms of non-monetary goods [16]. The value of

majority of the total voting power. Before the amendment of the Articles which took effect on July 28, 1969, a simple majority was required, and the Executive Board could act independently. Since 1969 this power *not* to maintain the gold value of the Fund's assets – in the said fairly imaginary situation of a uniform proportionate change in all par values – is listed among the powers of the Board of Governors (in Art. XII) and cannot be delegated to the Executive Directors.

14 On the 'General Account', see the following section, in particular footnote 22 below.

15 Art. XXI, Section 2 of the *Fund Agreement* reads: 'The unit of value of special drawing rights shall be equivalent to 0.888 671 gram of fine gold'.

16 H. J. Stokvis seeks to attach to the expression 'money standard' the meaning of a fixed relationship between a monetary unit of account and one ore more non-monetary goods (*Bretton Woods en het international monetair bestel* (Leyden, 1948, Chapter I). The idea of fixing the exchange rate between a monetary unit of account and a composite unit of commodities is an interesting one. Taking *all* goods into such a unit gives us, according to Stokvis, 'the only meaningful sense of the concept

money is the result of human valuation of the things which can be done with money. As as subjective human act, this valuation can *per definitionem* not be of an 'objective' (in the sense of 'generally valid') character: human acts differ because human beings and their responsibilities differ. For the rest it seems to me that the use of the word monetary standard outside the field of *monetary* accounting complicates things unduly from the linguistic point of view. It is best to confine the term 'money standards' to units for accounting *monetary* amounts rather than the *value* of money, just as standards of lengths measure distances [17].

It may be that before long the SDR will become so firmly established as an international currency and become such an *integrating factor* in international economics, that it may turn into a generally applied unit of account, not indirectly *via* gold, but directly as a common denominator of national currencies, to be used by the monetary authorities of the countries that participate in the Special Drawing Account.

In the longer run it might be possible when the SDRs become a legal and *de facto* currency denominator to uncouple them completely from gold, or at least to make their gold value subject to deliberate change. A modification of the SDR parity of the dollar would then be possible while maintaining the dollar's *gold* value; such an arrangement would probably diminish the resistance of the U.S. Congress to a possible dollar adjustment. Gold would thus keep its 'dollar character', i.e. it would remain being a claim on a fixed amount of dollars. The only difference is that it would no longer serve as a hedge against dollar depreciation. In practice, however, it does not serve that purpose at present either.

Speculation on possible changes in the gold value of SDRs is not much to be feared or expected: SDRs are not directly convertible into gold; they may not be used for a mere change in the composition of a country's reserves; and holding them is ruled by collectively agreed principles.

As long as the U.S. dollar is widely used as an intervention currency in the exchange markets, a change in its exchange rate vis-à-vis other currencies is only possible through action by the monetary authorities

---

of money standard' (p. 21). Such a concept cannot be valid, because both people and their valuations differ; no one is interested in the money value of a basket wherein all the goods in the world are represented in a particular set of ratios. Nevertheless, the idea of a fixed relationship between a commodity unit of a more restricted and subjectively established composition and a monetary unit, put forward in particular in connection with the commodity currency proposals, is very interesting in many respects.

17 This is why it seems to me preferable to speak of 'commodity (reserve) currency plans' than of 'commodity *standard* proposals'.

of other major currency countries. While this does not mean that a change in the parity of the dollar is impossible [18], it does mean that it requires an agreement with other countries. In passing, international deliberation would, in fact, be no less desirable if the dollar were not the principle intervention currency.

As things now are, a 'de-internationalization' of the value of monetary gold stocks by pegging it unchangeably and exclusively to the dollar would, of course, be unacceptable. But this would change if the gold component of world reserves decreased relatively to the SDR component as part of the gradual demonetization of gold [19], and the financial functions and significance of SDRs were enhanced. Possible ways of improving the status of SDRs as a reserve asset outlined in chapter V.

III. SDRS VERSUS OTHER RESERVE ASSETS

In this section we will briefly pay some attention to the characteristics of the main kinds of reserve assets by IMF members. This is not the place to enter into detail concerning the functioning of the Special Drawing Account; for this, reference may be made to the official documents and numerous other publications [20].

18 See on the dollar as intervention currency: *The situation of the key currencies*, Remarks by Otmar Emminger at the International Financial Conference on the Financial Outlook, Geneva, 19th May 1970, published in: Deutsche Bundesbank, *Auszüge aus Presseartikeln*, 5th June 1970, in particular p. 5: 'It is probably true to say that the United States, because of its inevitably passive role in the exchange markets, could change its parity in a meaningful sense (that is to say: against other important currencies) only by some sort of an agreement or understanding with other major countries. But, still, from a technical point of view it is not entirely unable to change it'. On the use of the dollar as the 'fixed centre of the system': 'I doubt whether in the longer run this is a viable system, except if the dollar also sets an acceptable standard of stability in terms of purchasing power'.
19 In addition, a downward parity adjustment of the dollar would be more acceptable than at present, as the *dollar* component of global reserves by the SDRs will be put down; it is the use of the dollar as an *international* reserve asset rather than its being a financial claim on the United States that causes the greatest objection to dollar devaluation.
20 Besides the sources mentioned in footnote 6 to chapter I, I may refer to the IMF publication *Allocation of special drawing rights for the first basic period*, Washington D.C., 1969, which contains the official text of the proposal by the $ 3.5 billion), January 1, 1971 (approx. $ 3 billion) and January 1, 1972 (approx. $ 3 billion). Two excellent short articles on the background and contents of the Special Drawing Account facility are: Otmar Emminger, 'The Brave New World of SDRs', *International Currency Review*, 1969, pp. 3-12, and Martin Barrett,

IMF statistics [21] distinguish four categories of international liquid stores of value held in the world's monetary reserves: gold, foreign exchange, reserve positions in the Fund and SDRs. The unit of account of all these categories is the U.S. dollar, though behind the dollar stands gold, as we saw in the previous section.

It is interesting to note that not all these categories do perform all the three monetary functions mentioned in the first section of this chapter. Reserve positions in the Fund have only one function: that of a liquid store of value. Foreign exchange is the most 'all round' kind of money: in all international monetary transactions it is involved as a means of payment, while it generally serves as unit of account and store of value. It is not only central bank money (in the sense of money used for settlements between central banks); it is also used outside the official circuit, so that it can be an instrument with which central banks can intervene in foreign exchange and national money markets.

Gold and SDRs are mainly significant as a store of value. The use of gold as a means of payment is mainly restricted to the official monetary circuit; SDRs as a means of payment and as a store of value are exclusively money for central banks and unlike gold, they are restricted to participants in the Fund's Special Drawing Account. SDRs and reserve positions in the Fund are the assets having the most specific and limited functions: they circulate only between official monetary institutions. Unlike these IMF moneys (and foreign exchange), gold has a double function as money and commodity.

SDRs are used as a direct and automatic claim on convertible currencies; they replace currencies as a store of value. Thus is it just as true to say that SDRs are a store of value (monetare 'reserve') as to say that they are a means of payment between central banks; central banks may use SDRs to buy currencies from each other. If SDRs are 'held', their store of value character prevails; if they are 'spent', they function in their means of payments role (see footnote 18 to chapter V). Of course SDRs are fully intended to be 'reserves to hold' – in the sense that they

---

'Activation of the special drawing rights facility in the IMF', Federal Reserve Bank of New York, *Monthly Review*, February 1970, pp. 40-46. A more critical comment is given in another short article: Gerhard Kolb, 'Vorzüge und Gefahren der IWF-Sonderziehungsrechte', *Zeitschrift für das gesamte Kreditwesen*, August 1, 1970, pp. 709-714. A detailed explanation of the functioning of the Special Drawing Account is to be found in: Joseph Gold, *Special drawing rights* (56 pages), Washington D.C., 1969 (IMF *Pamphlet Series*, No. 13).
21 See *International Financial Statistics*, monthly issued by the IMF, Washington D.C.

will not belong to any central bank's (currency) working balances. To the extent that SDRs are earned, they are a kind of compulsory investment of currencies; when they are spent, disinvestment takes place. A direct use of SDRs as a means of payment, however, can be made in certain transactions with the General Account of the Fund (Fund Agreement, Art. XXV, Section 7).

The differences between reserve positions in the Fund and SDRs deserve more attention, especially as misunderstandings often rise about their relationship.

It may be stressed that the 'old' IMF account – the General Account – and the Special Drawing Account operate quite separately [22]. It is purely a matter of convenience that the SDRs, which are a novelty in the history of international monetary cooperation, are administered by the Fund. The Fund has the technical and professional facilities for it. The negotiations were carried out to a large extent within the Fund organisation; and the agreement establishing the Special Drawing Account has been put into the form of an amendment to the Fund Articles of Agreement. A participant in the Special Drawing Account must be a member of the Fund, but not all IMF members need be Special Drawing Account participants. The only link between the two accounts is that allocations of SDRs are made

22 The *Outline of a facility based on special drawing rights in the Fund* which constituted the basic agreement on the principles of the new facility which was adopted unanimously at the Fund's Annual Meeting in September, 1967, states: 'The operations of and resources available under the Special Drawing Account will be separate from the operations of the present Fund, which will be referred to as the General Account'. The *Report of the Executive Directors* of April 16, 1968, explains: 'The separation of the two Accounts does not create a new legal entity. The Fund will continue to be the same institution with a single international personality' (see IMF, *Annual Report* 1968, p. 171 and p. 135 respectively).
As finally worked out, the Special Drawing Account was not kept entirely separate from the General Account. There is an interrelationship with respect to both quotas and voting power. Shortly after the completion of the 'Outline' Mr. Schweitzer could still state: 'Each participant (in the Special Drawing Account) will have a quota, which will *most probably* be the same as its quota in the General Account; and it is *on this quota* that both its entitlement to share in any issue of special drawing rights and, *at least initially* its *voting power* will be based' ('New arrangements to supplement world reserves and their implications for the developing countries', Arthur K. Salomon Lecture delivered by Pierre-Paul Schweitzer, reprinted in *International Financial News Survey*, December 15, 1967, p. 416; my italics). A certain separation as to voting power exists: Section 2 of the 'By-Laws of the International Monetary Fund' presently reads: 'In matters pertaining exclusively to the Special Drawing Account the references in these By-Laws (...) to members of the Fund or to Governors and Executive Directors shall be understood to refer only to members that are participants and Executive Directors appointed or elected by at least one member that is a participant'.

at rates which are expressed as a percentage of participants' Fund quotas, the percentage being the same for all participants in the Special Drawing Account. The fact that the General Account of the Fund can also hold SDRs – and actually does so – does not invalidate the principle that the General Account and the Special Drawing Account are separate.

The specific purpose of the Special Drawing Account is 'to meet the need, as and when it arises, for a supplement to existing reserve assets' [23]; the purpose of the General Account of the Fund is 'to give confidence to members by making the Fund's resources *temporarily available to them under adequate safeguards,* thus providing them with opportunity to correct maladjustments in their balance of payments without resorting to measures destructive of national or international prosperity' [24].

Thus, the main differences are follows:

The General Account is an international credit institution through which the IMF finances members' balance-of-payments deficits for three to five years; the Special Drawing Account represents reserves which can be used by participants without repayment within a fixed period (provided that, according to the present rules [25], the average of a country's daily holdings of SDRs in each period of five years may not be less than 30 percent of the average of its daily net cumulative allocation of special drawing rights over the same period).

Drawing rights in the General Account are backed by the resources of the Fund, raised out of contributions of members (quota subscriptions) and possible borrowings; these resources are made available by the Fund only under 'adequate safequards'; Fund credit, therefore, constitutes 'conditional' liquidity. The drawing country has to fulfil certain conditions, notably the adoption of a sound economic policy program which will enable it to repay the Fund credit in due time. The use of drawing rights which do not go beyond the 'reserve position in the Fund' is, however, unconditional; these can be called on automatically.

---

23 *Fund Agreement,* Art. XXI.
24 *Ibid.,* Art. I (v); my italics. See for a historical discussion of the General Account: 'The International Monetary Fund: use and supply of resources', Bank of England, *Quarterly Bulletin,* December 1968, pp. 37-51; for excellent explanations of the functioning of the Fund: *Introduction to the Fund,* IMF *Pamphlet Series* No. 1; J. Marcus Fleming, *The International Monetary Fund, its form and functions,* IMF *Pamphlet Series,* No. 2; Rudolf Kroc, *The financial structure of the Fund,* IMF *Pamphlet Series,* No. 5. The 'reform of the Fund' (General Account) that took effect with the amendment of the Fund's Articles of Agreement that became effective on July 28, 1969, is described in Joseph Gold, *The reform of the Fund,* IMF *Pamphlet Series,* No. 12.
25 *Fund Agreement,* Schedule G, 1 (a) (i) and Art. XXV, Section 6.

A reserve position in the Fund consists of: 1) the original, so-called 'basic', gold tranche, 2) the so-called 'super' gold tranche, 3) credit claims against the Fund [26]. On joining the Fund a member may draw its gold tranche (normally 25 percent of its quota [27]) automatically and unconditionally [28]); after that it may, on certain terms, draw a further 100 percent of its quota, subject to the drawing policies laid down by the Fund's Executive Board [29]. The SDRs, on the other hand, are unconditional. They are not backed by a central *fund* of resources for which an executive

---

26 The three components have in common that they are automatically and unconditionally available for drawing, provided that the country claims a balance-of-payments need to draw; the same holds true for the SDRs. As the reserve position in the General Account and Special Drawing Account both are reserve assets, it is understandable that they are sometimes confused. It may therefore be interesting to sum up the differences between them, as has been done here.
The three components which may add up to a reserve position in the General Account are not entirely similar to each other. Drawing the basic gold tranche means *net* use of the Fund's resources, and, therefore, can only be temporary. Drawings in the super gold tranche mean use of the Fund's resources, but no 'net' use, because essentially it means recycling of financial resources which the country earlier made available to other Fund members through its quota; super gold tranche drawings do not need to be repaid. (The expression 'net use of the Fund's resources' was used in the original text of Article VI, Section 1 (a) of the Fund Agreement). The same holds true for mobilizing loan claims against the Fund, which legally cannot be seen as drawings but as the unwinding of formal creditor positions. Most loans presently outstanding were granted to the Fund under the 'General Arrangements to Borrow', which entered into force on October 24, 1962 between the IMF and the countries of what afterwards became known as the 'Group of Ten'. Loan claims carry some interest (presently 1½ percent), as do super gold tranche positions (normally 1½ percent; this is called 'renumeration'). Basic gold tranche positions do not earn anything.
27 See *Fund Agreement*, Art. III, Section 3 (b) (ii), and Art. XIX (j), where the legal definition of a (basic or super) gold tranche drawing is given.
28 The term 'unconditional' means that no specific conditions as to the future behaviour of the member have to be met; a country that wishes to draw, however, is expected to do so only in case of payments need. This is not a 'condition'; it only means paying due regard to the character of Fund positions as a (source of) *means of payments for member countries.* The same point was made in section 1 of this chapter: a *country* has only to pay something if it has a 'payments deficit'.
29 Drawing rights in the *General Account* thus normally amount to 125 percent of the quota (in which case the Fund's holdings of the member's currency will equal 200 percent of quota; for drawings take the form of purchases of other member's currencies against the currency of the drawing (= purchasing) country. The Fund may waive the 200 percent limit in certain cases). A country can be *drawn upon* for 75 percent of its quota, being the amount of its currency originally held by the Fund (unless it lends additional amounts of its currency to the Fund). The drawing limits in the *Special Drawing Account* are 100 percent of the cumulative allocations to the *drawer,* and normally 200 percent of the cumulative allocations to the *drawee* (unless it consents to a higher limit). (*Fund Agreement,* Art. V, Section 3, 4 and Art. XXV, Section 4).

board has a daily responsibility; the backing for special drawings rights consists of the obligation of participants in the scheme to 'provide on demand currency convertible in fact' [30].

A fundamental difference between the General Account and the Special Drawing Account is the way that they lead to *reserve creation*. The Special Drawing Account has been set up as a means for the deliberate creation of monetary reserves, through an internationally organized process of decision-making, which takes into account the actual need for supplementing world reserves as it is seen by the participants as a whole. On the other hand, an increase in Fund quotas or payment of a subscription to the Fund by a new member, does not of itself increase world reserves. The new member does receive a gold tranche position, but, by the same token, it loses gold, because 25 percent of the subscription has normally to be paid in gold, the remainder being paid in its own currency. The gold tranche rights amount to the difference between 100 percent of the quota and the Fund's holdings of the currency of the country in question below that figure [31]. Reserve creation through the General Account occurs as a *by-product* of net use of the Fund's currency resources in the case where a drawing by a Fund member causes the Fund's holdings of the currency of another member to fall below (or to fall further below) 75 percent, thus creating new reserve assets for the member whose currency is drawn [32]. To the extent that total net drawings decrease

30 *Fund Agreement*, Art. XXV, Section 4; see on the term 'convertible in fact' also Art. XXXII (b) and IMF *Annual Report* 1970, p. 31).
31 *Ibid.*, Art. XIX (j).
32 Several cases have to be distinguished.
1. When the country drawn upon is a *non*-reserve currency country of whose currency the Fund holds not more than 100 percent of its quota, reserve creation occurs to the extent of the *drawing*. The new reserve either accrue to the countries that earn the foreign exchange from the drawing country, which needed the currency for current payments to those countries or they are held by the drawing country to make good earlier reserve losses. Normally the drawee country does not see any change in the level of its reserves, because the currency drawn from its Fund quota is immediately presented to its central bank for conversion into dollars or sterling; its foreign exchange holdings decrease, but the loss is matched by an increase of its super gold tranche position.
2. When the drawee is a *reserve* currency country of whose currency the Fund holds not more than 100 percent of its quota, the amount of new reserves being created in the process is *twice* the amount of the drawing (unless, of course, the currency drawn is converted by the ultimate receiver(s)); the reserve currency country will acquire a super gold tranche position which is not offset by a loss of a same amount of gross reserves.
3. When the drawee is a non-reserve currency country of whose currency the Fund holds more than 100 percent of its quota because the country has made a drawing in the credit tranches (i.e. beyond the gold tranche), *no* new reserves are created

(net repayments take place), reserve positions in the Fund also diminish [33]. The operations of the General Account are not primarily meant to be a technique for reserve creation [34].

to the extent that it is drawn upon for an amount equal or less than its still outstanding credit tranche drawings, because the drawee does not acquire gold tranche rights in exchange.

4. When, in a similar case, the drawee is a reserve currency country, the amount of new reserves that are created is only 100 percent of the drawing instead of 200 percent.

It has been assumed that in each of the four cases the drawing country draws *beyond* its gold tranche; when it draws within its gold tranche it simply uses one of its reserve assets: the reserve creation amounts 0, 100, -100 and 0 percent respectively in the four schematic cases that just have been mentioned.

Outlining these different cases I have, of course, followed the conventional method of counting the liquid liabilities of the monetary authorities of reserve currency countries – on a gross basis – as world reserves, except for the holdings of their currencies by the Fund.

33 The lack of stability of the total level of reserve positions in the Fund is not much of a disadvantage. First, drawings and repayments cancel out against each other, so that net drawings or net repayments are *relatively* small. Since 1962 net drawings have increased annually, with the exception of 1967 when the United Kingdom made large repayments. Second, when net repayments take place, there can be no reason for worrying about an imminent global shortage of reserves: it is a sign of an improvement in world balance of payments positions as a whole.

34 There has been a second way in which the Fund has *incidentally* created international liquidity, that is, by investing $ 800 million worth of gold in U.S. securities and funds. The IMF sold $ 200 million worth of gold to the United States in 1956, $ 300 million in 1959 and $ 300 million in 1960 (see: *Federal Reserve Bulletin,* issued monthly, Washington D.C., table A 74). Upon termination of each investment the Fund can reacquire the same quantity of gold. The United States counts the gold in question as part of its gross monetary reserves. The reason for which the Fund originally decided to invest some of its gold holdings in this way was that it needed the proceeds to pay for deficits in its administrative budgets. That problem no longer exists: since the Fund started operating on a larger scale (roughly since the introduction of internal convertibility for the important European currencies in 1961) it has been earning substantial net income, which has been accumulated in the 'General Reserve'. The General Reserve stood at $ 350 million on April 30, 1970, and the 'Special Reserve' (accumulated earnings from the gold investment) at $ 366 million on the same date (see the balance sheet of the Fund, *Annual Report* 1970, p. 203). In 1970 the Fund withdrew half of the gold investment ($ 400 million).

Thirdly, the Fund has incidentally created reserves through the General Account on the occasion of the last two general rounds of quota increases, when it decided to mitigate the effects of gold subscriptions for quota payments on the gold stocks of the reserve currency countries (which were to be called upon to offer gold in exchange for dollars and sterling to countries needing gold for their IMF subscriptions) by selling gold from its own holdings in an amount not exceeding $ 150 million and $ 700 million respectively. (See *Annual Report* 1965, p. 127 and 1970, p. 180). These measures *prevented the decline* in world reserves which would have resulted from using sterling for buying dollars or gold and dollars for buying gold from the United Kingdom and the United States respectively. *(cont. p. 54)*

The establishment of the Special Drawing Account was an excellent step forward in improving the supply mechanism of international reserves. Its purpose is indeed to get rid of the process of uncontrolled reserve creation which is a *by-product* of other financial developments, notably the balance-of-payments deficits of reserve currency countries, or of the availibility of gold, and hence is not a satisfactory and reliable source for the creation of adequate amounts of world reserves. If the world remains dependent on a reserve center running deficits for the creation of the reserves it needs, the lack of proper international control of the procedure of international liquidity creation is more serious than the possible loss of confidence in the strength of the reserve currency in question. The international community must avoid being dependent on purely national policies, an unsatisfactory situation that can easily give rise to international conflicts. This is why the Special Drawing Account is an historical development in the right direction.

The process of creating SDRs is an international procedure. This makes the SDRs in some ways superior to gold, the more so because the creation of monetary gold reserves is not infinitely variable, because of the physical and economic limits on supply.

Another characteristic of SDRs is that they are the most 'durable' asset. Unlike gold, they cannot be 'demonetized' by individual holders; unlike convertible currency they do not vanish when spent in a particular country (dollars spent in the United States disappear as international reserves). SDRs can only be destroyed by collective 'cancellation' decisions (besides withdrawal of individual participants from the scheme); otherwise they are absolutely permanent.

Once they have entered the international monetary circuit, both SDRs and gold are international money in the full sense of the term; they 'bear not the mark of a particular country' – to use the words of President de Gaulle. SDRs are meant in particular to be a supplement to *gold. Both*

Fourthly, the 1965 quota resolution allowed the Fund also to deposit amounts not exceeding $ 250 million and $ 100 million worth of gold as 'General Deposits' in New York and London respectively, to compensate for the actual reserve losses incurred by the United States and the United Kingdom as a result of the general quota increase.

Fifthly, the Fund has created reserves through the General Account by paying remuneration on super gold tranche positions and making distributions of net income, or payment of interest on loans.

The Fund has never invested any part of its reserves. This would, of course, be a sixth method of reserve creation; a 'link to development finance' through lending some part of the Fund's reserves to the IDA or investment in World Bank bonds is conceivable.

SDRs and gold serve to finance the possible positive difference between the world total of balance-of-payments surpluses and the world total of deficits.

Gold, in the meantime, still plays an important role. It is the *most* unconditional and most liquid asset that exists; it can be used throughout the world, East or West. Many countries attach great value to it, and not only in view of the possibility of military conflicts [35]. One of the reasons why I consider SDRs superior to gold is their relation to the U.S. dollar. Dollars can be converted into gold or SDRs [36], and they generally have to be so converted, unless the dollar holding country sees no harm in the political implications of holding a large dollar component in its reserves. When dollars are converted into gold, the

---

35   The French prime minister Chaban-Delmas made the following statement in an interview with the financial weekly '*La vie française*' (January 30, 1970): 'La monnaie est l'expression d'une souveraineté et, dans les règlements internationaux, l'or seul est politiquement neutre et indépendant des relations politiques qui lient les états. La plupart des grands pays du monde le comprennent parfaitement, qui maintiennent sous forme d'or une fraction appréciable de leurs réserves. Les États-Unis eux-mêmes, malgré la pré-éminence du dollar dans les transactions courantes, veuillent à éviter que leur stock de métal ne se reduise et cherchent plutôt à le reconstituer'.

Also illustrative are the utterances of E. Reinhardt during a lecture in Essen, October 1970, according to which 'jeder Staat das natürliche Bedürfnis hat, seine Währungsreserven in einer Form zu halten, die ihm einen maximalen Grad an Konvertibilität und Stabilität in Friedens- und Kriegszeiten sichert.

Dieser Anforderung entspricht das *Gold* grundsätzlich viel besser als Devisen oder Sonderziehungsrechte; denn deren Wert hängt entscheidend von der Haltung der grossen Schlüsselwährungsländer ab, während das Gold diesen Einflüssen praktisch nicht ausgesetzt ist und deshalb für *mittlere und kleine* Staaten ein wertvolles Mittel bildet, die eigene wirtschaftliche und finanzielle *Unabhängigkeit* gegenüber den Grossen dieser Erde zu verteidigen. Darum waren die Nationen, soweit sie nicht in politischem Abhängigkeitsverhältnis standen, stets bestrebt, einen nennenswerten Teil ihrer Währungsreserven im gelben Metal zu halten. Die Diskussion um die Demonetisierung des Goldes kommt somit einige *politische Tragweite* zu, welche bei der Meinungsbildung über diese Frage nicht übersehen werden sollte.' (*Neue Zürcher Zeitung,* October 26, 1969).

Quite in contrast with the views just quoted and also rather typical is the following U.S. comment on the gold arrangements between the IMF and South-Africa (and, behind the scenes, the United States) concluded in December 1969: 'Gold's power to disrupt the international monetary mechanism has now been greatly reduced, and possibly ended. Under-Secretary of the Treasury Volcker has voiced the hope that this latest move will dispose of gold as a 'contentious problem'.' (*New York Times,* January 5, 1970). (See for the full text of the arrangements between the IMF and South-Africa: *International Financial News Survey,* January 16, 1970, p. 13/14).

36   See *Fund Agreement*, Art. XXV, Section 2 (b) (i): 'A participant, in agreement with another participant, may use its special drawing rights to obtain an equivalent amount of its own currency held by the other participant'.

burden (loss of interest) of this disciplinary act is carried entirely by the country that offers its dollars to the United States for final settlement [37]. To the extent that dollars are converted into SDRs – also a final money instrument, not having the character of an IOU – this burden is *distributed* over all the countries which have creditor positions within the SDR system [38]. The burden also is lighter, because excess holdings do carry some interest (1½ percent), unlike gold.

The creation of SDRs gave rise to an entirely new problem for the international community. Not only the amount to be created each year, but also the manner in which the newly created reserves should enter into the system, required deliberate collective decisions. Unlike that of new monetary gold or newly created dollars, the *distribution* [39] of SDRs could not be left to a more or less spontaneous process (sometimes called 'free economic forces'). Distribution indeed seems to be the major unsatisfactorily resolved issue relating to special drawing rights.

37 The former President of the Netherlands Bank, Mr. M. W. Holtrop, wrote in his *Annual Report* 1964 (p. 22): 'It is the 'gold' countries, including the Netherlands, that confine their stock of currencies to (no more than) an ample cash supply which, by sacrificing interest, bear the burden of preventing the gold exchange standard from becoming a pure currency standard, the inflationary or noninflationary character of which would be solely determined by the reserve currency country's internal policies uninhibited by any external consideration.'

38 The creditor positions in the SDR system ('excess holdings' of SDRs, i.e. holdings beyond the net cumulative allocations) are over time distributed according to a ratio which in principle is uniform for all countries holding excess balances. *(Fund Agreement,* Art. XXV, Section 5 (b) and Schedule F). See on the harmonization of SDR holdings also chapter V, section 6, second paragraph.

39 I.e. not the distribution of excess holdings of SDRs referred to in the preceding footnote, but the distribution of the initial holdings, the allocations of SDRs by which the SDRs are *created.*

IV. The present distribution of newly created special drawing rights

I. THE CRITERION: THE FUND'S QUOTA STRUCTURE

The rates at which SDR allocations are made are expressed as percentages of quotas on the date of each decision to allocate, or other dates on which the Fund may decide; the percentages are the same for all participants [1].

In this chapter we will pay some attention, therefore, to the structure of the Fund's quotas and its determinants, with special reference to developing countries.

When judging the financial adequacy of quotas of individual countries or country groups, we have to bear in mind that quotas perform more than one function. This is one of the reasons why the original quotas and the later [2] quota changes have been *compromises;* different *weights* had to be applied in view of the several functions of quotas. The other reason was that the quotas have been the result of a negotiation process in which the interests of a great number of members had to be harmonized.

---

1 *Fund Agreement,* Art. XXIV, Section 2 (b) and (c) (iii).
2 Decisions to increase total quotas were taken in 1959 (about 54 percent), and in 1965 (about 33 percent), and in 1970 (35.5 percent). Article III, Section 2 of the Fund Agreement lays down that 'The Fund shall at intervals of not more than five years conduct a general review, and if it deems it appropriate propose an adjustment, of the quotas of the members. It may also, if it thinks fit, consider at any other time the adjustment of any particular quota at the request of the member concerned (. . .)'.

The Fund's quotas determine the following rights and obligations of members:

1. Payment of subscription, equal to 100 percent of the quota: normally 25 percent in gold and 75 percent in the national currency of the member [3].
2. Extent of drawing rights, normally 125 percent of the quota [4]. In addition, the Fund's special drawing facilities are expressed in terms of quota tranches (see section 3 of this chapter: Compensatory and Buffer Stock Financing Facilities).
3. Extent of obligation to allow drawings upon the members' own monetary reserves, namely 75 percent of the quota [4]. (Legally, this obligation is implied in the payment mentioned under *1* above: when a country is drawn upon, all that happens is that the Fund makes use of *its own resources* (i.e. its holdings of the currency of the drawee country; in most cases, however, the drawing country converts the currency drawn into a reserve currency, so that the former country loses foreign exchange)).
4. Voting power; each member has 250 votes (the so-called 'basic votes') plus one additional vote for each part of its quota equivalent to $ 100,000 [5].
5. Distribution of the Fund's net income after payment of (presently) ½ percent of the average super gold tranches to the holders of super tranche positions [6].
6. Extent of allocation of SDRs (see footnote 1).

At the Bretton Woods conference in July, 1944, where the original Fund Agreement was drawn up, the first five (virtually four) factors listed above

3 *Fund Agreement*, Art. III, Sections 3-5.
4 See footnote 29 to chapter III.
5 *Fund Agreement*, Art. XII, Section 5; a related provision with respect to the size of quotas is Section 3 (b) (i) of the same Article, which states that five out of the Executive Directors (at present 20) shall be appointed by the five members having the largest quotas. Section 3 (c) provides that the two members having the largest super gold tranche positions over the two years preceding the regular elections of directors have the right to appoint a director. Being entitled to *appoint* instead of to *elect* does, of course, not alter the voting power in the Executive Board of the *country* concerned; it may however diminish the number of votes the individual *Executive Director* can cast. A director who has been elected by countries A, B, C and D represents more votes in the Board, than he does when he has been *appointed* by country A alone.
6 *Fund Agreement*, Art. XII, Section 6 (b). Super gold tranche holders receive a regular 'renumeration' of 1½ percent (see Art. V, Section 9). Distribution of net income to all members has not taken place as yet.

were taken into account in the process of drafting and negotiating. Hence, while the discussions on quotas, may have started from a uniform formula concept, the multipurpose character of the quotas prevented them from being determined rigidly by any one formula, or by exclusive attention to economic data [7]. Just as in the case of the general reviews of quotas approved by the Board of Governors in 1959, 1965 and 1970, at Bretton Woods the 'negotiations and compromises took place within the limitations imposed by a number of generally accepted principles. It was assumed that the Fund would ultimately have assets of about $ 10 billion, but that the quotas of the Bretton Woods participants would amount to about $ 8 billion, thus leaving $ 2 billion for new members. Account also had to be taken of the relationship of the U.S. quota to the U.K. quota, and of the relationship of the quotas of other large countries to these two. It was clear that the United States had to supply a major part of the Fund's assets and that the major postwar demands would be for gold or dollars. Moreover, it was realized that countries that could pay the largest amounts of gold and convertible currencies to the Fund would not necessarily be those that would wish to make the largest use of its resources. Given this general framework, it would have been helpful to have a base line, more or less sharply defined, from which to start negotiation and discussion' [8]. 'Tentative quota calculations based on economic data, according to the so-called Bretton Woods formula [9], were made at Bretton

7 See Oscar L. Altman, at the time Advisor in the Research and Statistics Department of the Fund, in his interesting article 'Quotas in the International Monetary Fund', *Staff Papers,* August 1956, pp. 129-150. He also mentions literature on the subject.
8 Altman, 'Quotas', p. 136.
9 Altman *(ibid.,* p. 138/139) mentions the 'real' Bretton Woods formula (quoting also some literature of the years 1945 and 1946, including the report of the Norwegian Bretton Woods Delegation to the Norwegian Parliament, which contained less 'real' descriptions of the formula). According to Altman, 'The complete formula was: *Determine the sum of*
(1) 2 percent of national income for 1940 (if this year was available and appropriate);
(2) 5 percent of holdings of gold and U.S. dollars as of July 1, 1943 (if this date was available and appropriate);
(3) 10 percent of average annual imports, 1934-38;
(4) 10 percent of maximum variation of annual exports, 1934-38.
Increase this sum by
(5) the percentage ratio of average annual exports, 1934-38, to national income'.
Rather illustrative is Altman's quotation from (p. 141/142) Professor R. Mossé, a member of the French delegation at Bretton Woods: 'The Chinese and the Indians would have liked a large weight for population. For the British, the figures on foreign trade were the only truly important ones. The Americans were more interested in national income. The French recommended a formula giving strong

Woods for many, but not for all, of the countries that took part in the Conference. The formula was generally, though informally, known at Bretton Woods. At no time has it had any official status and, (. . .) it is not mentioned in the Bretton Woods Agreement. The calculations that were made, and the data that were used, are nowhere officially recorded [10]. It is known that, in the nature of the case, many of the formula calculations were made hurriedly, that they may have contained errors, and that of necessity some of the data were fragmentary or inaccurate. Nevertheless, calculations of greater or less authority and accuracy were made for many countries, and these were often used as a starting point for discussion. The practical difficulties of making formula calculations in some cases, e.g., the U.S.S.R., could hardly be overlooked, and a quota of $ 1.2 billion was agreed for the U.S.S.R. 'almost entirely in recognition of its political and potential economic importance' [11].'

It is interesting to compare this historical statement with the view of the U.S. experts in 1943 that a quota for each member country should be computed by '*an agreed upon formula* which gives due weight to the important relevant factors, e.g., a country's holdings of gold and free foreign exchange, the magnitude and the fluctuations of its balance of payments, its national income, *etc.*' [12]. The provision for 'an agreed upon formula', Altman remarks, 'was later dropped. It does not appear either in the April 1944 Joint Statement by Experts on the Establishment of an International Monetary Fund or in the Articles of Agreement drawn up at Bretton Woods in July 1944' [13].

It is curious to note, however, that the outcome of these negotiations,

weight to population, including the population of overseas territories, and to gold holdings. With respect to the Soviets, it was generally admitted that any advantageous formula had to give weight to a coefficient K, representing their sacrifices and heroism. In the end, quotas were established more or less arbitrarily by the United States in a series of deals. Certain quotas (China and the U.S.S.R., for example) simply corresponded with the current military and political situation. In any event, while it must be admitted that the scale of quotas does not correspond in any precise way with the resources and the needs of the different countries, it nevertheless reflects in a general way the hierarchy of economic importance of the nations concerned. (*Le Système Monétaire de Bretton Woods et les Grand Problèmes de L'Après-Guerre*, Paris, 1948, pp. 47-48).'

10   The same holds true for the later calculations on general quota adjustments, which were not officially published either.

11   Altman, 'Quotas', p. 137/138.

12   *Preliminary draft outline of a proposal for an International Stabilization Fund of the United and Associated Nations* (Revised July 10, 1943), Section II, 4, quoted by Altman, 'Quotas', p. 137. In the end, the Soviet Union did not join the Fund.

13   Altman, 'Quotas', p. 137.

carried on as they were *without* the application of an agreed formula, did *later* appear to be an 'agreed general formula'! This, at least, is what seems to have happened during the discussions preceding the adoption of the agreement on special drawing rights. In the report of the Deputies of the Group of Ten, issued July 1966 [14], paragraph 43 reads: '(As stated in paragraph 37), there is general agreement that distribution of additional reserve assets should take place in accordance with an *agreed general formula.* Most members consider that allocations of newly created reserve assets should be determined on the basis, either of *IMF quotas,* or of *IMF quotas plus G.A.B.* [15] *commitments,* or of a *formula similar to the one on which present IMF quotas are based*' (my italics).

Apparently, the Deputies believed that the 'Bretton Woods formula' did in fact primarily determine the Fund's quota structure. Admittedly, to the *extent* that the mysterious formula did play a role, its impact on the quota *structure* has been more or less preserved until now. The three general quota increases that have taken place since Bretton Woods were to a large extent uniform for each country; 'selective' increases were agreed for those cases where economic developments had made quotas 'clearly out of line' [16]. But in these reviews too, statistical data and in- genious calculations (numerous *variations* of the 'Bretton Woods for- mula' [17]) served only as a reference point, a starting point for the negotia- tions.

I would not deny that the allocation of newly created SDRs must be made on the basis of an *agreed* formula, expressed in economic terms, but then it must be an appropriate one. In the next chapter we shall

---

14 See footnotes 5 and 20 to chapter I.
15 General Arrangements to Borrow, see footnote 20 to chapter I.
16 The 1959 increase was almost totally a 'general' (i.e. uniform) increase of 50 percent; except for Canada, the Federal Republic of Germany and Japan, which received increases of 83 percent, 72 percent and 100 percent respectively; (shortly after the general increase, 14 smaller countries also requested and received special increases). On the occasion of the 1965 adjustment of quotas, the general increase was 25 percent, but 16 countries received larger, so-called 'selective' increases. In 1970 percentages varied widely, from 25 percent upward; the one exception was the U.K. (increase: only 15 percent). This was to align its quota to some extent to post-war economic developments (Source: IMF *Annual Reports* 1959, 1965 and 1970). The quota of China has remained constant ever since 1945 in view of the separation, shortly after the war, from Mainland China. Even at Bretton Woods the Chinese quota was already 'somewhat inflated by American ideology' – to use the words of Roy F. Harrod, quoted by Altman ('Quotas', p. 141).
17 See J. Keith Horsefield, 'Fund quotas', *Finance and Development,* September 1970, pp. 7-12, and David Williams, 'The fifth general review of quotas', *ibid.,* pp. 13-18.

discuss a formula which, although extremely simple, has a more rational basis than those referred to by the Deputies. The SDR negotiatiors did in fact not study the distribution problem any more thoroughly. The Fund's quota structure was considered at least a distribution criterion everyone was used to; it had a respectable history, and had proven to be workable in the Fund; it presented itself as a readily available solution that was in fact already in being. There was, for that matter, not much time available for entering into secondary problems. The main thing at stake was the creation of a mechanism for handling *total* world reserves; the *distribution* of SDRs was not considered as having a bearing on the *total* to be created.

The point, however, which they overlooked was that the *purpose* of the new system of reserve creation was to be different from that of the old Fund, where, as we have seen, reserve creation took place, not as a *purpose* but only as a by-product. It ought not to have been accepted without debate that the distribution of Fund quotas would *also* provide the right distribution for allocating new reserves, even if it were agreed that the quota structure of the *General Account* was ideal in purely economic terms. The main purpose of the original Fund was the creation of *conditional credits for the financing of short-term or medium-term balance of payments deficits;* the size of these credits was (and is) limited by the ability of the Fund members to repay, i.e. the prospects open to them for restoring their payments equilibrium through internal adjustment processes; the need for these credits was (and is) directly related to the short-term or medium-term balance of payments fluctuations that they generally might expect [18].

II. OBJECTIONS TO THE USE OF THE FUND'S QUOTA STRUCTURE AS A BASIS FOR ALLOCATING SPECIAL DRAWING RIGHTS

Reserve creation was not one of the purposes of the old Fund. These were directed primarily to ensuring sound behaviour by *individual* members; reserve creation, however, is necessary because of the *structural deficiences in the global reserve supply mechanism.* The General Account deals with drawings by individual countries; an activation of the special drawing rights facility, on the other hand, respresents one big 'drawing' by the world as a whole, so to speak.

18 In the event of 'fundamental disequilibria', of course, exchange rates have to be corrected. The philosophy of the Fund prohibits financial support for unrealistic parities.

This does of course not mean that the two are not interrelated; through the Special Drawing Account the Fund has 'to meet the long-term global need, as and when it arises, to supplement existing reserve assets', but this has to be done 'in such manner as will promote the attainment of its purposes' [19]. The purposes of the Fund [20] are served both by the General Account and the Special Drawing Account. Thus, the latter must prevent a global shortage of reserves, at the same time as favouring 'the expansion and balanced growth of international trade' and contributing 'to the promotion and maintenance of high levels of employment and real income and to the development of the productive resources of all members' as well as promoting exchange stability, *etc.* These purposes of the Fund since Bretton Woods would receive a setback if a shortage of global reserves should occur. Countries would resort to such practices as restrictions in their international transactions, competitive exchange depreciation and the like, in their scramble for reserves.

While the establishment of the Special Drawing Account itself is a splendid example of the 'collaboration on international monetary problems' referred to in the first paragraph of Article I of the Fund Agreement [21], the important difference between the General Account and the Special Drawing Account is that the former grants *short* or *medium term credits* with a view to each country's *individual* situation, while the latter has been set up to put the creation of *world reserves* on a proper basis, and to control the *long run* development of the total of world reserves. This primary occupation with the level of total world reserves explains the fact that the initial *distribution* of special drawing rights got little attention.

First objection

In considering the *total* amount of reserve creation, the distribution aspect cannot be totally neglected. My first objection to the chosen formula is that it does not *economize* the reserves to be created. This is a major disadvantage of the present system. As SDRs perform the function of

19 *Fund Agreement*, Art. XXIV, Section 1 (a).
20 These are listed in Article I of the *Fund Agreement;* the Article mentioned in the preceding footnote adds to that list the avoidance of 'economic stagnation and deflation as well as excess demand and inflation in the world', a purpose with which the Special Drawing Account is supposed to be closely related.
21 The following is the first purpose listed in Article I: 'To promote international monetary cooperation through a permanent institution which provides the machinery for consultation and collaboration on international monetary problems'.

'owned' reserves, their steady accumulation will constitute in the long run a huge mass of purchasing power that, unlike 'conditional' liquidity, may be unloaded by individual countries without any international control. International monetary policy lacks the instruments that domestic monetary authorities have at their disposal to influence the monetary impact of the level of the money stock.

'Deliberate reserve creation should be neither geared nor directed to the financing of balance of payments deficits of individual countries but rather (. . .) it should provide for the global needs of the system' [22]. But this does not prevent the participants in the Special Drawing Account, especially the larger ones, from pressing for the creation of substantial reserves, when they are or expect to be in deficit, simply because the deficits are theirs! There is a real danger that countries will try to secure the maximum possible allocation for themselves (for these are gratuitous), thus forcing up total SDR creation proportionately. In other words, under the Fund's quota structure it is to the advantage of (the major deficit) countries to argue systematically in favor of a large amount of SDR creation; and the fact that allocations are to be made proportionately to all countries [23] spreads this tendency throughout the whole process of reserve creation.

Assuming, as the negotiators of the Fund Articles on special drawing rights seem to have done, that the best method of distributing reserves is to allocate them to *countries,* they could have chosen a better formula. They were right in their assumption that reserve creation should not be geared to the deficits of individual countries, but it might be better to say that reserve creation should not be geared to the deficits of *any given individual* country. The fact is that *from the global economic point of view all countries are not similar,* and that, when considering the best criterion for the distribution of special drawing rights, we may on *economic* grounds distinguish between different *groups* of countries. It may then appear that there is one group that is eligible for SDR allocations and another group that is not. What are the criteria for placing countries

22 Group of Ten, *Report of Deputies,* 1966, paragraph 37.
23 It is true that SDR creation requires a majority of eighty-five percent of the total voting power in the Fund and that this provides a certain guarantee against excessive allocations, but in practice the political influence of the large members on the decision should not be underestimated. In any event, the amount of creation is the result of negotiations in which some large countries have more weight than a number of small countries together, although the total voting strength of the small countries may be substantial. One country for instance has nearly a quarter of total Fund quotas, and this surely means that national motives cannot be abstracted from the position which that country takes in SDR negotiations.

in one or other of these groups? Individual deficits or any other criteria pertaining only to the short term or medium term are excluded. They must be long-term differences between countries.

There are two criteria which *both* happen to result in the same classification of countries. The first has directly to do with the *need for reserves*, the second has a more general, though still economic, character. The two criteria for SDR distribution I have in mind are: *distribution of adjustment costs* and *distribution of wealth*. The fact that they have not been taken into account gives rise to two other objections to the use of the quota structure criterion.

Second objection

If one wishes to apply an economic criterion for SDR distribution to *countries,* the most accessible is the criterion of the *distribution of adjustment costs*. It is Benjamin J. Cohen who pointed out the connection between 'Adjustment costs and the distribuition of new reserves' [24].

Monetary reserves are held to enable countries with balance of paymets deficits to survive the period they need for the fundamental adjustment of their external payments position at minimum costs. This process of restoring balance of payments equilibria is a global one. The *cost* of adjustment is distributed throughout all countries concerned, but *not proportionately to their disequilibria*. The cost – i.e. 'the amount of real national income foregone during and on account of the adjustment process' [25] – can even be near zero for one country involved in the process and approaching 100 percent for another country.

A large country generally is able to *transfer* its adjustment costs to a small one. The proportion of the adjustment cost which a country must pay in the event of external imbalance is called '*adjustment vulnerability*' by Cohen [26]. Four *structural* attributes of countries are considered by him particularly important in determining the international distribution

24   Title of his essay in the series 'Princeton Studies in International Finance', no. 18, 1966 (35 pages).
25   Benjamin J. Cohen, *Adjustment costs and the distribution of new reserves,* Princeton, 1966, p. 9. He calls this 'transitional cost of adjustment' as distinct from 'continuing cost of adjustment', which is always borne entirely by the deficit country, because, after restoring international equilibrium the former deficit country receives a smaller proportion of the combined output of all countries together. There is therefore no *distribution* problem at this point. I doubt whether it is useful to call this an 'adjustment cost'. It can only be an offset to 'benefits' received earlier when the country was in deficit.
26   *Ibid.*, p. 17.

of adjustment costs: 1) diversification of production, 2) degree of industrialization, 3) international investment status (extent to which the country is a regular exporter of capital) and 4) secular growth rate. Countries having a highly diversified production structure, a considerable degree of industrialization, large capital exports, or a high rate of economic growth over an extended period, have a relatively small adjustment vulnerability, just like a large country vis-à-vis a small country *(ceteris paribus)*. For a discussion of these structural characteristics of national economies I may refer to Cohen [27].

The vulnerability of the weak countries is enhanced by the fact that strong countries (i.e. countries with low vulnerability during the adjustment process, and which can *transfer* their adjustment cost simply by initiating the adjustment process), are likely to be more tolerant of internally generated disturbances than nations lacking such capabilities. This is an extra source of instability in the international economic system [28].

The structural weaknesses mentioned above happen mainly to apply to *developing countries.* 'What we see here is another in the series of vicious circles enmeshing the less developed countries. Because they are over-specialized and concentrate on primary production, developing nations have a relatively high adjustment vulnerability. To reduce their vulnerability they seek to diversify and industrialize. Because of the inadequate supply of development resources available to them, they fall back on their exchange reserves to finance many of their capital imports. But, with their reserves diminished, they find themselves no less vulnerable to external pressures than before' [29].

My second objection, therefore, to the present distribution of SDRs is the same one as Cohen's, namely that, assuming that the *method of allocating SDRs to countries* as such is the best, not all the newly created reserves are distributed to developing countries, whose 'adjustment vulnerability approaches infinity' [30] and which ' until now have been obliged to pay the highest price for the privilege of membership in the (international monetary) system' [31].

I would like to stress that the argument that the developing countries

27 *Ibid.,* pp. 16-29.
28 *Ibid.,* p. 12. See also p. 31: '... the international economy is almost always in transition, with new disturbances always emerging to keep the system in a state of more or less constant flux. For countries with high adjustment vulnerability, such a situation is intolerably costly'.
29 *Ibid.,* p. 33.
30 *Ibid.,* p. 31.
31 *Ibid.,* p. 34.

as a group should be the beneficiaries of newly to be created reserves is intrinsically an economic one. (The daily confusion between expressions like 'economic', 'political', 'humanitarian', 'ethical', will be briefly discussed in chapter VIII.) This argument is based entirely on monetary grounds. It is an economic argument. But there is also in it an element of *justice,* in view of the difference in economic status of developing and developed nations. If this is taken into account in the international monetary cooperation, the economic aspect is *deepened* in the sense meant in section 2 of chapter II. The economic meaning of life receives a greater content than would be strictly necessary to form a *mere concept* of economics. Nevertheless, this additional meaning moment (to use the terminology of Dooyeweerd), is fully economic in nature. We have here an example of what he calls a 'juridical analogy' within the economic law-sphere.

In addition, the argument that world adjustment costs, like all costs, must be kept to a minimum may be considered economic. This argument is only invalid, if one is not interested in the world as a whole. But then part of the content of economics is lost, and one falls back on an individualistic (nationalistic) position, which as we have seen in section 4 of chapter II conflicts with the very core of economics. If SDRs were distributed to developing countries instead of to industrialized countries, those wo are generally the least able to apply '*positive*' adjustment techniques, to use the expression of Staffan B. Linder, quoted by Cohen [32], would at least receive some benefit. Negative adjustment techniques (such as those involving unemployment) are costlier than positive ones (such as those involving technological innovation). Total world adjustment costs would be minimal, therefore, if developing countries were able to handle their balance of payments deficits to a relatively large extent through financing, while the developed countries did so mainly through internal adjustment.

Third objection

My third observation is that we cannot remain indifferent to the fact that wealth is not distributed equally throughout the world. While such inequality may not be very significant with respect to the quotas governing the operations of the General Account of the Fund, the position is different when it comes to SDR allocation. SDRs are intended to be 'owned

32   *Ibid.,* p. 11.

reserves' (as distinct from 'borrowed reserves', e.g. conditional Fund credit or swap credits between central banks). This special feature of SDRs is connected with the rules for 'reconstitution', meaning the rules governing the repayment of drawings on the Special Drawing Account. At present, 70 percent of any SDRs that are allocated may be used without repurchase. In other words, they give the right to permanent acquisition of this amount of real resources from other countries.

It is clear that any theory based on the equalization of wealth and the balanced development of the world economy would lead to allocating SDRs in such a way that the direct benefit will go exclusively to the poorer countries. This is a clearcut economic proposition, but its acceptance implies that the rich countries will refrain from taking a purely nationalistic view. If balanced economic growth were to be an agreed goal of international economic cooperation – and it is one of the explicit purposes of the IMF [33] – there would be little argument against allocating SDRs exclusively to poor countries. Such an arrangement would help to free the world economy from the many interrelated deficiences which as vicious circles keep large sectors of it underdeveloped.

The same argument may be advanced from the ethical point of view. It is interesting that this provides a good illustration of the coherence of (in Dooyeweerdian terms) the modal structure of reality. It is indeed no wonder that the economic and the ethical arguments point to the same practical conclusion. For both the ethical aspect and the economic aspect of reality are universal within their own province, to use Dooyeweerd's terminology [34]. This implies that, ethically speaking, goods should be used as *economically* as possible. In other words, goods should be used in such a way that they have a maximum effect, earn a maximum ethical 'profit'. This is an 'economic analogy within the ethical aspect'. At the same time, under the lead of the ethical principle, the *economic* aspect itself will be 'deepened' ('expanded') by the disclosure of its anticipatory ethical moment (see chapter II, section 2).

SDRs are, in a sense, 'manna from heaven' [35]. The poor are more in

33 *Fund Agreement,* Art. I: 'The purposes of the Fund are: (. . .) (ii) To facilitate the expansion and balanced growth of international trade, and to contribute thereby to the promotion and maintenance of high levels of employment and real income and to the development of the productive resources of all members as primary objectives of economic policy. (. . .)'.
34 *Inleiding tot de encyclopaedie der rechtswetenschap,* Amsterdam, n.d., p. 60.
35 *A proposal to link reserve creation and development assistance.* Report of the Subcommittee on International Exchange and Payments of the Joint Economic Committee, Congress of the U.S., (hereafter to be called: 'Subcommittee'), Washington (U.S. Government Printing Office), 1969, p. 10.

need for it than the rich, not only because they are poor and SDRs mean wealth, but also because, as we have shown earlier in this section, they happen to bear the greater part of the costs of global balance of payments adjustment.

Fourth objection

Even *assuming* that the Fund's quota structure is accepted as a reasonable basis for the allocation of special drawing rights, there is still the difficulty that the economic data on which the quota formulae are based are bound to be taken from the past. *No target is implied.* The *status quo* is made a norm, and the dynamic character of reality is neglected. This objection does not apply to the *General* Account, because it concerns only the short or medium term, unlike the Special Drawing Account which influences in a direct sense members' long-term positions.

It is sometimes said that reserve creation is a matter for the 'major' industrial countries alone. These countries do indeed deserve a good deal of credit for initiating the discussions and studies which ultimately led to the entry into force of the SDR system; this may have been because liquidity and related problems were felt mainly within that group. But this does not mean that only these countries should be considered 'real members of the international monetary system' and thus rightly the main beneficiaries of SDRs. The fact that poor countries play a relatively small role in international monetary affairs is in part due to the unwillingness of rich nations to give them opportunities to trade. If country shares in international trade are to be a determining factor in the allocation of SDRs, it is hardly respectable for the most powerful nations first to prevent the developing countries from raising their exports and then to use the supposedly 'objective' criterion of trading shares as the basis for the distribution of SDRs. Naturally, this criticism scarcely applies to drawing rights in the *General* Account, where what counts is a country's ability to repay short-term or medium-term credit through an internal adjustment process. The relative inability of poor countries to make such an adjustment in the short run must be taken into account. The size of quotas, for that matter, does not rigidly determine the amount of credit to which members of the Fund have access, which is a matter for the Fund Board to decide, according to agreed policies and practices.

Fifth objection

My main argument against using the Fund's quota structure as the basis for the allocation of SDRs is related to the nature of international cooperation, or, as Dooyeweerd would call it: the 'individuality structure' of international cooperation.

As we have seen in chapter II, international policy rests upon voluntary association. International agreements, other than decisions leading to complete integration of national political structures (so that international cooperation is replaced by national policy), are 'functional' ones having *specific* purposes [36].

Global reserve creation is intended to meet the needs of the balance-of-payments adjustment process, in which every country is involved. It would therefore seem only logical that the obligations undertaken by the countries participating in the reserve creation system should serve the interest of the whole international community as such and not any given national policy purpose over which other countries have no control. Participants in the Special Drawing Account – and indeed all countries maintaining free international trade relations – expose themselves to great losses of real resources in the first spending round of newly created SDRs. The more SDRs are created, the greater are the losses of real resources possibly suffered by individual countries. The lack of international control over the purposes for which these resources are used by the countries receiving them is quite lamentable. For national purposes may well conflict with the sound development of the world economy, which is the very purpose of reserve creation. Therefore, as Robert Triffin has said on several occasions recently: *'Internationally agreed SDRs should serve internationally agreed purposes'* [37]; distributing SDRs among countries on the basis of their Fund quotas is *'morally repugnant, economically wasteful and politically unviable'* [38]. I agree with this statement and would therefore oppose all those proposals for linking reserve creation to development assistance that maintain the principle of allocating SDRs to *countries,* even if all future SDRs are allocated to *developing* countries.

---

36 An interesting intermediate form between 'functional' cooperation and complete political integration is provided by the structure which was adopted in 1954 by the three countries constituting the Kingdom of The Netherlands: Art. 3 of the 'Statute' declares a number of specific political areas 'matters of the Kingdom'.
37 Very eloquently explained in Triffin's statement at the hearing before the Subcommittee (see footnote 35) which was held on May 28, 1969, Washington (U.S. Government Printing Office), 1969, p. 41.
38 *Ibid.,* p. 40.

Sixth objection

The direct coupling of the allocating of SDRs with quotas in the General Account distorts the negotiations on quota increases on the occasion of the periodical quota reviews. It sets a premium on high upward quota adjustments: the higher the new quota, the higher the SDR allocations to the country concerned if any allocations are made. Given the different purposes of the General Account and the Special Drawing Account, this pressure for upward revision of quotas is contrary to the principle that the two accounts should be operated separately [39]; it is a factor that is alien to the proper functioning of the General Account itself.

A high SDR allocation will be welcomed by deficit countries in the first place; however, it cannot properly be considered a *dis*couragement for persistent surplus countries either: first, for such countries, too, the SDRs are 'manna from heaven' which is by no means to be sneezed at and, second, the extent to which they will obtain a creditor position in the special drawing rights system i.e. to which they accumulate 'excess holdings' of SDRs beyond their original holdings (= allocations), is determined not primarily by their cumulative allocations, but by their official holdings of gold and foreign exchange [40].

Seventh objection

A seventh, related, objection can be raised. The encouragement for over-large SDR creation built into the present system and the allocation of SDRs proportionally to quotas in the General Account, together mean that there will be less use of *conditional* Fund credit than there might otherwise have been. The same effect would have been achieved by extending the automatic and unconditional 'gold tranche' rights in the General Account, a method of reserve creation that was rejected during the early discussions about deliberate reserve creation. The present SDRs may be used even for longer periods than gold tranche rights, since 70 percent of the former may be used permanently.

The falling off in the use of *conditional* credit may result in impairing the Fund's most important role of 'multilateral surveillance'. Member countries now receive SDR allocations that are substantial in relation to their Fund quota. Thus they are able to finance existing deficits or indeed to afford further deficits, while instead the use of traditional Fund re-

39 See footnote 22 to the preceding chapter.
40 *Fund Agreement*, Schedule F (a).

sources might be entirely proper and sufficient for meeting 'legitimate' payments needs. The present automatism of SDR allocation 'is in contradiction with the emphasis that must be placed on adjustment mechanisms' [41].

III. SUITABILITY OF THE FUND'S QUOTA STRUCTURE FOR THE OPERATIONS OF THE GENERAL ACCOUNT, WITH SPECIAL REFERENCE TO THE DEVELOPING COUNTRIES

This section will deal at greater length with Fund quotas and the General Account. The impossibility of finding a formula which is absolutely satisfactory to all countries concerned must not be taken too seriously, it has in fact been endeavored to base quotas on sensible data [42]. Moreover, though I do not mean to say that no improvement is possible, four general remarks on the question of quotas seem to be justified.

First, as has been noted already, the quotas do not function as automatic determinants of the amounts which member countries can draw or for which they can be drawn upon; they only set *limits,* and even these limits can be exceeded if the Executive Board of the Fund so decides. Fortunately, the Board has *discretionary* powers as to the use of Fund resources. (Naturally, it tries as far as possible to apply general principles). It may also borrow from its members in order to replenish its currency holdings. Second, no grants are given. Fund credit is temporary, i.e. in practice three to five years. (If in special circumstances, a member wishes to prolong the maturity of its debt, renegotiation is necessary.) Thus, any 'inadequacy' in the amount of *credit* will automatically be removed when the debt expires. Similar observations do not apply to allocations in the Special Drawing Account.

Third, insofar as objections to the Fund's quota structure are based on the voting power of members (which is predominantly set by quota size), it is only fair to say that improvements could be made without changing the quotas themselves, for example, by altering the size of the 'basic' vote of each member [43].

---

41 Triffin, *The fate of the pound,* p. 55.
42 See J. Keith Horsefield, 'Fund quotas', *Finance and Development,* September 1970, pp. 7-12, and David Williams, 'The fifth general review of quotas', *ibid.,* pp. 13-18.
43 See page 58. Cr. the following remark of Tiémoko Marc Garango, President of the West African Monetary Union, at the 1969 Annual Meeting of the Fund: '... one may well wonder if, twenty-five years after Bretton Woods it would not be

Fourth, if the quotas of the developing countries ar taken as a whole it will be found that they are relatively high, despite the claims of many developing countries to the contrary. By 'relatively high' I mean high compared to the statistical data on which they are based. On the occasion of the quota increases decided upon in 1970, the Group of Ten countries acted in concert to prevent the reduction in the total share held by the developing countries, which would otherwise have resulted from the automatic application of the statistics. Since the previous review the relevant economic data, particularly the foreign trade figures [44], had risen faster for the developed countries than for the developing countries. The new maximum quotas agreed upon [45] in fact meant a slight reduction in the combined quota share of the Group of Ten countries from 61.1 percent to 60.7 percent; the quota share of the developed countries remained virtually unchanged at 28 percent (strictly there was a slight reduction from 28.2 percent to 27.7 percent); the share of the remaining countries (other developed countries) rose from 10.7 percent to 11.6 percent [46]. (These figures are based on the assumption that all quota changes agreed upon will become effective, through the appropriate procedures).

In December 1967 the Managing Director of the Fund drew attention to the fact that the quotas of the developing countries were higher than they would be if they were strictly proportional to their share of total world reserves and international trade [47]. The following figures are illustrative:

	World * total	Less developed countries	
	U.S. dollars (millions)		percent
Fund quotas **	*21,349*	*6,030*	*28.3*
Imports (cif) ***	254,400	47,600	18.7
Export (fob) ***	243,000	47,300	19.5
Reserves **	76,920	15,190	19.8
Reserve positions in the Fund **	6,726	619	9.2
Use of Fund credit ** ****	4,011	1,167	29.1

Source: *International Financial Statistics*
* Excludes Albania, Bulgaria, China (Mainland), Cuba, Czechoslovakia, East Germany, Hungary, North Korea, North Vietnam, Poland, Rumania and the U.S.S.R. As to Fund quotas, other countries that are non-members are of course also excluded.
** December 31, 1969.
*** 1969.
**** Excluding gold tranche drawings.

In addition to possessing relatively high quotas when measured against certain yardsticks, the developing countries also have open to them two special *facilities* in the Fund. These are for the *Compensatory financing of export fluctuations* (established in 1963, amended in 1966) [48] and for the *Financing of international buffer stocks of primary products* [49]. Use of these *extra* facilities does not diminish the amount of the 'normal' drawing rights.

These facilities are not in a formal sense facilities for developing countries; developing and developed countries are not legal categories in the Fund [50]. The compensatory financing facility is intended to 'assist members, particularly primary exporters, encountering payments difficulties produced by temporary shortfalls'; 'such members can expect that their requests for drawings will be met where the Fund is satified that (a) the shortfall is of a short-term character and is largely attributable to circumstances beyond the control of the member; and (b) the member will cooperate with the Fund in an effort to find, where required, appropriate

desirable to raise the number of basic votes of each member country, a principle that the founders of the Fund had themselves considered necessary to write into the Articles of Agreement in their concern for reconciling the exigencies of a weighted voting system with the elementary rules of international law that sees equality for all states' *(Summary Proceedings,* p. 142).

44   See Second Chamber of the States General of the Netherlands, Session 1970/ 1971, document No. 10935 (R 750), 3, p. 5.

45   See International Monetary Fund, *Annual Report* 1970, p. 183/184.

46   See the document referred to in footnote 44, p. 5.

47   'New arrangements to supplement world reserves and their implications for the developing countries', Arthur K. Salomon Lecture delivered by Pierre-Paul Schweitzer, December 5, 1967, reproduced in: *International Financial News Survey,* December 15, 1967, pp. 413-420; see p. 418.

48   See *Compensatory financing of export fluctuations,* A report by the International Monetary Fund, Washington, 1963 and *Compensatory financing of export fluctuations – Developments in the Fund's facility,* A second report by the International Monetary Fund, Washington, 1966. The 1966 decision doubled the maximum amount to which members may use the facility from 25 percent to 50 percent of their quota.

49   See International Monetary Fund, *The problem of stabilization of prices of primary products,* Report of the Executive Directors: Scope for action by the Fund, Washington, 1969.

50   Even the provision (Art. XIV of the *Fund Agreement)* concerning a member's exemption from the convertibility obligations of Art. VIII is related *not* to the possible lack of *development* in its economy, but to 'the post-war transitional period'. In practice, however, the Fund naturally takes the special problems of its developing members into account, as far as is possible within the framework of the Articles of Agreement.

solutions for its balance of payments difficulties' [51]. Thus, no distinction is made according to the kind of *members* of the Fund, but to the kind of *problems* facing the Fund's membership. In principle, 'developed' countries can also use the facility, and this has in fact been done by New Zealand, a 'developed' but 'primary exporting' country. The provision that the export difficulties must be 'largely' attributable to circumstances *beyond the control* of the member leads in practice to an almost exclusive use of the facility by developing countries. Thus the Fund does in practice pay regard to the *structural* differences between the economies of its members with respect to its policies pertaining to the General Account.

The limit up to which a member may draw on the compensatory financing facility is 50 percent of its quota; the buffer stock facility has the same limitation, but the combined use of both facilities may not exceed 75 percent [52] of quota. No use has yet (November 1970) been made of the buffer stock facility; in the period May 1, 1966 – April 30, 1970 total drawings under the decision on compensatory financing as amended amounted to $ 303 million [53].

One reason often put forward for higher quotas in the Fund by the developing countries is that they 'do not enjoy access to the wide range of credit facilities outside IMF that is open to developed countries' [54]. In this respect, however, it must be considered, that since convertibility became wide-spread the major developed countries have been facing special problems relating to the stability of and confidence in their currencies. They need their 'wide range of credit facilities' (notably the inter-central-bank credit arrangements) to cope with possible sudden but massive movements of short term capital. The stability of the international monetary system as a whole requires much greater credit facilities for the developed countries than for the developing countries; indeed, they are in the interest of the latter as well.

It seems doubtful whether it would be desirable to liberalize the Fund's credits terms for developing countries, especially with respect to the size and duration of compensatory financing drawings. The purpose of the

51 Paragraph 5 of the Fund's 1966 decision; see the Second Report mentioned in footnote 41. See for a short explanation of both facilities: J. Keith Horsefield, 'The Fund's Compensatory Financing', in: *Finance and Development*, 1969, No. 4, pp. 34-37.
52 See the publication mentioned in footnote 49, in which the text of the decision concerned is reproduced on the page preceding page 1.
53 International Monetary Fund, *Annual Report,* 1970, p. 140.
54. See for instance *International monetary reform and cooperation for development*, Report of the Expert Group on International Monetary Issues of the UNCTAD, New York, 1969, p. 9.

Fund is not to finance individual *items in* its members' balance of payments which may be in deficit, but *overall* deficits. Furthermore, the Fund must be primarily concerned not with the adequacy of *special* drawing facilities, but with the adequacy of *quotas*. Paragraph (3) of the Compensatory Financing Decision itself reads: 'The quotas of many primary exporting countries, taken in conjunction with a reasonable use of their own reserves, are at present adequate for dealing with export fluctuations such as have occurred during the past decade. In those instances, however, where adjustment of the quotas of certain primary exporting countries, and in particular of countries with relatively small quotas, would be appropriate to make them more adequate in the light of fluctuations in export proceeds and other relevant criteria, the Fund is willing to give sympathetic consideration to requests for such adjustment' (see footnote 48).

Making an exception for developing countries with respect to the maximum duration [55] of Fund credit, regardless of the underlying cause of the payments imbalance, would not be wise. A solution to the balance-of-payments problems of those countries can hardly be sought in a further accumulation of short-term and medium-term indebtedness. It is when they are faced with unfavorable structural trends in their external position – trends that are by definition *beyond their control* – that the developing countries need most to undertake *fundamental adjustments*. The purpose of Fund assistance is primarily to enable members to restore their balance of payments equilibrium, not simply to finance deficits. In practice, several members, some of them developing countries, appear to have remained indebted to the Fund for periods longer than five years; apparently this is possible without infringing the *principle* of a five-year maximum for individual drawings.

That developing countries have substantial liquidity needs is unquestionable. The separation of their 'balance of payments' problems from their 'development' problems is often artificial and dogmatic. The more capital that is transferred to the poor countries, the less will be their balance-of-payments problems. This is one of the reasons why collaboration between the IMF and the World Bank Group is valuable. The following chapter will deal with the possibility of long-term development financing, through the *Special Drawing Account* of the Fund, without in any way impairing the attainment of the purposes for which it was created.

55 See for instance *International monetary issues and the developing countries*, Report of the Group of Experts of the UNCTAD, New York 1965, p. 13.

V. Putting the SDR system on a truly international basis and on a sounder monetary footing

I. THE 'LIMITED GROUP' IDEA AND ITS AFTERMATH

The problem of the *distribution* of SDRs has not received any thorough attention during the preparation of the scheme. Indeed the section entitled 'Allocation of newly created reserves' is one of the few sections in the 1966 Report of the Group of Ten that was only a single paragraph in length (paragraph 43).

The experts concerned need not be blamed for this; in any event, 'the officials of the Fund and of the negotiating governments showed a courage far greater than the academic economists have had' [1], and the distribution problem can be considered to some extent as secondary. The lack of interest in the distribution of SDRs can be explained by the history of the negotiations. During the early Group of Ten discussions the idea of creating reserves within a *limited* group of 'important' countries found most favor. The Ministers and Governors of the Group of Ten countries decided during their meeting in The Hague in July 1966 to instruct their Deputies to talk with the Executive Directors of the IMF, because they 'thought it appropriate to look now for a wider framework in which to consider the questions that affect the world economy as a whole' [2].

---

1   A remark made by Fritz Machlup, in view of the fact that it was the officials themselves who 'scuttled the Myth of 'Backing'' (*Remaking the international monetary system*, p. 65). See below in this section.
2   *Communiqué of the ministerial meeting of the Group of Ten* on July 25 and 26 in The Hague, paragraph 7.

It is therefore quite understandable that, when in the discussions that followed the idea of reserve creation in a limited number of countries was dropped, and the much larger number of IMF members, represented by the Executive Directors [3], came into the picture, the IMF quota structure suggested itself from the outset as the 'natural' formula for the distribution of any new reserves. It was indeed on any count an improvement on the limited group.

How has it been possible to consider the *world's* monetary system to be an affair of a *limited* group?

This too is understandable in the light of the events. Although the system of international reserve creation has been a matter of regular study by the IMF since 1963 – its first published report on this particular subject dates from 1953 [4] – it has also been a matter of regular concern to the 'Group of Ten' countries as a group since 1963; without that deliberate, intensive and effective concern, SDRs would have never come into being. It all started when in October 1963 the Ministers of Finance and Central Bank Governors of the Group of Ten decided that meetings of their Deputies should become a permanent forum for discussion. 'It appeared to them to be useful to undertake a thorough examination of the outlook for the functioning of the international monetary system and its probable future needs for liquidity' [5].

The outcome of the SDR negotiations cannot be explained without recognizing the effect of 'the cavalier way in which the outsiders were treated until 1966 by the exclusive Group of Ten' [6]. Probably, 'the Group of Ten countries would not have taken as much trouble as they did to devise a new reserve asset if they had not feared that *they* could run short of liquidity in the near future and/or if some of them had not

---

3 Four joint meetings of the Deputies of the Group of Ten and the Executive Directors of the IMF were held in 1966/67. These enabled the developing countries to participate in the discussion, though against a double representation of the Group of Ten countries. It was the Ministers and Central Bank Governors of the *Ten* who, after these joint meetings, negotiated the final 'Outline' of the scheme during their two sessions in London (August 1967). The Board of Governors of the IMF granted formal approval in Rio de Janeiro, September 1967.

4 See footnote 5 to chapter I.

5 *Communiqué* of the Ministers and Governors of the Group of Ten, October 2, 1963; I quoted from the *Ministerial statement of the Group of Ten and annex prepared by Deputies,* August 1964, p. 4.

6 These words are quoted from the essay of Javier Márquez, 'Developing countries and the international monetary system', *The future of the international monetary system,* edited by Hans W. J. Bosman and Frans A. M. Alting von Geusau, Leyden/Lexington, 1970, p. 133.

considered that they were already short of it, with little prospect of 'earning' additional reserves' [7].

On the other hand, the limited group approach may seem to be justified as 'the industrial countries may (. . .) claim that they, as the chief holders of reserves, should be allowed to create additional reserves without having to 'earn' them through transfers of real resources (. . .)', says Professor Machlup [8].

However, if consultation and cooperation with the developing countries is considered irrelevant for the functioning of the system, and the 'system' is, as has been shown in chapter II above, essentially an expression for 'the way *countries cooperate* in the monetary field', it follows logically that either developing countries do not maintain external monetary relations, *or* developing countries are no real countries.

If the *global* need for reserves is considered of *global* concern, the argument that the Group of Ten countries, having a majority of votes within the IMF, are free to deliberate only among themselves is not necessarily useful. In fact, the Group of Ten, while not violating the letter of the Bretton Woods agreement, has acted against its spirit by establishing a *two-stage decision-making procedure* in Fund matters. For it makes a great difference whether non-Ten countries are able to contribute views during the formative stage of discussions, or whether they are only informed when the Group of Ten have already agreed among themselves [9].

Not only the developing countries could not influence the opinions of the Ten through an *exchange of views about the studies* that were undertaken, but also they have been at the same disadvantage as the Liberal Party in regard to the election system of the United Kingdom. As a result of the establishment of a separate 'constituency', – namely the Group of Ten – certain 'votes' (individual positions) in favor of the interests of the developing countries, which might have had an impact on the outcome of the discussions if they had been held in the hearing of the *whole* Fund membership, have probably been lost. (In a similar way, votes of the

---

7 *Ibid.,* p. 131.
8 *Quarterly Journal of Economics,* 'The cloakroom rule of international reserves: reserve creation and resources transfer', August, 1965, p. 355.
9 Cf. the statement of Governor Jha (India) of the International Monetary Fund at the 1969 Annual Meeting *(Summary Proceedings,* p. 73): 'A good deal of the discussion and the more crucial negotiations have taken place outside the forum of the Fund where no one from the developing world was present. *As a result,* the question of a formal link between the creation of international liquidity and development finance has been shelved' (my italics).

British Liberal Party are systematically lost as minorities in individual constituencies do not count for the outcome of the national elections of the House of Commons). An example may illustrate this point. Suppose that there are 20 participants in a discussion, and there is a *two-stage* procedure: 10 out of the 20 have *advance* deliberations in order to decide on a *common* view. Suppose, further, that within this 'limited group' six persons are *in favor* of a certain viewpoint, two are against and two are indifferent. What matters in the *second* stage is only the 'consensus' of the group. If among the *other* 10 parties four favor the agreed view of the separate group, four are against and two have no 'strong feelings', the agreed view will be adopted by the wider group. If the original discussion had taken place in the wider group, there would have been no majority for the supposedly common views, but the *individual* positions of all twenty participants would have been decisive.

There were also faults in the 'economic' reasoning behind the 'limited group' approach to reserve creation. Of course, a limited group of countries can create reserves, but it is economically impossible to consider such an activity a matter of internal concern only. For *internal reserve creation also increases the means of financing for purchases of external real resources,* just as the allocation of SDRs within the limited group of participants in the Special Drawing Account may lead to more real resources being drawn from, say, the Soviet Union. This is due to the fact that a change in the composition of reserves within the limited group frees other internationally acceptable funds for spending outside the group. The creation of liquidity within a limited group of rich countries would only 'imply that poorer countries were being expected to earn the increase in their liquidity (...), while richer countries were given an increase free of charge' [10].

What then were the reasons for which the Group of Ten countries saw global reserve creation primarily as their particular affair? Where they moved by paternalistic or moralistic feelings – the 'larger industrialized countries sharing the responsibility for the working of the international monetary system' [11] while the other countries could ask only for *special* 'benefits' [12]? However interesting and valid these questions may be,

10 *International monetary reform and Latin America,* Report to CIAP by the Group of Experts, Washington D.C., 1966, p. 21.
11 *Ossola Report,* paragraph 118. See also paragraph 120: 'Assets which are specifically created to fulfil the reserve function should, consequently, be distributed only to countries (. . .) which are (. . .) able to assume the obligations as well as the rights entailed in the convention and its working'.
12 *Ibid.,* paragraph 120: 'A system which meets the reserve needs of the larger

this is not the place to answer them. The economic justification of the 'limited group' approach was given in the 'Ossola Report' (1965), paragraph 117-122 and in the 'Report of Deputies' (1966), paragraph 56-67. The *main* idea behind the 'limited group' concept, however, was the 'myth of the need for backing' which, in the meantime, in fact has been scuttled by the Group of Ten itself (cf. footnote 1). While most of the early schemes for reserve creation had incorporated the notion of a central debtor whose liabilities were to be backed by the currencies or securities of its own debtors, the SDR scheme disposed of this idea entirely.

The reason why I dwell rather extensively on the question of the 'limited group' is immediately related to the question of backing for deliberately created reserves. The argument still put forward by the Group of Ten in 1966 was that 'full acceptance of (such) reserve units requires that they be backed by major trading and financial countries which, in the event of liquidation or withdrawal, would be able to convert them into other usable assets' [13].

Yet SDRs were created essentially for one original reason: to overcome a supposed shortage of gold. They were intended to be a 'supplement to gold' or, in newspapers terms, 'paper gold'. Has anybody ever worried about converting gold? Who expects the scheme to be liquidated? [14]

nations will, in practice, benefit all countries'. A not unusual answer to the proponents of a *link between SDR creation and development* is that there is already an 'indirect' link because developing countries *benefit* from SDR creation, which forestalls the emergence of a reserve shortage with all its consequences, namely, balance of payments restrictions, deflation and aid-cutting by the industrial world. Hence the so-called 'benefit' only means the avoidance of hardships which would admittedly be greater for developing than for developed countries if a liquidity shortage were to arise (see chapter IV, section 2 under 'Second objection'). No 'net' benefit is at stake, only the possibility of unreasonably large losses. Logically, this argument would entail saying that the poor countries must be content with their disadvantages; for the greater these disadvantages, the greater the 'advantage' if they are prevented. In the same line of thought it is possible to call the desires of developing countries for a *true* 'link' a request for 'special privileges', as was done quite recently by an important authority in international affairs.

It is rather curious that Gerald M. Meier, a development expert, in his *The international economics of development,* London/Tokyo, 1968, stresses the indirect beneficial effect of reserve creation 'from the standpoint of contributing to development' (p. 308). On the direct 'link to aid', he sticks with 'orthodox financial opinion', thus neglecting the fundamental change in that opinion that took place with the death of the 'backing' myth (see below in this section). I owe this reference to Mr. R. C. Carrière.

13 *Report of Deputies,* 1966, paragraph 60.

14 The more SDRs that are created in the future, the less it would make sense to liquidate the scheme for the purpose of bringing down the level of world reserves.

Admittedly, a country may wish to withdraw. If it has a creditor position in the scheme on the moment of withdrawal, the other participants will have to redeem its SDR holdings. But why should such a redemption be possible only by industrial countries and not by developing countries? Contrary to the claim of the Group of Ten, the developing countries are not necessarily net spenders of monetary reserves. Their combined reserves grew steadily and uninterruptedly from $ 8,725 million at December 31, 1962 to $ 17,485 million at July 31, 1970 [15]. In the first half of 1970 they did use SDR 282 million, but 'at cost of' the General Account of the Fund itself (SDR 244 million)[15], rather than of the developed countries (SDR 38 million).

Those who are concerned about the 'full acceptance' of the new asset or say that the SDR *must be 'firmly established' as a reserve asset before being linked to development assistance* seem to forget that the *acceptance* of the SDR is already assured by international agreement.

In the meantime, to repeat Professor Machlup's expression, the Myth of Backing has died. Ten years ago Professor Triffin yet suggested that Fund members should make *deposits* as a *source* of liquidity creation by the Fund [16]. Such *backing* is, however, not needed for creating money. 'Money needs takers, not backers; the takers accept it, not because of any backing, but only because they count on others accepting it from them' [17].

The view apparently adopted by the experts of the Fund and the Group of Ten meant that they were in fact establishing a *final* reserve asset being not in need for redemption with any other monetary means; there was therefore no *liquidity problem* in the generally accepted sense. Hence, there could be *no conflict between 'long-term' development financing and the 'short-term' character of SDRs*. It is true that ideally reserve assets should be used and recovered within a comparatively short period, or at

What would take place is a replacement of 'excess' holdings of SDRs by other reserve assets such as foreign exchange and reserve positions in the Fund, which would probably have to be additionally *created* for the purpose. If no other solution was available, holdings of SDRs would no doubt be exchanged for holdings of the 'illiquid' currencies of former debtors under the SDR scheme. If this happens, it is clear that liquidation would be no solution for problems caused by a lack of liquidity in the SDR scheme. Indeed, the very idea that a lack of liquidity in the SDR scheme could occur, resulting in 'impairing' the SDR as reserve asset, is almost a contradiction in terms (see also footnote 82).

15 *International Financial Statistics,* October 1970. The supposition that developing countries would be always and automatically spenders of any new reserves accruing to them was a reason for the earlier 'limited group' idea (see also section 3 below).

16 *Gold and the dollar crisis,* p. 103.

17 F. Machlup, *Remaking the international monetary system,* p. 66.

least it should be possible to use them in this way, but this has nothing to do with the mechanism for reserve *creation,* as will be shown later. The Group of Ten experts, who resisted the establishment of a 'link' with development financing on the grounds of the short-term nature of the new asset, have in fact invalidated their argument by dropping the suggestion that backing is required for the asset. They just did not carry through consistently enough this principle. SDRs are a 'supplement to gold'; no one has ever considered that the quality of gold as a reserve asset would be undermined when its first monetary use possibly had been for 'long-term' purposes. It is totally irrelevant with respect to the money character of gold. The same applies for SDRs.

The resistance to the principle of a 'link' is primarily an aftermath of the old 'limited group' philosophy. The movement from the idea of 'reserve creation within a limited group' – with or without special credit lines to outside countries [18] – to 'reserve creation in the Fund' will certainly not stop there. The point of interest is how this trend should continue. The next sections are more specifically devoted to this topic.

II. OSTRICH POLICY-LIKE ATTITUDE TO THE PROBLEM OF REAL RESOURCES

Now that some experience has been gained with the working of the SDR scheme, the problem of the distribution of newly created reserves may recently be put on the agenda once again. The whole SDR scheme has in fact repeatedly been described as open to review.

It was often stated by representatives of the negotiating countries, notably those from the richer ones, that the purpose of creation of international liquidity should not be, using the words of M. W. Holtrop, to 'bring about a transfer of real resources to the countries that might, on the basis of some agreed formula, be the beneficiary of such creation, whether they are industrialized or developing nations' [19]. What Mr. Holtrop had in mind in using the phrase 'transfer of real resources' obviously was a *permanent* transfer, as it was put in the Report of the Group of Ten, 1966 [20].

---

18 Cf. *Report of Deputies,* 1966, paragraph 64 and Scheme B.
19 International Monetary Fund, *Summary Proceedings,* Annual Meeting 1965, Statement by the Governor for the Netherlands, p. 148.
20 *Group of Ten, Report of Deputies,* 1966, paragraph 40: 'We are agreed that deliberate reserve creation is not intended to effect permanent transfers of real resources from some countries to others'.

The argument seems to be that, though in general there would be nothing wrong with matching transfers of money for transfers of real goods, *international* money – in the sense described in chapter III [21] – should not be allowed to bring about a *permanent* transfer of resources, because the existence of a permanent deficit on current account in one single country or group of countries conflicts with the goal of international payments equilibrium. At least, I presume this is one of the reasons behind the frequently-mentioned concern with the real recources; the peculiar thing is that the non-transfer requirement is nearly always put as an axiom, without further justification [22].

If the proposition is generally valid – and it may reasonably be argued that persistent current account imbalances may increase inflation in the world, enhance cyclical instability, exchange rate risks, and so forth – a reasoned reply is still possible. This is, basically, that those countries whose balance of payments show a *structural* deficit on current account, like most of the developing countries, are completely ignored. One of the functions of international money is to act as a means for transferring real resources from rich to poor countries through matching capital transfers. There is no reason why international monetary equilibrium should be endangered merely because there are *structural differences* between balances of payments provided that there is no major disturbance in the balances taken as a whole. Permanent or long lasting current account deficits or surpluses need not be an impediment to sound monetary relationships.

Admittedly, it has never been maintained that the use of international reserves should not lead to permanent transfers of real resources from one country to another, but only that reserve *creation* should not do so. Nevertheless, I criticised the view that *reserves* should not permanently influence the international flows of real resources, because it makes more

---

21 Chapter III, section 1, first paragraph.
22 To avoid misunderstandings I wish to do full justice to the sources quoted. Holtrop and the Group of Ten report said only that reserve creation is not *intended* to effect permanent transfers of real resources. Naturally, reserve creation *always has* an effect on the distribution of real resources (sooner or later financial resources must command *real* resources). I can understand the view that changing this distribution need not be the primary goal of reserve creation; but I do feel that the Group of Ten did in fact try to hide the fact that liquidity creation almost *per definitionem* has a bearing on movements of real resources, and that this was something on which there ought to have been an agreed purpose. If the belief was that net transfers would tend to cancel out in the long run, this may rather be called a pious wish, for, there is no guarantee that any such thing will happen. *The choice is between a controlled transfer of resources and a uncontrolled one.*

sense to put the problem in such general terms. The question of reserve creation, then, is implied. For even though the initial distribution of newly created reserves may be without any effect on the international distribution of real wealth, any net *use* of the money, once created, would have such an effect, and this effect may be permanent. Reserve creation means producing money, and the essential thing one can do with money is to pay for real goods with it. Hence, if one wants to prevent money from being used in this way, one has to refrain from creating it. The concerns about the effects of reserve creation on real resources therefore run counter to the very idea of creating money itself. Creating money means creating claims on real resources. Real money may be spent 'permanently', that means, without being earned back. (According to the present rules this may be done with 70 percent of the SDRs allocated to any participant in the scheme. (See footnote 25 to chapter III.)).

At this point the fundamental disadvantage of using the concept of 'system' as an independent set of 'technical' relationships, brought forward in chapter II, can be clearly seen. The 'monetary system', according to Holtrop in the statement already quoted, should 'give the maximum guarantee of being a politically neutral framework, with no aims of influencing the distribution of wealth among its member countries' [23]. However, there cannot in practice be a *politically neutral* monetary system because, as we have seen in chapter II, the 'international monetary system' is only a vague expression for 'the way in which *countries cooperate* in the monetary field'. There is no neutrality about this cooperation. The particular points to be made here are that: 1) reserve creation is bound to have an influence on the distribution of wealth, and 2) having no intentions with regard to this distribution is an end in itself since it implies approval of the particular outcome of the *chosen policy* for the distribution of the newly created reserves, i.e. of the absence of any deliberate policy on this matter.

III. WHEN DO THE NEWLY CREATED SDRS ENTER THE MONETARY CIRCUIT?

During the years immediately preceding the establishment of the Special Drawing Account both official and academic economists often made a distinction between reserves 'to hold' and reserves 'to spend' [24].

23 IMF, *Summary Proceedings*, Annual Meeting 1965, p. 149.
24 See, for instance, Fritz Machlup, 'The cloakroom rule of international reserves:

To many of these theorists the idea of spending newly created reserves was abhorrent, quite apart from the fact that, depending on the mechanism by which the reserves were created, the spending might lead to reserve destruction and thus run counter to the very purpose of reserve creation [25]. These fears about reserve spending were connected with the argument that reserve creation should lead to the least possible movement of real resources. Taken to extremes, the idea apparently was that the world demand for 'reserves to hold' manifested itself in *individual national* demands for reserves, and that these demands were felt only in 'the larger industrialized countries', i.e. 'the countries which principally hold and use reserves for international monetary purposes', and whose reserve needs, in the words of the 'Ossola Report', 'are a primary concern of the international monetary system' [26]. According to this line of argument, the major countries (in general members of the Group of Ten) felt a need for additional reserves, but not for additional means for spending. If they acquired newly created reserves, they would behave in a 'disciplined' way, i.e. they would not use them forthwith, or they would repurchase them within a short time.

This view can, for instance, be read between the lines of page 18 of the Fund's Annual Report for 1965. There the distinction is made between 'countries with a high propensity to hold reserves, such as the industrial countries and certain primary producers' on the one side, and 'countries with a weak tendency to hold reserves' on the other. The observation is made, that 'where reserves were distributed directly to less developed countries (which on the whole have a weak tendency to hold and accumulate reserves), the creation of reserves would also involve a long-term movement of real resources from the more developed to the less developed countries. An important question to be considered is whether a mechanism which involved such transfers of real resources would be desirable'.

reserve creation and resources transfer', *Quarterly Journal of Economics,* Vol. LXXIX, August 1965, p. 350, where he speaks about 'the purpose of satisfying a growing world demand for international reserves, that is, for reserves to hold rather than to shuttle back and forth'. Also the same author: *Remaking the international monetary system,* p. 57: 'The idea of creating a new reserve asset for only the rich countries (. . .) rested on the propositions (1) (. . .) and (2) that new reserves should be created only for those who could be expected to hold them rather than to spend them'.
25 Spending dollars in the United States, for instance, means reserve destruction: the reserves of the spending country decrease with the amount of spending, while the *gross* reserves of the U.S. do not increase.
26 *Ossola Report,* paragraph 118.

Generally, among the rich countries, the view was more or less accepted that an 'early turnaround' of new reserves would *not* be desirable, as it was in contradiction with the very philosophy of reserve creation. The 'Ossola Report' for instance contained the following sentence: 'A reserve asset is characterized by the expectation that, if it flows out, it should ordinarily be reconstituted in due time' [27]. In the arrangements as finally adopted, however, the reconstitution requirement was very mild (see footnote 25 to chapter III).

In this connection I like to raise a conceptual question: is it correct to speak of a 'first spending round' when new money is used for the first time, essentially similar to second and further rounds, or can the first spending be considered an *integrate part of the mechanism of creation?* In other words, is it useful from the viewpoint of monetary analysis that the money is considered money before *it has effectively entered into the monetary circuit?*

Here a parallel may be drawn with national monetary theory. Cash balances held by monetary institutions with the power to create money are not counted as part of the national stock of money. Neither are cash balances held by treasuries or other state agencies. Some authors argue that treasuries are money-creating institutions [28]; others prefer to consider the government as distinct from the banking system, but agree with the exclusion of money held by the state from national money supply figures [29]. There are obvious reasons for this: it is the *spending* policy of the state that has a major monetary impact, *not* the fact that it may hold large unused cash balances. Moreover, it is not the amount of cash in existence that limits government spending, but the power of the government to force monetary institutions to create money on its behalf [30]. Cash balances owned by the state are therefore not of statistical significance; they do not tell much about changes in the quantity of money in the country and they are not part of the currency in circulation. As

27 *Ibid.,* paragraph 120.
28 For instance C. F. Scheffer and M. J. H. Smeets, *Geld en overheid,* Utrecht/ Antwerpen, 1961, p. 41, who state that the central government is also to be considered a money-creating institution. ('Aangezien ook de centrale overheid tot de geldscheppende instellingen wordt gerekend, behoren ook de saldi, welke zich in de Rijkskassen bevinden, te worden afgetrokken').
29 See Korteweg and Keesing, *Het moderne geldwezen,* p. 89-91.
30 This power, whether it only exists *de facto* or *de jure* as well, is related to the nature of the state described in chapter II. The extent to which it is used depends on collective political decisions, which ought be guided by the principle of public interest. *One* of the objectives which need to be taken into account under this principle is, of course, monetary stability and the avoidance of inflation.

the state-held cash balances are easy to identify, it is not difficult to exclude them from national money stock figures.

At the national level the creation of money through credit expansion nearly always gives rise to immediate additional spending. Newly created money can therefore be counted as belonging to the national stock of of money, because it enters the circuit without delay. In most countries (the United Kingdom is an exception) money creation through credit expansion only appears in the statistics when credits are actually drawn upon. However, when the state acquires additional cash, monetary analists do not count it as money until it is actually spent. Cash holdings by the state – unlike cash holdings by private persons and institutions – are not part of the money supply. Thus one is justified in saying that government *spending* is an *integrate part of the process of creating money.*

International liquidity differs from the national currency in many respects [31]; but there are still similarities. Just as the national money supply is controlled in the (national) public interest, so the international money supply should be controlled in the (international) public interest. Although the latter takes the form of voluntary cooperation, it is no less real than the former. Indeed, it can be even *more* powerful because the Special Drawing Account makes it possible deliberately to create and cancel money at will, and the system contains very few participants. Thus SDR creation, *which is money creation in the international public interest,* can have a relatively greater impact on the international money supply than the creation of national money will have on the domestic money supply.

The *spending* of newly created SDRs is of much more significance than their allocation which, under the present arrangements, is really like opening an unconditional line of credit. This being so, SDRs could be accounted for in the same way as domestically created money in behalf of the state by excluding them from international accounts until they are *spent.* For any given country there is no telling when special drawing rights will be spent, if at-all. Such a treatment would be in line with the accounting practice for swap facilities or stand-by credits in the Fund: they do not influence total world reserves until they are actually used.

There is, however, one important respect in which special drawing rights differ from national currencies. Although they are events of international interest, allocations of SDRs do not take place in behalf of an international *treasury.* The beneficiaries are all participating countries, who may choose when to spend them freely and unpredictably. In these circumstances it does seem most practical to consider SDRs as being created at the moment of allocation.

This situation – it will be argued below – is, however, not satisfactory from the monetary point of view; and the fact remains that allocations of SDRs are in fact analogous to lines of credit that have not yet entered the monetary circuit. It would be desirable to establish a procedure more clearly parallel with that for creating money in national treasuries. An arrangement of this sort is described in the following section, which adumbrates a method for linking SDR creation with an internationally sponsored activity, namely development cooperation.

It will be clear from what has been said that the *fear* that a 'link' between SDR creation and development finance would lead to 'immediate spending' of the newly created money is unjustified. On the contrary, the spending should be considered as a natural element of the creation mechanism, just as it is in national economies, and indeed always has been in the international monetary system too. In such a system the developing countries would not receive *reserves*-to-spend; they would instead increase their indebtedness to the International Development Association. Developed countries would be able to earn the additional reserves and to hold them or spend them to acquire real resources from other developed countries *or from the developing world,* as they wish. In the latter case the developed countries would suffer no net loss of real resources at all.

IV. PUTTING THE SDR SYSTEM ON A TRULY INTERNATIONAL BASIS

As has been pointed out in chapter IV, section 2 ('Fifth objection'), some elements in the SDR system remain outside international control, and are thus out of line with the very character of the system as a framework for international cooperation. As long as there is no truly international control of the system, it might operate in a way that comes into conflict with the international interest. For instance, SDRs may be used to finance balance of payments deficits caused by 'fundamental disequilibria', and thus perpetuate a monetarily undesirable situation. Or the deficits to be financed may be caused by such activities as aggression or economic imperialism, which are surely contrary to any concept of international justice. Internationally created money ought clearly to be used for internationally agreed purposes [32]. Otherwise, there is no international cooperation in the full sense. Improving the functioning of the SDR scheme to take in more adequately the idea of public international interest means 'deepening' the economic law-sphere in which special drawing rights function by opening juridical anticipatory moments of the economic aspect of international cooperation [33] so as to enable the SDRs to serve as a means for international economic cooperation in an extended way.

Just as objections may be made to the use of *nationally* controlled reserve currencies for *international* purposes, so may they be raised against the use of internationally controlled special drawing rights for strictly *national* purposes.

As has been remarked in chapter IV, section 2, participants in the Special Drawing Account expose themselves to great losses of real resources. The losses are not necessarily suffered by the particular countries that accumulate SDRs under the system (they only change the composition of their reserves [34]), but by the countries with balance of payments surplus positions that are the counterpart of the current account deficits *financed* by SDRs. The *distribution* of earned special drawing rights is not strictly proportionate to the *distribution* of real resource losses. The building up of SDR holdings does not by itself cause any loss of real resources. It is rather the other way round: if a country's reserves are increasing because of net exports it is likely to be designated for holding more SDRs. The likelihood of real losses becomes greater as total world holdings of international money increase, and these may affect participants and non-participants alike. It is quite possible for a participant in the Special Drawing Account to finance its deficit vis-à-vis, say, the Sovjet Union by using its SDRs in transactions with other participants [35].

Losses of real resources arise in those countries that accumulate external monetary reserves, i.e. in the first instance, foreign exchange, as the consequence of current account surpluses. The creation of additional monetary reserves in the form of SDRs representing automatic claims on foreign exchange increases the extent to which individual countries may suffer real losses. In comparing SDR creation by allocation to individual

32 See footnote 37 to chapter IV.
33 See chapter II, section 2 on this Dooyeweerdian terminology.
34 See the beginning of section 6 below, the second paragraph.
35 Fund members not participating in the Special Drawing Account are: Ethiopia, Iraq, Kuwait, Lebanon, Libyan Arab Republic, Nepal, Portugal, Saudi Arabia, Singapore and Thailand. China is a participant but did not wish to receive an allocation of SDRs to be allocated to it for the first period, 1970-1972 (IFS, March 1970, p. 7).

participants with creation by allocation to an international agency, it may be wondered why the second – under which real resource losses are inevitable – should be considered superior to the first, where they are not.

Apart from the fact that allocation to an international institution most probably will economize on SDRs [36], and thus cut down the effect on real resource movements, the following points may be made. First, *any* money creation must result sooner or later in a transfer of real resources to a certain extent. The very fact that the money is created means that it *will be taken in exchange for real goods,* when it is spent on those goods. To the extent that SDR creation leads to additional international spending, the spending country compels (speaking in terms of market forces) the international community to deliver real goods. When domestically the money supply is increased, this means that people are holding more non-interest bearing [37] assets, *'and the Government is getting the benefit of the real resources involved'*[38]. By contrast, under the present SDR system, when the international money supply is increased, the real benefit goes to those who are ready to take it. While domestically the real benefit of money creation accrues to the community, which can moreover control the *direction* of spending through its political processes, internationally, the direction of spending can be made entirely subservient to purely national interests [39], even though the decision to create SDRs is

36 See chapter IV under the heading 'First objection'.
37 The fact that SDRs which have been earned under the present system bear interest does not mean that they have to be considered a form of 'credit' *instead of* 'money'. The interest paid – 1½ percent – has nothing to do with market conditions; it is in the nature of symbolic remuneration. Of course, any holding of earned reserves does represent a credit which the country grants to the rest of the world. This credit claim is held in the form of international money. Investments on a short-term basis (securities, bank deposits) do not impair the money character of the reserve holdings. The liquidity criterion for a country's monetary *reserves* allows for longer-term investment than would be acceptable by a private person wishing to have liquid cash balances at his disposal. Hence, the earnings on official monetary reserves can be greater than those on private short-term investments. A 1½ percent rate on SDRs is thus very low; *giro* balances, which are as liquid as cash in the Netherlands, now earn 2½ percent.
38 Remark of Harry G. Johnson during the Hearing before the Subcommittee, 1969 (see footnote 37 to chapter IV, p. 70). For the sake of completeness it has, of course, to be added that also real benefits accrue to the money creating banks, which have the same status in public law as any other citizen or private legal person. These real benefits arise to the extent that money creation takes place through 'transformation', i.e. monetization of assets that do already exist in the national economy; the monetization occurs when banks acquire such assets from non-banks (see F. de Roos, *De algemene banken in Nederland,* 3rd edition, p. 47). The benefits from money creation meant here are of course small in relation to those of Governments.
39 Nationally, when additional money creation is deemed economically justified,

a collective one. This is an anomaly: the liquidity of SDRs as a medium of exchange is 'backed' by the whole community of nations, on whose mutual real resources they represent a claim; the beneficiaries of their *creation*, therefore, must be chosen in accordance with internationally agreed policies.

Second, allocation to an international institution rather than to countries is to be preferred on purely monetary grounds (i.e. apart from the question of who receives the real benefit). The monetary argument is the following. The present SDR system has the disadvantage that not only is the *direction* of spending not controlled; neither are the *moment* or circumstances of spending within the purview of the community of nations. The system of controlled reserve creation thus leaves the major initial impact on the world economy at the mercy of uncontrolled action. Certain large countries or groups of countries may unload special drawing rights allocated to them at any moment they choose to allow their balance of payments to move into deficit.

The present method of creating SDRs makes collective control either of the monetary effect of the operation itself or of the direction of use of the special drawing rights impossible. In these circumstances something similar to the monetary powers of national governments will have to be created. There is no need for a real supranational authority, but the shaping and coordination of international economic cooperation does require the intervention of international agencies, if SDRs are not only to meet the world's reserve needs but also to finance internationally agreed purposes (to use the words of Triffin) while so doing.

While there may be many such purposes, any activity to be financed through SDR creation should preferably 1) represent a widely accepted agreed purpose; 2) be *controlled* by the same wide circle of countries as the SDR scheme itself; 3) require *substantial* amounts of money (at least of the same order of magnitude as sufficient supplements to world re-

---

the additional spending is either collectively controlled by the political process (government spending) or controlled by market forces. Banks are simply allowed by the monetary authorities to increase the volume of lending. Those who receive the benefit in real resources pay for their loans according to market conditions. Internationally, liquidity creation can also be the result of market forces, but the international community has no control over the operation, as may be seen by examining the history of dollar creation, or bilateral central bank credits. In the present system, special drawing rights are created even if there was no immediate demand, and are thus quite different in nature from domestically created credits. No country creates money by simply granting it so citizens. The only way in which citizens themselves receive newly created money is by *borrowing* from commercial banks, a process that clearly differs from SDR allocations.

serves are likely to require so that no situation will occur in which several kinds of spending purposes have to compete for the same funds); 4) be relevant to *economic* international objectives, which require international financing; 5) have a positive influence on global monetary equilibrium; and, 6) require only a limited amount of funds.

The World Bank Group, consisting of the International Bank for Reconstruction and Development and the International Development Association and the International Finance Cooperation [40], does in fact carry on activities of this sort. Those of the IDA are particularly appropriate for collective international financing, and proposals for using SDRs for the financing of the IDA operations, therefore, deserve full support. I may quote the Pearson report in this connection: 'The great demand for concessional development finance and the interest in greater internationalization of the aid system converge on IDA. It has a proven record, and it is impossible to imagine the succesful creation at this time of another agency, with greater capacity to combine the disbursement of soft money on a global scale with committed leadership in aid stategy' [41] [42]. In addition, the *de facto* ties between the IDA and the IMF would be most valuable, especially if SDRs were allocated to IDA.

Finally, it is essential for international economic policy aims to be in harmony with each other. The major problems of the world economy cannot be treated in isolation, as has been done in creating the SDR system. There is only one world community; and yet the nations committing themselves to the attainment of goal A have possibly committed themselves yesterday to goal B, which is inconsistent with A. The public interest requires the harmonizing not only of individual interests but also of the various public objectives themselves. What holds true for the *national* public interest, does so equally for the *inter*national public in-

40 IFC was set up in 1956 to deal exclusively with the private sector in developing countries; IDA was established in 1960; it operates in the same sectors and with the same policies as the Bank, but its loans are provided only to the poorer developing countries on easier terms than conventional World Bank loans.
41 *Partners in Development,* Report of the Commission on International Development, Chairman: Lester B. Pearson, New York/Washington/London, 1969, p. 223.
42 There would probably be not much disagreement on this point. In *Shaping the world economy* (1962) Tinbergen wrote: 'A major decision confronting the non-Communist countries concerns the organ which will have to disburse the considerable larger development funds to be advocated below' (a doubling of development aid from developed countries). 'For the time being the Internatoinal Development Association (IDA) seems to be the most appropriate organ, since it is operated by the experienced staff of IBRD. Its policy will have to diverge from the Bank's at several points, however, and it may turn out that an independent organ would be better suited to the task' (p. 114).

terest. If the international community commits itself to certain development targets, it must also earmark the financial means for attaining them.
The desirability of a substantial flow of real resources from the rich
countries to the poor countries is generally agreed. National budgets and
capital markets have been shown to be unable to finance a sufficient
flow of resources in that direction. Hence, opposition to a link between
special drawing rights and development financing on the one hand and
acceptance of any development target beyond the world's traditional
financial resources on the other would be incompatible; they logically
exclude one another.

Reference may be made in this connection to Mrs. M. J. 't Hooft-
Welvaars' comment, that it would be senseless to aim at closing the trade
gap between the developing and the developed countries in the next few
decades. As long as developing countries have relatively large supplies
of labor – and sometimes land – and very little capital at their disposal,
it will make sense for their current accounts to be in deficit. The emphasis in this direction will increase as the population reaches higher levels
of education [43]. To illustrate this point further I can do no better than
quote the statement by the Governor of the Fund for the Democratic
Republic of Congo, Albert Ndele, at the 1970 Annual Meeting of the
World Bank and the IMF.

'An industrial country, as a rule, expects to show a surplus in its current transactions for reasons inherent in the unequal degree of industrialization in different
regions of the world. Furthermore, this surplus is materially indispensable in order
to obtain the resources that the industrial countries have undertaken to place at the
disposal of the developing countries, which resources should represent, by present
standards, 1 percent of the national product.

It is to be expected that this surplus of the industrial countries for current transactions will amount within five years to some $ 15 billion, if we take into account
the anticipated expansion of the national product and the results obtained during the
decade now ended. Now, this surplus anticipated by the industrial countries implies
an equivalent deficit for the less developed countries. Since, from the point of view
of these latter, the deficit represents financing in the form of real resources indispensable for rapid growth, the accumulation of a large surplus by the industrial
countries and the interests of the developing countries are, therefore, fundamentally
compatible and complementary. But this complementarity implies that the industrial
countries cannot obtain the expected surplus unless they are prepared to finance
the deficit of the less developed countries without thereby excessively aggravating
those countries' burden of debt, either by transferring existing savings to the developing countries *or by creating new instruments of payment for their use.*
(. . .) If the structure of the payments balances in our various countries is a

43 See the introduction to her article 'De grondstoffenproblematiek met betrekking
tot de ontwikkelingslanden' (The problem of primary commodities with respect to
the developing countries), *De Economist*, 1965, no. 7/8, p. 509/510.

normal and even desirable one – since it enables the savings of the industrial world to be used for purposes of development – this can be a reality only insofar as the international payments mechanism effectively ensures an adequate flow of funds toward the developing countries. If, without recognizing this need, the industrial countries nonetheless continue to strive in their activities for surpluses on current transactions, they will inevitably find it necessary to establish exchange restrictions, or even quantitative restrictions. Their policy would result in a contraction of international trade that is incompatible with the aims of the Fund and, very likely, in deflationary pressures by which the less developed countries would not be the only ones affected.

(...) *The obvious links between the functioning of the international payments system and the development of the third world countries now make it necessary for development aid to be incorporated within the organization of the international monetary and financial system. (...)* A satisfactory method for distributing new forms of international liquidity, *when these are created,* would very likely contribute to the solution of this problem' 44.

Minister Ndele's point that the interests of the developing and the industrial countries as to the link between reserve creation and development finance, far from being incompatible, are *complementary* is of fundamental importance. The purpose of reserve creation is to forestall a scramble for reserves accompanied by generally applied restrictive balance of payments practices, deflationary measures, competitive devaluations, and the like. But for this purpose to succeed, not only the *reserve* aims of the major countries should be accommodated but also their *export* aims. Both the actual and the probable future export aims of the industrial countries do not only call for mere reserve creation, but for reserve creation through the 'link'. As the industrial countries as a group systematically strive after substantial export surpluses and do so *regardless* of their – probably much smaller – capital outflow to the developing world, the need for the 'link' is undeniable.

V. IMPROVING THE MONETARY IMPACT OF DELIBERATE RESERVE CREATION; THE NEED FOR RESERVES

One of the historical explanations as to how precious metals like gold and silver have come to assume monetary functions has been based on their *limited availability.* The fact that the money could not be created *ad libitum,* at the wish of the powerful, was a guarantee against depreciation of its exchange value. As only a limited quantity of gold could be newly

44 IMF/IBRD Annual Meetings 1970, *Press Release No. 10,* Statement by the Hon. Albert Ndele, Minister of Finance and Governor of the Fund and the Bank for the Democratic Republic of Congo, pp. 1-3 (my italics).

produced, only a limited quantity could be *monetized*. Interested parties could not influence these circumstances which were of a non-monetary nature.

The development of fiduciary monetary assets called for the invention of a non-physical check on the unlimited expansion of money. This took the form of monetary policy which was based, like all state policies, on the ultimate compulsory powers of national governments. The main concern of ministers of finance and central bankers in this respect has always been to keep money creation within due limits [45], and the central control of the production of money is generally considered as a necessity.

The advantage of gold as a form of money – namely, that its supply was limited – became a disadvantage, when it was found to be *too* limited. There are also good reasons for accepting the view that gold has been in unduly short supply even as a reserve asset for central banks. It seems clear therefore that in the future a supplement to gold, like the Special Drawing Account, is certainly needed. But this is not to deny that there were some major advantages in a limited and, *from the standpoint of individuals, largely uncontrollable* supply of money. One does not need to go so far as President de Gaulle in glorifying without any reservation 'the invariability, the impartiality and the universality that are the privileges of gold' [46], and yet it is still possible to feel that gold did have an 'impartiality' that is lacking in a reserve currency system or the present SDR system. Large countries with an interest in substantial SDR creation have a significant influence in the decision-making process as to the amount to be created. There is no effective authority, as there is on the national scene, and there cannot be. *In these circumstances it would surely be appropriate for the countries concerned to agree that the determination of the amount of SDRs to be created annually should be based on an 'impartial' formula, such as the amount of financing required by multilateral development effort, however this may be defined.* SDRs could then be considered as *monetized development effort;* and there would be a non-monetary check on money creation, just as there was with gold.

The objection may be raised that the outcome of such an 'automatic' formula would not necessarily be in conformity with 'scientifically' deter-

---

45   In this respect, 'conservatism' on the part of ministers of finance and governors of central banks can only be *professional*.

46   President de Gaulle during his press conference on November 27, 1967 (see *Le Monde,* November 29, 1967; the international monetary system is described as 'fondé sur l'immobilité, l'impartiabilité, l'universalité, qui sont les privilèges de l'or').

mined global reserve needs [47], which may well fluctuate. But any so-called scientific determination is surely open to doubt. Even if a need for the creation of, say SDR 2 billion or SDR 5 billion annually could be 'proven', the impact of the interests of the nations concerned and their respective weight in the decision-making process would determine the actual outcome of the negotiations on the amount to be created. Only once that process was complete would the final result be rationalized in 'scientific' terms [48].

The reasoning followed in the 'Proposal by the Managing Director of the International Monetary Fund' concerning the 'Allocation of special drawing rights for the first basic period' [49] is rather questionable. After admitting that none of the 'great many different ways' of setting about the measurement of normal growth in the need for reserves is 'very satisfactory', the Managing Director's official 'Proposal' nevertheless selected some out of a number of possible calculations as the basis for action. Apparently, the fact that more than one (admittedly 'highly tentative') calculation was taken into account, so that 'a set of estimates' was provided, warranted the attachment of a certain value to the average of the results obtained, even though individually they might not be acceptable [50]. This kind of logic lends fuel to the argument that a so-called 'scientific' case for any concrete proposal to create a certain amount of SDRs is likely to be no more than a 'rationalization' [51]. The Managing

47 See also chapter VI, section 1.
48 'There is no way of measuring the 'need' by scientifically tested rules and formulas' (Machlup, *Remaking the international monetary system*, p. 45).
49 Title of the IMF publication mentioned in footnote 20 to chapter III, see p. 14/15 of it.
50 The appropriateness of the methods is left open to judgment; possibly no single method is right; nevertheless the combination of a *number* of methods may be right. This is tantamount to attaching qualitative meaning to a quantative datum, a method not unknown to current social sciences.
51 Something may be said about the particular methods mentioned by the Managing Director: It is said that 'an approach based on the rate of growth of world trade, using for this purpose the growth of imports over the 1952-68 period, could lead to an estimate that the long-term trend in required reserves would increase at a rate of 7 percent per annum' (p. 14). Implicit in this argument is the dubious *assumption* that the relation between trade growth and the growth of reserve needs is 1 to 1. Another mathematical formula might be better, if in fact there is a suitable precise formula at all. The other methods mentioned are also based on *extrapolations* of certain trends in the past. Attaching normative value for present and future policies to past factual relationships, without any judgment as to the particular circumstances that prevailed at the time when those relationships were identified, is a strange way to proceed. For any one method suggesting that a high rate of reserve growth is required, there might be another indicating that a low rate, or even a negative one, would be desirable. If reserve growth had been the

Director himself, for that matter, said in his 1967 speech quoted already earlier (see footnote 22 to chapter III): 'There is not now, and probably never will be, any scientific method of gauging precisely the global need for reserve growth'.

In view of the impossibility of establishing precise figures for global reserve needs and the dangers inherent in any kind of rationalization, another approach should rather be followed. For the need for a new deliberately created reserve asset only appeared when the *structural* deficiencies of the long-term supply mechanism for the traditional reserve assets (gold, dollars, sterling) had become manifest. The primary problem was that the supply was likely to stagnate, apart from any difficulty in estimating the volume of future reserve needs. The shortcomings to be overcome were in fact qualitative rather than quantitative in nature.

In particular, the danger of *gold* shortage called for action. Gold was the only reserve asset financing the difference between world balance of payments surpluses and world balance of payments deficits. The mere availability of such an asset is important. It means that surpluses can accrue *without corresponding deficits,* because these surpluses can be financed by the amount of gold that has entered the monetary circuit. The extent to which this is possible is less important than the mere fact that it happens at all. Both economically and psychologically what is important is that reserve growth should be clearly visible. The very existence of new gold and new SDRs to finance the gap between total surpluses and total deficits makes for a smoother process of reserve distribution. This gap must be clearly visible, but it cannot be too wide without damaging the anti-inflationary adjustment processes. The net creation of international money to the equivalent of $ 1-2 billion in gold and SDRs means that reserve surpluses will exceed reserve losses up to that amount.

It is preferable for analytical reasons to measure this gap between total surpluses and total deficits by leaving out SDR *allocations* and counting only 'earned' SDR balances (in the present system called 'excess holdings'). SDR creation through allocations to countries is a new balance of payments category quite different from the traditional main categories:

---

same as trade growth, say, since 1950, reserves would nowadays amount to many times the present figure, with which the world does in fact manage. At the other extreme, Professor Goudriaan calculates 'the minimum amount of aggregate national reserves required for the world as a whole' at the end of 1964 at *half* of the actual figure at that time. (See the appendix (in English) to his article 'De goudwissel-grondstoffenstandaard' in *De Economist,* November/December 1966).

those creating a surplus on international transactions and those financing it [52]. Changes in the level of national monetary reserves caused by SDR allocations have no liquidity effect on the national economy (unless the treasury sells the SDRs to the central bank and spends the proceeds, a kind of behaviour which would be certainly against the philosophy of the SDR system). An important feature of the creation mechanism proposed in this chapter is that *the SDR-financed gap between the world total of surpluses on international transactions and the world total of deficits, which is the essential thing that matters, becomes directly manageable.* This is a major advantage compared to the present system.

With SDR creation in the order of magnitude of SDR 1-2 billion, relatively few countries are likely to suffer unduly large deficits, so that it should be possible to avoid an illiberal world climate, 'with governments pursuing policies restricting imports, prohibiting capital movements, cutting down aid to poorer nations, manipulating interest rates, and controlling incomes and prices' [53]. Naturally, if certain countries wish to acquire reserves beyond the new gold and SDRs available, they will be dependent on the willingness of other countries to pay (i.e. to move into deficit). However, this is only in accordance with the economic law that every seller needs a buyer.

The paradoxical conclusion is therefore that while a need for reserve growth may be claimed to exist on psychological and economic grounds, it cannot be quantified. Any method that pretends to be able to 'prove' a reserve need of a more or less precise figure is based on an assumption regarding the reserve acquirement aims of the countries concerned. These aims thus become 'data', and are not subject to adjustment. Hence there may be some conflict with the very idea of international cooperation, which implies that conflicting aims should be harmonized. It is surely not in the international interest that inconsistencies between national reserve aims should be ironed out through reserve creation rather than through adjustment of the aims themselves. From the international point of view one must distinguish between 'legitimate' and 'illegitimate' liquidity needs, as Javier Márquez rightly does in the following words: '(. . .) The shortage of reserves of individual countries is not always independent of policies, whether they are wise or foolish, and if the 'illegitimate' liquidity needs are satisfied, they are likely to persist, and new illegitimate needs

52 See John S. Smith and Arie C. Bouter, 'The treatment of reserves and of reserve creation in the balance of payments accounts', IMF *Staff Papers*, Vol. XVI No. 2 (July 1969), pp. 204-207.
53 Machlup, (*Remaking the international monetary system*, p. 45) states that a 'rather illiberal' world is likely when 'many countries suffer deficits'.

may arise, all of which would lead to an inflatonary spiral throughout the world. This is well-explored ground and leads to the rejection of any automatic mechanism for the creation of liquidity according to the 'needs' of individual countries' [54]. I agree fully with this statement, for the reasons set out in chapter I, section 3. Although Mr. Márquez may not be quite right when he says 'that there is no such thing as an abstract 'world need for reserves' ' [54] – for it can be argued that the world money supply mechanism must provide for reserve growth for financing the positive difference between total surpluses and total deficits – it cannot be said too often that the need for reserves is made visible in the form of demands by particular countries, on the legitimateness of whose claims we have to pass judgment.

The 'reserve needs' of a country are not an autonomous factor; they depend on its plans for growth, its adjustment policy, its desire for prestige or other objectives. A determination of world reserve needs on the basis of the needs of individual countries is only possible if specific assumptions are made with respect to policies in these fields. However, as the world's reserves needs cannot be represented by an absolute figure, such a procedure is not necessary, even if it was practicable.

It will thus be seen that the advantage of creating SDRs only as the monetary counterpart of multilateral development efforts, namely, that the pressures of *individual* countries in behalf of their *direct* interest would be eliminated, would not be offset by the disadvantage that the 'existing' reserve need might not be met. On the contrary, SDR creation is provided with a ceiling, something that is essential in any form of money creation.

Two things must be borne in mind, in this respect. First, the proportion of international assistance to be monetized can be made greater or smaller, and the amount of SDRs to be created can be adjusted accordingly. A smaller or greater portion of IDA operations could be financed through SDRs; in addition, gross disbursements by other multilateral development agencies to less developed countries could be financed in that way [55]. SDRs might even be used to finance other internationally agreed purposes, such

54 Javier Márquez, 'Developing countries and the international monetary system', p. 132.
55 In 1968 these were as follows (in millions of U.S. dollars): World Bank 605, International Development Association 215, International Finance cooperation 31, Inter-American Development Bank 233, Asian Development Bank 20, African Development Bank 2, European Development Fund 121, European Investment Bank 10, U.N. Institutions 300; total 1537. The total figures were in the years 1960-1967 respectively: 483, 548, 725, 950, 1112, 1248, 1421, 1551 (Source: *Pearson Report*, p. 390).

as 'United Nations peace-keeping and other agreed objectives' (Triffin [56]) or the operation of 'the entire United Nations and its specialized agencies' (Byron L. Johnson [57]). But the World Bank Group alone is able to finance projects in a scale that would make reserve creation in this way worthwhile. In his speech at the 1968 Annual Meeting, the President of the World Bank said: 'I believe that globally the Bank Group should during the next five years lend twice as much as during the past five years' [58]. One reason why preference may be given to using SDR creation for *development* financing is that the increase in the world volume of money is coupled with an increase in productive capacity, that may give rise directly or indirectly to additional trade movements later, so that part of the SDRs created can be spent again by the developed countries in the developing countries. After all, development is one of the Fund's purposes [59].

Second, liquidity can also be created through the General Account of the IMF. A relatively small creation of SDRs would have the great advantage of not impairing the multilateral surveillance of balance of payments policies which is the corollary of requests for drawings in the credit tranches of the Fund [60].

From the monetary point of view there are still other arguments in favor of the creation of SDRs through development financing by the IDA. First, the initial beneficiaries will be those countries that have the biggest need for reserves (the developing countries), and it would be possible to meet their needs without allocating the same proportional amounts to countries that have no legitimate need for additional reserves (see chapter IV, 'First objection'). The developed countries can *earn* additional reserves if they

56 See Subcommittee, *Hearing 1969*, p. 29.
57 *Ibid.*, p. 88. Johnson observes that this currently amounts to $ 550 million a year (p. 92). He suggests, in an article in *War/Peace Report,* February 1968, 'seven novel ways to increase the total budget of the world organization from $ 550 million to $ 14 billion, allowing for a vast increase in assistance to underdeveloped nations' (*Ibid.*, p. 87 ff).
58 Robert S. McNamara, President, World Bank Group, *Address to the Board of Governors,* Washington D.C., 1968, p. 5. World Bank lendings should increase to about $ 1.6 billion a year. In his 1970 address, the President stated: 'Should we succeed, it will mean that we will have approved loans, credits and investments during these five years that aggregate $ 12 billion for high-priority development projects – projects whose total cost will approximate $ 30 billion. (. . .) I can report to you that we are on schedule' (p 2). These figures relate to the whole Bank Group and the period 1969-1973.
59 See chapter IV, section 2, second paragraph.
60 See the document mentioned in footnote 44 to chapter IV, p. 6.

feel a need for them. The following remarks by John R. Karlik are worth mentioning [61]: 'The need to earn additional [62] SDRs through payments surpluses would tend to check their distribution. General distributions of SDRs under the existing (system) will be based on what nations say their reserve needs will be in the future; the willingness to earn reserves through payments surpluses is a far more substantial demonstration of a perceived need. Conservative [63] Fund members fear the unrestrained creation of fiduciary reserve assets. The requirement that need be demonstrated through net external earnings should ease these fears'. To summarize: linking SDR creation to IDA operations would *economize* on the SDRs that are required to meet any presumed 'global need for reserves' (See chapter IV, section 2, 'First objection').

Second, the fact that the primary beneficiaries of SDR creation would generally be the countries with structurally weak payments positions can only be considered a direct step toward the first goal of international monetary collaboration: the promotion of global equilibrium between national payments positions. The *balance of payments problems* of most of the world would be alleviated in the process. (See chapter IV, section 2, 'Second objection' [64].)

Third, multilateral 'aid' agencies would be able to expand their operations, and thus stimulate international competition, which is not encouraged by tied bilateral aid. Thus world inflation is likely to be checked because the international bidding process tends to ensure that orders are placed with the lowest bidders. The result is likely to be an increase in economic activity in those parts of the world where productive capacity is less fully occupied then elsewhere, a process more in accord with general economic principles than the present method of allocating SDRs. This method has been described as being akin to establishing some 'new

61 Subcommittee, *On linking reserve creation and development assistance,* a staff study (written by John R. Karlik), Washington D.C., April 1969, p. 11.
62 The word 'additional' here relates to Mr. Karlik's own proposal: 'to provide a special issue of SDRs that Fund members desiring additional reserves could purchase at their own volition with the foreign exchange proceeds of earlier payments surpluses' *(Ibid.,* p. 9). The present allocation system would remain unmodified.
63 Reference may be made to footnote 45.
64 The following remark by Tinbergen *(Shaping the world economy,* p. 122) may be quoted: 'The favorable impact of investment aid on the balance of payments of the receiving countries deserve more attention than has so far been given to it. Many institutions are now engaged in dealing with exchange controls and trade restrictions; they will find their problems largely solved if more aid is given for development. This is particularly true of the activities of the International Monetary Fund'.

bank which would be committed by its very character to allot its credits automatically among all prospective customers in strict proportion to their height, or to their waistline, so as not to have to bother the Management about deciding on the comparative usefulness of alternative uses of the bank's lending capacity' (Triffin [65]). If the proposed system were adopted and developed countries could only acquire reserves by earning them, the outcome would be anti-inflatory; for those countries would only succeed in capturing their share of the new monetary resources if they are competitive in the world market, and they can be so only if they keep inflation under control as least as well as their competitors. Distributing the whole of the new reserves in this fashion would be 'fully consistent with the principle of multilateral trade and with the high degree of competitiveness that should prevail in world trade' (Prebisch [66]). On the other hand, allocating SDRs to *countries* regardless of whether they have relatively stable prices or whether they allow inflationary price trends to remain unchecked can only stimulate inflation. IDA-linked SDR creation could of course, have an inflationary impact on countries supplying real resources, just as in the present system. But it would not be possible for countries with an inflated economy to use SDRs newly allocated to them for sustaining their export of inflation to the world. Developing countries generally have exchange systems that largely isolate them from the world economy. They cannot afford to maintain exchange systems that allow domestic inflation to cause current account deficits. SDRs would be used on (internationally agreed) development and not as a consequence of domestic inflation. In the present system, however, the use of new SDRs by developed countries is likely to aggravate world inflation not only by perhaps causing inflationary tensions in the countries from which they import goods, but also because domestic inflation is facilitated, which again may stimulate world inflation.

Finally, the creation of SDRs only through the monetization of development activity would enable us to improve some of the present rules on the holding and use of special drawing rights, a matter that will be discussed further in the next section. It may be added that the quality of SDRs as reserve assets will improve because all SDRs will have been earned, and hence have a psychological significance which may be lacking with SDRs that are obtained in the cheapest possible manner, by way of allocation.

65 See Subcommittee, *Hearing,* 1969, p. 40.
66 *Ibid.,* p. 31.

VI. FITTING THE NEW CREATION MECHANISM INTO THE PRESENT RULES OF THE SPECIAL DRAWING ACCOUNT

One of the possible ways of establishing a link between SDR creation and development financing would be to allow individual developed countries to use SDRs for what they see as their aid obligations. This proposal has been made on many occasions [67]. One objection to it has been that the image of SDRs would suffer. The fact that any country that wished to get rid of SDRs could easily do so by using them instead of traditional aid financing would impair the balanced distribution of SDR holdings around the world, and, hence the 'credibility' of the asset.

I mention this argument, not because I advocate such a 'voluntary' link, but because the criticism is not valid.

The Fund's rules governing the 'Designation of participants to provide currency' [68], which were framed by analogy with the existing practices of the General Account with respect to 'Currencies to be drawn and to be used in repurchases' [69] are such as to make it impossible for countries disliking SDRs to get rid of them on those grounds alone. The Executive Board would immediately restore their SDR holdings, by *designating* the country concerned to provide currency in exchange for *new* SDRs which it would have to accept (unless its balance of payments and gross reserve position was not 'sufficiently strong'). 'Participants shall be designated in such manner as will promote over time a balanced distribution of holdings of special drawing rights among them' [70]. The result is intended to be the *harmonization of the composition of official monetary reserves around the world,* in as far as these are held with the International Monetary Fund, whether in the General Account *or the Special Drawing Account.* This can be considered as a marked historical development in international monetary cooperation. Harmonization of reserves should greatly improve monetary stability by decreasing the scope for shifts between reserve components, a traditional threat to confidence in reserve assets.

This important feature of the SDR scheme must, of course, be maintained. There should be no difficulty in doing so; the Fund could still designate participants, and the use of SDRs by participants could still be

---

67 See chapter VII, section 3.
68 *Fund Agreement,* Art. XXV, Section 5.
69 See International Monetary Fund, *Selected decisions of the Executive Directors and selected documents,* 4th issue, Washington D.C. 1970, p. 37–43 (also reproduced in the Fund's *Annual Report* 1962).
70 *Fund Agreement,* Art. XXV, Section 5 (a) (i) and (b). See also Section 3 of the same Article.

governed by the same rules [71]. The only differences would be that there would be only one first user of SDRs: the International Development Association. The IDA would have to become an 'other holder' of SDRs [72], to which exclusively allocations are made on January 1 of each year, *in accordance with the creation decision for the basic period concerned.*

For any loan by IDA to a developing country, IDA would be able to use SDRs up to the amount needed. The Fund would then designate participants in the Special Drawing Account to provide the currency required, as at present. There would be no need to create SDRs *(i.e. to designate the participants that will be the first countries to hold the newly created SDRs)* before expenditures have to made in the developing countries. The IDA would incur a formal debt position in the books of the Fund, just as the developing countries become debtors of IDA [73].

The existing *designation* technique is a reply to those who argue that a link between SDR creation and development must not come too early because the SDR *must first become 'firmly established'* as a reserve asset. The provisions in the SDR agreement concerning the *obligation* of members to provide currency in return for SDRs are a sufficient guarantee in themselves.

The obligation of members to provide currency against SDRs could remain proportional to *Fund quotas,* as it is now. At present, participants need not accept more than twice their net cumulative allocation of SDRs, an amount that itself is related to their Fund quota [74]. Under the system here proposed the principle of proportionality to quotas could be retained. The 200 percent limit could be retained also: 200 percent of that portion

---

71   Some relaxation of the Fund's attitude toward the 'requirement of need' as a condition for using SDRs (Art. XXV, Section 3) might be possible. The principle as such would, however, survive because it is implied in the Fund's designation technique.
72   Art. XXIII, Section 3, enables the Fund to prescribe 'as holders, non-members, members that are non-participants, and institutions that perform functions of a central bank for more than one member'. The wording would need some adjustment or addition. At present, *allocations* can be made exclusively to participants and not to 'other holders'. The principle Article in which the IDA should appear would of course be the present Article XXIV, which governs the way in which SDRs are to be allocated.
73   The terms of the debt positions of developing countries vis-à-vis IDA would, in my opinion, not require any change. The present conditions are: repayment within 50 years; grace period 10 years; 0.75 percent interest. A 'poverty test' has been applied since 1964. Members with per capita GNP above $ 300 are ruled out. Those members are not ineligible for 'hard' IBRD loans. (See *Pearson Report,* p. 161 and 226).
74   *Fund Agreement,* Art. XXV, Section 4.

of the total amount of existing (circulating) SDRs, which corresponds to the ratio of the participant's quota to total Fund quotas. As the SDR is a reserve asset in the full sense, however, there would be no objection to raising this limit, or dropping it entirely. The essential thing is that 'earned' SDRs are distributed according to the gold and foreign exchange positions of eligible participants.

I would consider it an improvement in the SDR system to drop the *'reconstitution'* rules. The present provision to the effect that a participant shall maintain average holdings amounting to 30 percent of net cumulative allocations over a five-year period is rather ambiguous. The provision has no great significance as 70 percent of allocated special drawing rights can be considered as being entirely equal to money. Why should we not make 100 percent of it? Application of the rule requires difficult calculations and procedures. On the other hand, if country holdings of SDRs were fully *earned,* and were thus similar to gold, dollars and other traditional reserve assets, there would no longer be any psychological reason for the reconstitution provision. The position would be covered by the designation principles already in force [75].

The money-like character of SDRs could also be enhanced in another way. Under the present provision countries making net use of their allocations must pay interest of 1½ percent [76]. Moreover, countries that acquire SDRs beyond their allocations ('excess holdings'), receive interest at the same moderate rate [77]. This is low in comparison to the present return on liquid investments; it would improve the attraction of SDRs – whose primary function is to be a *store of value,* and hence an investment medium (as has been observed in chapter III, section 3) – if the interest rate to be earned on holdings could be increased. (Countries would not have to *pay* interest on the *use* of SDRs, as in the proposed system all country holdings will have the same character as the present 'excess holdings').

Now, the rate of return on SDRs could be raised if not only IDA operations but also IBRD lendings were to be financed through SDR

75 Article XXV, Section 6 (b) of the *Fund Agreement* provides for abrogation of the rules for reconstitution by an eighty-five percent majority of the total voting power in the Fund.

76 *Fund Agreement,* Art. XXVI. Interest to be paid by a participant is considered as a 'charge', as in the General Account of the Fund.

77 Loans to the Fund (such as under the General Arrangements to Borrow) also presently bear 1½ percent interest; in addition, the 'renumeration' received by Fund members on their *super gold tranche positions* amounts to 1½ percent per annum *(Fund Agreement,* Art. V, Section 9; see also Art. XII, Section 6 (b)).

creation (see footnote 55). The World Bank would borrow newly created SDRs (or rather SDRs *to be* created, cf. chapter V, section 3) from the IMF, perhaps through IDA, and lend the currency proceeds of the Fund's designations to developing countries, in the same way as it has been suggested above could be done by IDA. The World Bank would have to continue borrowing and lending on market terms. Thus it would be able to pay a high rate of interest to the Fund, which could in turn pay a higher rate to its SDR holders than at present. The rate would of course be lower than the one paid by the World Bank because IDA itself could not pay interest (perhaps a very small 'service charge'); but, depending on the 'blending' of Bank and IDA loans to be financed, the rate could closely approximate market rates for liquid investments. Assuming that SDR 2 billion a year were created, of which SDR 1.5 billion were in favor of the Bank and SDR 0.5 billion in favor of IDA, if the Bank paid 8 percent interest, SDR holders could receive an over-all return of about 6 percent. There is nothing financially unsound in this conclusion. The Fund could every year decide to *distribute the net income from SDR operations to participants,* just as is now done with the General Account. Such an arrangement would become particularly significant over the longer term. As per capita income rises, the time will come when the need for soft development loans will decline. Investment on market terms is, however, unlikely to cease. The role of the World Bank as a leader in international investment will thus continue to be of great value for the world economy.

The improvement of the 'reserve status' of SDRs in the way described could lessen the likelihood of participants withdrawing from the scheme. If a member still wishes to terminate its participation it could perhaps be repaid by the Fund when the World Bank redeemed part of its debt to the Fund [78].

If SDRs had a better reserve status, it might be more attractive for the communist countries to become participants. Their adherence to the scheme could greatly expand its 'backing', and thus enhance the usability of SDRs. Politically, communist countries may find SDRs preferable to dollars as a reserve asset. The Articles of Agreement prevent non-members of the Fund from becoming participants in the Special Drawing

78 The Fund could also use repayments by the IDA or the World Bank to designate itself when a participant wishes to use SDRs. (The Special Drawing Account would become like a real bank if the system described in this chapter is adopted.) Holdings of SDRs by the Fund and cancellations of SDRs are examples of reserve destruction. Of course, as long as the World Bank and IDA continue to expand their operations it will be possible to create reserves through these institutions.

Account [79]. But as long as communist or other non-member nations see difficulties in becoming members of the Fund (the multilateral surveillance of members' internal policies being probably the major stumbling-block), the Fund might allow them to participate in the Special Drawing Account as 'other holders' in the sense of Article XXIII, Section 3 of the Fund Agreement [80]. After all, the Special Drawing Account is intended to be a fully independent affair, not directly related to the General Account (the Special Drawing Account being a reserve creation institution, and the General Account only a 'cloakroom' of reserves [81]). Most non-members of the Fund are not only UN members, but also have an interest in the development of the weakest parts of the world economy; moreover, they might see an advantage in holding 'supplements to gold' in their reserves.

Finally, to revert to an earlier point, if SDR are created in connection with IBRD operations and not by way of allocations to countries, objections may be raised as to the possibility of liquidating the Special Drawing Account. However, even in the present setting any plan for liquidating the scheme after large amounts of SDRs have been created would cause problems. The likelihood of liquidation is however rather 'theoretical'. While liquidation provisions must perhaps be embodied in the Fund Articles (cf. Art. XXXI) for legal reasons, it is hardly conceivable that the scheme would be liquidated on economic grounds. The 'need' for reserves may not be quantifiable, but if such a thing exists, it will only increase in the future. As the scheme is world wide, there are no 'liquidity' problems. Balance of payments deficits are always matched by surpluses that automatically generate the 'demand' for the existing 'supply' of SDRs [82]. Nevertheless, if does become necessary to liquidate,

79 *Fund Agreement,* Art. XXIII, Section 1.
80 Non-members are allowed to become 'other holders'. The use of currencies of non-member countries that are of course not convertible in the sense of Art. VIII of the Agreement might cause some difficulties; but there is nothing to prevent these countries from accepting SDRs in exchange for gold or dollars.
81 A cloakroom cannot create coats and umbrellas but only deliver those that earlier have been put in it. 'The IMF (. . .) does play a role in the creation of international reserves, though this role is confined to putting into circulation the currencies created by national monetary authorities. It remains true that the IMF is a warehouse, transfer agent, and rental service for national currencies received from member countries' (Machlup, 'The cloaksoom rule of international reserves', *Quarterly Journal of Economics,* August 1965, p. 341). (See also chapter III, section 3 on the creation of reserves as a 'by-product' of the operations of the General Account).
82 Although the following quotations do not speak of the SDR system itself, they are fully relevant to the question of 'liquidity'. 'For international payments in the same world, the assets (amount, quality, composition, liquidity) of the reserve bank (or an appropriately organized IMF) are irrelevent; they become relevant only for

the difficulties would probably not be greater than they would be after the creation of large amounts of SDRs under the present system. The World Bank and IDA would resume their present fund-raising techniques on a full scale; they would have to reach an agreement with the Fund for the settlement of their debts out of repayments from the developing countries and new capital and contributions. A similar but easier case would arise in the event of a partial cancellation of special drawing rights under Article XXIV of the Fund Agreement; but this too seems to be very unlikely in practice.

Paragraph 138 of the 'Ossola Report' (1965) contains the following reference to the 'link': 'Most members also hold the view that the character of an asset depends to some extent on its quality in case of liquidation of the scheme or of withdrawal of members. In case of liquidation of the scheme, participants would receive long-term IBRD bonds, which might not meet the requirements of liquidity demanded by a central bank. For these reasons, therefore, the idea of combining asset creation with development finance was not widely favored'. One might observe, however, that fears about 'liquidation' were more appropriate when the idea of reserve creation within a limited group of countries still prevailed than they are now. Second, the IBRD bonds would be only one possible method of liquidating debts and claims. If that technique were to be used, why could the bonds not be made temporarily transferable? (IBRD bonds do already play a role in central bank reserves, although mostly only with maturity limits of no more than two years [83]).

---

payments to persons, banks or reserve banks on other planets, that is, for *interplanetary payments*' (Machlup, *ibid.*, p. 343).

'The world pool of reserves being destined to grow overtime, with little or no probability that circumstances would ever require a sudden or massive contraction, the Fund should never face any drastic reduction of its deposit liabilities, forcing it to liquidate any substantial portion of its global assets. Balance of payments settlements among IMF reserve holders will reshuffle the Fund's deposit liabilities among its members, but should not reduce their total amount'. (Triffin, *Our international monetary system, yesterday, today, and tomorrow,* New York, 1968, p. 137/138).

83 Cf. World Bank/International Development Association, *Annual Report* 1970, p. 35/36: 'The principal supplier of new borrowed funds in fiscal 1970 was the Bank of Japan, which lent a total of Y 72,000 million (U.S. $ 200 million equivalent) to the World Bank. (...) The Bank of Japan stated that it had decided to extend them on the basis of recent developments in Japan's balance of payments which had added materially to the country's monetary reserves. The Bank of Japan added that further factors influencing its decision regarding the loans were 'the great contribution toward the development of the Japanese economy' made by the World Bank, and a desire on the part of Japan to 'help the World Bank's activities and thereby strengthen international monetary cooperation'. Lending by the Bank of

VII. CONCLUSION

The conclusion of this chapter is that the Special Drawing Account of the Fund must be used as a credit-creating financial institution. On the asset side, it should operate like an investment bank, financing the world's economic development where it is most needed. On the liability side, the balance sheet would consist of compulsory deposits: the SDR holdings of designated countries. This would not be a substitute for the future 'world central bank' with fully discretionary powers. The Fund would be unable either to acquire deposits from any source it wished, or to invest its money according to an independent policy. A detailed set of Articles would continue to be in force to govern the limits of credit creation, the beneficiaries of such creation, and the holding and use of the deposits by members, all in the name of international public interest, sound monetary cooperation, and the development of the world's productive resources.

The Special Drawing Account *is* already a banking institution, as it acquires compulsory deposits (i.e. 'excess holdings') in an internationally agreed manner. However, at present there is no active international policy with respect to the distribution of credit. At the beginning of each allocation period the participants decide to hand out money to each other according to their respective 'waistlines' (i.e. their 'economic status' as reflected by their Fund quotas [84]). What is needed is to allow the Special Drawing Account to operate actively not only on the liability side but also on the asset side in line with an *international policy*. As things stand now, 'the arbitrariness of the new facility is alarming, as it enables an international agency to supply its members with new means of payments, without an objective criterion regulating their distribution in any serious manner' [85].

Japan to the World Bank was divided into two separate loans of Y 36,000 million each, in February and March 1970. (...) Terms (...) included interest at a rate of 7.14 percent a year and repayments of principal serially over the period 1973-75. (...) At June 30, 1970 the Bank's outstanding funded debt stood at $ 4,568 million equivalent (...). 20 percent is held largely by central banks and other governmental accounts in some 75 countries'. (One of the most important creditors in the recent past has been the Deutsche Bundesbank).

84 R. Triffin, 'Prepared statement' for the Subcommittee *etc.*, *Hearing*, 1969, p. 40.
85 Pierre Mendès-France, 'Opbouw van een stabiel monetair systeem', *Nieuwe Rotterdamse Courant*, September 30, 1969. Personally I find the term 'objective' most confusing; I would rather say 'adequate' in the quotation above.

VI. Discussion of arguments against the principle of a 'link'

I. INCOMPATIBILITY OF OBJECTIVES?

In the following chapter it is intended to deal with a number of recent arguments against the *principle* of linking SDR creation with development financing. Most of the answers to the questions that will be mentioned have already been implicit in the earlier chapters.

What might be called a 'classical' argument against linking liquidity creation with development activity is that they are 'separate issues, each with its own economics and, more important, with its own politics' [1]. On closer examination, however, this is rather a strange criticism, for two economic reasons.

First, on the domestic plane it is quite conceivable that additional government spending deliberately takes the form of deficit spending

---

[1] These words are taken from Harry G. Johnson (*Hearing* before the Subcommittee on International Exchange and Payments of the Joint Economic Committee, Congress of the United States, May 28, 1969, p. 16), who, however, adds the following remark: 'One can argue that the linkage of these two problems in policy discussions is really a matter of willingness of governments to link them, and that perhaps at the present time this possibility is greater than it has been in the past, and that is a matter on which I am not competent to pass a judgment'. Other places are the Group of Ten reports of 1965 ('Most members believe that the provision of capital to developing countries is a problem quite distinct from the creation of reserves and should be achieved by other techniques', paragraph 138, first sentence) and 1966 ('We have treated reserve creation as a problem distinct from the provision of capital for developing countries', paragraph 7 (f), last sentence).

financed through money creation, when both the spending itself and the resulting increase of the money stock are desirable. In cases where the latter is the *primary* goal, the resulting rise in total spending will be a corollary that may be distinguished from the money creation but cannot be separated from it. Creation of additional money always has an effect within the real sphere. Governments do not use to create money simply by handing it out to all possible holders of money, i.e. all citizens. Second, the argument that two or more goals may not be served by one instrument is the last to be expected from an economist! Nothing more economical can be imagined, than serving one goal and gaining another desirable effect 'automatically' in the process. Not to grasp this opportunity would be like producing gas and wasting the coke which is automatically produced at the same time [2].

The problem is not how to choose between a 'link' or 'no link'. Money creation always has certain effects within the 'real' sphere; and there has always been a link between international liquidity creation and international spending, including spending on development. In the past dollars and pounds have accumulated in foreign hands largely as the result of American and British payments deficits brought on by giving aid to less developed countries. This is the reason why Robert Triffin speaks of the *traditional* link 'between the creation of fiduciary reserves and development financing' [3]. To quote: 'Far from constituting a revolutionary innovation in international monetary practice, the 'link' would merely preserve an essential feature of the gold-exchange standard. The accumul-

---

[2] The following observation of John Karlik (*On linking reserve creation and development assistance,* a staff study prepared for use of the Subcommittee *etc.,* p. 2) may be quoted: 'Opponents of any link between these two goals have generally pointed out that the objectives are distinct, that there is no direct interrelationship between them, and, therefore, that each problem should be solved independently according to its particular facets. Such a distinction between objectives and the means used to attain them is normally a sound analytical and practical device. Occasionally, however, two problems can be solved more easily if considered together rather than independently. The linking of separable issues is perhaps most commonly used as a political tactic, but occasionally examples also occur in the area of economic policy. For instance, both domestic monopolies and persistent external surpluses can be attacked through the removal of tariff barriers, even though there may be no causal link between the two problems'.

Mr. Sidney Dell mentions other examples: a devaluation affects exports *and* imports; 'a high tax on tobacco tends to restrain a harmfull consumption at the same time as it adds to government revenue'. 'It is difficult to see why the fact that a particular measure may achieve two different types of results at the same time should be regarded as invalidating it' (*Hearing* before the Subcommittee *etc.,* 1969, p. 8).

[3] *Ibid.,* p. 42.

ation of sterling balances as reserves by foreign central banks traditionally helped Britain finance a larger amount of capital exports – particularly to less developed countries – than it could have sustained otherwise. The same was true of the dollar balances accumulated, in the same way, by foreign central banks, and particularly by the surplus countries of continental Europe since the end of World War II' [4].

The basic problem is how to *control internationally* the spending, whether for development or other purposes, of SDRs that are created *by international agreement.*

Separating the use of money from its creation would be tantamount to denying the economic character of monetary economics [5]. At this point I may refer back to what has been said in the previous chapter (sections 3 and 4) about the desirability of providing the combined Bretton Woods institutions, on the basis of voluntary *international* cooperation, with similar functions as are performed by *national* treasuries to control the first use of SDRs (their 'injection into the system').

Professor Tinbergen has commented most interestingly on the role of a central bank as distinct from that of a treasury [6], the former mainly handling 'monetary' policy, dealing with the *stock* of money, and the latter 'financial' policy, dealing with the *flow* of money. Since the depression of the Thirties, Tinbergen says, it has been discovered

'that the flow of money is more important than the stock of money. It is the flow which determines the volume of production and is the source of material well-being. We can observe that the relation between money flow and stock is a loose one, especially in the short run. Only severe restrictions on new credits have any direct influence on the flow of total demand; other instruments of monetary policy are of secondary importance' [7]. 'It follows that genuine and wholehearted cooperation between the 'two poles' is necessary: contradictory policies are intolerable. That being the case, the government must have the last word in any conflict between the central bank and the treasury: there cannot be two captains on one ship. At the same time, this final responsibility puts a heavy obligation on the government. Not all governments have been sufficiently aware of the role they should play and this explains why central bank experts and others tend to favor an independent central bank' [8].

4 *Ibid.*, p. 40.
5 Reference may again be made to Article I (ii) of the Fund Agreement where it is said that one of the *Fund's* purposes is 'to facilitate the expansion and balanced growth of international trade, and to contribute thereby to the promotion and maintenance of high levels of employment and real income and to the development of the productive resources of all members as *primary* objectives of economic policy' (my italics.)
6 See *Shaping the world economy*, Chapter 9 ('Financial and monetary systems and stability'), Section 9.1 ('Role of financial and monetary policies').
7 *Ibid.*, p. 168.
8 *Ibid.*, p. 168/169.

Now, if the flow of money is more important than the stock of money within a single country, it is even more so internationally. Here *a fortiori* it can be said that 'the relation between money flow and money stock is a loose one'. In a situation of near-equilibrium of payments throughout the world as a whole, movements of *monetary reserves* will be very small and there will be almost no net flow of money. (It is the *net* flow of money between countries in which we are primarily interested when dealing with the problem of reserve creation). Suppose, all over the world annual balances of payments are completely in equilibrium, and in this situation reserve creation does occur, thus setting up new international reserve flows; it is clear that it is the direction of the newly induced flow of international reserves (settling the payments balances) that determines its impact on international material well-being. In other words, what counts is the way in which the new reserves are spent. The fact that there are reserve flows as such does even not necessarily have any impact on the level of world economic demand. The important difference between national money and international monetary reserves is that there is no direct relationship between total world demand for goods and services and the size of the world stock of reserves, whereas there is such a relationship domestically. World economic activity may very well rise with a constant level of global reserves. International trade can even increase without restriction, provided that payments imbalances are avoided or limited; and if imbalances do occur, the extent to which they influence world demand will vary greatly, depending on the causes, and the policies adopted to counter them.

The conclusion must be, that, if domestic central banks cannot be really independent from treasuries either economically (cf. Tinbergen, quoted above) or legally, *mutatis mutandis* the same holds true with even greater force internationally. The IMF is normally considered an institution for facilitating cooperation between central banks and a 'purely monetary' affair. Paradoxically, however, decisions to create either SDRs or conditional liquidity through quota increases are made by *governments,* in which Ministers of Foreign Affairs play a certain role alongside Ministers of Finance. But, even more paradoxically, this being the case, no decision whatsoever is made about the flow of reserves or the direction of that flow. We could hardly imagine such an ambiguous political influence on the monetary policy of the central bank.

The point I wish to make is that if monetary cooperation between nations is concerned with four separate but interdependent problems, namely, liquidity, development, adjustment, and confidence, and *'all four problems can be formulated in terms of 'monetary reserves"* [9], what can be the objection to extending international collaboration to all four, instead of to the three of them on which everyone is already agreed? Why not kill two, three or more birds with one stone if possible? SDR creation in order to provide funds for multilateral development activity is certainly a form of money creation, and it serves 'development' *as well as* 'liquidity'. It is most probably more anti-inflatory than the present technique of reserve creation, and it fosters both balance of payments 'adjustment' and price 'stability'. Finally, 'confidence' is enhanced to the extent that the new reserves are captured by the United States and the United Kingdom, thus diminishing their enormous liabilities bolstering them in their valuable roles of providing key currencies for the operation of the world's payments system [10]. The question is: do we want to shape an international monetary policy for SDRs in the 'broad' sense [11], or not?

At the end of section 4 of the preceding chapter, we showed that it was not a link with development financing that would be incompatible with the smooth operation of the international monetary and financial system, but the absence of such as link. Besides Minister Ndele of the Democratic Republic of Congo, Minister Giscard d'Estaing of France has defended at least the *principle* of the link on the grounds of the connection between monetary economics and developments economics. 'We cannot claim to solve the problems of development', he said at the Fund's 1965 Annual Meeting,

'by taking almost exclusively the approach of investment financing. The whole of the economic relationship between strong and weak countries has to be organized as such. In my view, *the improvement of that relationship constitutes the indispensable complement to any progress in the international field of financial and monetary cooperation.* Therefore, an effort of imagination such as we propose to undertake in the reform of the world *monetary* system, and which, to be sure, concerns only the industrialized countries, should be dedicated to *increasing the resources of developing countries.* (...) It is conceivable that a distribution of additional reserve assets could take into account, among various criteria, the actual efforts made by each country in favor of developing countries. If there is a wish

9 Fritz Machlup, *Remaking the international monetary system,* p. 76.
10 The 'confidence' aspect was particularly stressed in the 'Stamp Plan'. See Maxwell Stamp, 'The reform of the international monetary system', *Moorgate and Wall Street,* Summer 1965, p. 11.
On the 'killing of the birds' the same author some years earlier made the following sensible remark: ' 'Killing two birds' at once ought to be an advantage, but in practice it smacks of black magic or gimmickry and anyone who thinks that either of the birds does not need killing will oppose it, without considering the other advantages' ('The Stamp Plan – 1962 version', *Moorgate and Wall Street,* Autumn 1962, p. 7.)
11 See chapter I, section 1.

that both the problem of reforming the monetary system and that of transferring resources in favor of less developed countries *should be dealt with simultaneously,* one single endeavor is not enough. There is a need for two. Let us impose upon ourselves the discipline of the mind together with the creative effort of the will' [12]

Mr. Schweitzer has rightly observed that one cannot say that a link between reserve creation and development assistance would not be feasible. In his statement of December 1967 he said:

'While *there was nothing technically impracticable about this way of getting new reserves into circulation among monetary authorities,* the idea was generally un-welcome to industrial countries who felt that the provision of aid and the creation of international liquidity called for two distinct decisions, each of which should be taken deliberately on its own merits by appropriate procedures, and that reserve creation should not provide a back door through which aid-giving could be freed, in some measure, from the restraints of parliamentary control over expenditure' [13].

As for parliamentary control, this argument would be disposed of if a link were to be established along the lines suggested in chapter V, section 4. There would no longer be any need for SDR-financed aid-giving on the part of a particular industrial country. Such a country would no longer have to give away a part of its monetary reserves. But nor would it acquire them free of charge: it could only get them by earning them. It is true that particular development efforts financed by newly created SDRs would not be under the direct control of particular developed nations. But that is exactly the purpose of international development financing through multinational institutions. If an industrial country were to yield up an amount of dollars equivalent to a certain proportion of SDRs that it had received free of charge, it could hardly call itself a donor nation. Such 'aid-giving' would only benefit the reserve positions of other developed countries that do not participate in the voluntary arrangement concerned, though these countries at the same time pay in real terms for the additional development assistance, if any (cf. p. 149/ 150).

Now what about the other argument mentioned by Mr. Schweitzer, namely, that 'two distinct matters' are at stake, on each of which decisions should be taken on its own merits? It will be clear from our discussion so far that nothing would prevent development policy from continuing in its present form just because it is financed by reserve creation, and it would not impair the SDR scheme to introduce an international policy on one of its most important aspects. On the contrary, there is a con-

12 IMF, *Summary Proceedings,* Annual Meeting 1965, p. 127/128; italics are mine.
13 Pierre-Paul Schweitzer, 'New arrangements to supplement world reserves and their implications for the developing countries', *International Financial News Survey,* December 15, 1967, p. 417/418; my italics.

tinuing *long-term* need for development outlays and a similarly continuing *long-term* need for new reserves. The situation thus suggests linking reserve creation with development financing rather than trying to keep them apart. Nevertheless, the authors of the 'Ossola Report' wrote:

'Most members (. . .) saw disadvantage in an attempt to combine objectives of long-term developed finance with the needs of flexibility required for monetary management. From the point of view of international monetary management, full flexibility of decision is called for as to whether assets should be created or not. From the point of view of development, on the other hand, planning both by donors and by recipients requires firm commitments over considerable periods. This would introduce an inflexibility into the monetary aspects of the scheme and thus impair the monetary quality of the asset' [14].

As has just been pointed out, however, 'firm commitments over considerable periods' are exactly what are needed in connection with reserve creation. The *'long-term* global need' must be fulfilled. What is required is a smoothing of the adjustment process, so that not every surplus requires a compensating deficit. But the precise *size* of the gap to be filled is not as important as the *direction* in which the world reserve level is visibly moving [15]. There is no way of telling whether the equivalent of $ 1 billion would be more appropriate than the equivalent of, say, $ 4 billion. But in any case no short-term flexibility is required; the Group of Ten itself stated a year later that 'decisions on the amount of reserves to be deliberately created should be taken for periods of some years ahead' [16]. It is a structural matter, not a cyclical one; the purpose is 'to strengthen *general* confidence in the system' and to 'allow the gold and exchange markets to operate on the basis of *more certain* expectations' [17].

The recognition of this principle has led to the adoption of the provision that decisions to create SDRs 'shall be made for basic periods which shall run consecutively and shall be five years in duration' [18]. With respect to possible 'unexpected major developments' [19] 'the Fund may change

---

14 It was added, however, that 'the difficulties might not be insuperable if (. . .) the amount of reserve creation associated with development finance were kept at a modest fraction of the total creation of reserves' (*Ossola Report*, 1965, paragraph 138).
15 See chapter V, section 5.
16 *Report of Deputies*, 1966, paragraph 41.
17 *Ibid.*, my italics.
18 *Fund Agreement*, Art. XXIV, Section 2. The Fund may deviate from this rule, as it has done for the current first basic period which runs only for three years.
19 Paragraph 41 of the Deputies Report of 1966 mentions the example of 'situations when actual additions to monetary gold differ widely from those anticipated at the time the decision was taken'.

the rates or intervals of allocation or cancellation during the rest of a basic period or change the length of a basic period or start a new period, at any time the Fund finds it desirable to do so' [20]. Such 'major developments' are hardly imaginable; but, as pointed out earlier [21], there is nothing to prevent the IMF from changing the amount of SDRs to be created by deciding to lend larger or smaller amounts to development institutions than originally intended. Planning for a basic period of five years, however, certainly seems to be feasible. Even an 'empty' basic period would be possible (though perhaps not necessary). In such an event, the IDA (and the possible secondary beneficiaries of SDR creation) would have to resume their traditional fund raising techniques. Neither would 'cancellation' of SDRs – a rather unlikely occurrence – be impossible [22]. As for the 'firm commitments over considerable periods' for development, if linked to SDR creation, they would be much firmer than at present, when contributions to IDA are subject to cumbersome renegotiation every three year.

It seems almost impossible to believe that if any need for flexibility in the level of international liquidity were to arise, this *could not be met by the operations of the General Account of the Fund*. It is for the very reason usually given for considering liquidity creation through the General Account inappropiate to meet 'the long-term global need' for durable world liquidity [23] that it is in fact the proper mechanism to provide the desired flexibility in the level of world reserves. For if liquidity became 'too great', credit tranche drawings would be repaid and super gold tranche positions in the Fund would decrease. If world liquidity became 'too small', net drawings would increase, and *any basic period could thus be bridged*. The rise in drawings could be a signal for the creation of more special drawing rights in the next basic period.

The argument regarding the need for flexibility is, to my mind, the result of applying national monetary thinking to international affairs. At the world level an inflexible generally agreed criterion for increasing the stock of money would be perfectly satisfactory. For, the relation of the *flow* of international reserves to the *stock* of international reserves is an extremely loose one. 'Flexible monetary management' is called for in a *monetary union,* such as exists within a single developed country. But

20 *Fund Agreement,* Art. XXV, Section 4.
21 Chapter V, section 5.
22 See chapter V, at the end of section 6.
23 Reserve creation through the General Account of the Fund occurs only as a by-product of temporary credit operations, see chapter III, section 3.

the community of nations is not a monetary union at all, regardless of the volume of special drawing rights that may be created. World inflation is no more than inflation in a large number of *countries*. World monetary policy is international cooperation in coordinating *independently managed* national money systems [24].

Even on the national scene, the effect of the level of money supply on total economic activity is uncertain, and the need for 'flexible monetary management' questionable. Reference may be made to the views of Professor Milton Friedman, who believes 'that an automatic policy under which the quantity of money would grow at a steady rate, month-in, month-out, year-in, year-out, would provide a stable monetary framework for economic growth without being a source of instability and disturbance'. He denies 'a rigid connection between monetary change and income change', admitting only that 'there is a close relation *on the average* between changes in the quantity of money and the subsequent course of national income' [25].

The relation between changes in the total stock of world reserves and world inflation is an extremely loose one, as recent experience has shown. Major reserve countries can export inflation to others with world reserves at any level, including or excluding special drawing rights. Furthermore, balance of payments imbalances may be financed by the use of many different credit arrangements. And in the unlikely event of the rate of SDR creation being considered too high in the light of the current inflation, 'flexible monetary management' could in any event only have an effect after the inflationary tendencies had already occurred.

The following quotation from Mr. Polak is illuminating on this point:

'The effects of the reserve situation on governments' policies are likely to be slow and cumulative – except where there is a sudden sharp decline in reserves. A judicious addition to the flow of reserves such as that provided by the activation of the special drawing rights facility did not overnight – on New Year's Eve of 1969 – change the degree of reserve ease that governments took into account as they set their economic policies. The impact is expected rather to be gradual and cumulative [26]. Thus flexibility, the ability to respond to changes in economic conditions in order to affect such conditions in the relatively short run, which is fre-

---

24 It is for this reason that Article XXIV, Section 1 of the Fund Agreement sounds very unrealistic; SDR creation is said to be intended to 'avoid economic stagnation and deflation as well as excess demand and inflation in the world'. A better wording would have been: 'help to avoid, *etc*'.
25 'The counter-revolution of monetary theory', *The Financial Times*, September 17, 1970, p. 12.
26 This stability of reserve policy behavior is likely to be even greater in the case of a link as described in chapter V.

quently claimed for domestic monetary policy, has no counterpart in international reserve policy. To this observation of substance one could add two more practical points. First, short-run appraisal of the relevant economic criteria on a worldwide basis is far more difficult than a corresponding appraisal in any one country; and second, the international decision-making process in matters of this magnitude and importance is almost certainly not capable at present of making short period decisions on world monetary policy.

(. . .) The conduct of world reserve policy, in contrast to monetary policy in individual countries, is deliberately focused on the trend, rather than on cyclical factors. This approach reflects a conviction that, whatever may be the ability of monetary policy within a country to respond to short-term developments in the economy, and in turn to influence them, such possibilities do not exist on the international plane' [27].

If these observations are accepted as true, it would hardly be possible to maintain any argument for flexibility in reserve creation at all. Both inflation and deflation and international payments imbalances, though matters of international concern, can only be dealt with through cooperation between individual countries and multilateral surveillance of those counties' actions. If it is said that too much use is being made of international reserves, what is meant is that this is done by particular countries. These countries would have to be persuaded to change their policies; and no variation in the growth rate of SDRs can seriously be considered as having a direct effect in this direction. After all, special drawing rights are not the only reserves that can be created and very large credit facilities are available outside the Special Drawing Account. But if there were good reasons for limiting the amount of SDRs allocated in any specific basic period, or for having a basic period when no special drawing rights were created at all, the adoption of the 'link' would not prevent the IMF from taking the decision 'on its own merits'. The proponents of the link between special drawing rights and development have always clearly realized this. The authors of the 1965 UNCTAD report wrote for instance: 'We are quite clear that the amount of any new reserve creation should be determined by the monetary requirements of the world economy and not by the need for development finance. But once the need for additional reserves has been demonstrated and the amount of the addition determined on the basis of monetary requirements, the introduction of a link with development finance is entirely proper and desirable. In any case, the need for leading industrialized countries to acquiesce in the creation of additional liquidity ensures that it will not be excessive' [28]. To mention another example, the Governor of the Fund and the World Bank for Ceylon, Minister Perera, stated at the 1970 Annual Meeting: '. . . we

27 J. J. Polak, 'Money – national and international', p. 184/185.
28 *International monetary issues and the developing countries*, p. 30.

fully accept with all its implications the proposition that the creation of SDRs should be determined solely by the monetary needs of the world economy and not by those of development finance' [29].

Would the creation of a substantial volume of special drawing rights for development purposes not create a precedent from which it would be difficult to depart? In my opinion, there would hardly be any greater danger of this than under the present system, and the use of this argument as an objection to the link would be an act not of policy but of fear. In any event there are ample means for achieving 'flexible management'. Special drawing rights could be used to finance the World Bank's operations as well as those of IDA; or IDA's alone; or only some part of either institution's commitments. There seems to be no real reason why an amount of SDR 500 million should not be created annually in any given basic period, even when this amount had been larger previously. Any reduction in the level of development-linked SDR creation would offer the opponents of the link an opportunity for channeling more *ex ante* savings into development investment. The 'flexibility' argument is no reason not to enhance the quality and possibilities of SDRs as an international financial instrument.

One final point should be made. The opponents of the link may argue that there would be no benefit to developing countries unless the aid made available through the creation of SDRs is *additional* to other aid. While it is a matter of judgment whether this would be the case or not, my own view is that the benefit would be substantial [30]. At any rate, not only would the urgent need for *soft* development loans be more adequately met, but 'aid' might become more an aspect of 'international development policy' than a 'gift'. One additional strong argument in favor of the link is that it would provide a means of absorbing any unused productive capacity in a situation of world deflation. Moreover, even if the volume

---

29 IMF/IBRD Annual Meetings 1970, *Press Release No. 45*, p. 5.
30 The Expert Group on International Monetary Issues in its report to the Secretary-General of the UNCTAD entitled *International monetary reform and cooperation for development* (New York, 1969), believes that total aid flows will increase because several direct impediments to aid increases would disappear: in particular, no more *reserve losses* or *budgetary costs* would be involved. Furthermore, the link would 'avoid the disputes about burden-sharing which tended to occur in international aid operations and which tend to make any such operations small-scale and slow-moving'. This process would be replaced by 'an automatic and unquestioned method of sharing the burden of additional aid' (paragraphs 52, 53). (See also Sidney Dell's statement before the Subcommittee *etc.*, *Hearing*, 1969, p. 10; there are many other places).

of 'aid' was not increased at-all, the strengthening of international cooperation and the benefit to the functioning of the special drawing rights system would still be worthwhile.

II. WOULD THE 'LINK' BE MORE INFLATIONARY THAN THE PRESENT ALLOCATION MECHANISM?

The main argument of the opponents against the 'link' between development activity and deliberate reserve creation is that the link would be more inflationary than the present system of allocating SDRs to participants in the scheme. The Governor of the IMF for Tanzania, however, spoke as follows at the Annual Meeting of the Fund in 1969: 'I regret that the opportunity has been missed to create a link between SDRs and the development needs of the world. Contrary to the belief expressed by the distinguished Governor of an advanced country [31], I believe that such a decision would have been less inflationary in its effects than the possible effects of the present decision' [32].

The volume of special drawing rights exclusively through the 'monetization' of multilateral development assistance is likely to be smaller than that under the present scheme. The inflationary impact will, therefore, in the long run also be smaller, especially because no SDRs are fully allocated to the major developed countries that are the main source of world inflation. Admittedly, *spending* by developing countries will be financed, but outlays of that type are mainly structural in nature so that, from the development point of view, the world economy should adjust to them. There might be an inflationary impact, but it would be more limited than in the event that SDRs are used to sustain major *cyclical* imbalances in developed countries that might thus be reinforced and have cumulative inflationary effects on the world economy. The creation of special drawing rights linked to development in the way described in chapter V will be

31 Statement by the Governor of the World Bank for the Netherlands, H. J. Witteveen, at the Bank, IFC and IDA Session during the combined Bank and Fund Annual Meetings, 1969: 'The function of international reserves is to be available in case of need for the financing of temporary maladjustments in the balances of payments of their holders and recipients, not to increase the flow of capital for development assistance which involves a long-term transfer of real economic resources that should be financed out of genuine savings. Otherwise it could become a source of inflation' (IMF, *Summary Proceedings,* Annual Meeting 1969, p. 98/99).
32 Statement by the Governor of the Fund for Tanzania, A. H. Jamal (*Ibid.,* p. 203).

less than in the present system because in so far as less SDRs will be created, this will be felt in the long run. Admittedly, in the present system SDRs may be 'held' for short periods after being 'created' because they have been created possibly without any need on the part of the particular countries holding them. The expansive impact will be felt in the long run, *and it is the long run that matters.* As has been argued in chapter IV, section 2, the 'link' will make more economical use of new SDRs than the present system. Under a link as proposed in the previous chapter, the main industrial countries are likely to be a little more modest in their views on the 'global reserve need', as they would have to earn their share in the total instead of freely acquiring the desired increase in their reserve levels.

Indeed, there is in a sense a premium on pursuing healthy non-inflationary policies as countries that want to acquire additional reserves must earn them, and to do so they must maintain price levels at which they can compete on the world market. IDA 'aid' is multilateral 'aid', so that IDA spending may be directed to the most appropriate source which would logically be a country where inflation is more under control than elsewhere. In general, only countries that really wish to have increases in their reserves capture part of the additional reserves created, whereas in the present system *all* participants receive them freely, regardless of the state of their economies (see chapter IV, section 2, 'First objection').

It is often argued that development assistance must be financed out of 'genuine' savings (cf. footnote 31), if it is not to be inflationary. On the other hand, if we suppose that country A makes financial contributions to multilateral development institutions, raising the funds either on the capital market or from the budget, two questions must be asked: 1) will this prevent inflation in country A? 2) will it prevent inflation in other countries B, C, *etc.* where some of the money may also eventually be spent? Or is this too an argument that does not really apply to international economics but rather to single countries?

The answer must be that inflation in A will only be avoided if total *spending* i.e. effective foreign *plus* domestic demand (money creation, cost push) is kept within proper limits. The way that aid contributions are generated is only of very partial importance.

Now suppose that inflation does not occur in A because aid is 'correctly' financed; in other words A undertakes domestic deflation equal to the financial resources that return to A in exchange for the real goods that are purchased with aid funds. This does not mean than inflation will be also avoided in countries B, C *etc.,* where some (perhaps most) aid money will also be spent. For by the same token, inflation can only be warded off in those countries too if the *use of the domestic means of production* is kept within proper limits. The way in which the original aid contribution of A is financed is *irrelevant*. If aid spendings in B do result in an overheating of the national economy, inflation may be exported to A as well as to other countries [33].

Moreover, the existence or absence of inflation in any of the countries concerned at the time that the aid flows are raised is irrelevant. What counts is the extent of inflation at the time (perhaps some years later) that aid funds are disbursed.

Anti-inflationary policies must always be pursued whenever and wherever *total* spending increases too much. This holds true nationally and *a fortiori* internationally, when purchases are made in country B or C, with funds that may be provided by A. *The fact remains that anti-inflationary policies can only be implemented at the national levels, where they form part of a country's over-all cyclical policy.* Inflation cannot possibly be imputed to particular single *items* of total effective demand, such as international development purchases.

The 'genuine savings' argument has some validity in the case of strictly *tied* bilateral aid, though not in the case of multilateral international aid, and even then only to the extent that total national spending is not properly controlled.

As tied aid is replaced by multilateral aid the industrial countries' inflationary problems will diminish. The *financing* of aid through the creation of special drawing rights in itself will not necessarily have an inflationary effect, whereas if funds are raised from capital markets interest rate increases with some inflationary effect may take place; additional credit creation may occur to meet remaining domestic capital demands. The real aid flows tend to come from countries where overspending is least likely or least present. 'The present distribution of SDRs like manna from heaven to everybody, whatever their policies are, is certainly contrary to one of the cardinal principles (. . .) always repeated, that the creation of new reserve assets should be linked to an improvement of the adjustment process' [34].

---

33 The same point was made by Maxwell Stamp as early as 1962. 'The effect of purchasing power created in this way' (through reserve creation) 'is *hardly different from* the present effects produced by International Bank lending or other untied aid. The surplus countries would hardly claim that these should be curtailed in order to ease their own domestic problems' ('The Stamp Plan – 1962 version', *Moorgate and Wall Street,* Autumn 1962, p. 14, my italics).
34 *Hearing* before the Subcommittee *etc.,* 1969, p. 65 (Triffin).

There are of course quite different instruments for making anti-cyclical policies effective, besides financing national or international aid contributions out of savings. If all the industrial countries were to finance their aid in a deflationary way, the inflation problem would to some extent be alleviated, but even if they do not demand does not become unmanageable in these countries [35]. One way of overcoming the tendency to inflation in the developed countries would be for them not to *hold* the additional reserves they earn from the developing world, but to *spend* them in exchange for real resources from that part of the world. In other words, they would have to allow international trade to develop without raising tariff and other protective barriers.

By definition, all money creation has an expansionary effect. In this sense the 'link' will certainly be 'inflationary', but it is likely to be less so than SDR creation in favor of individual countries, or than the traditional reserve creation of the past. And, for that matter, 'countries do not object to an inflationary impact if it comes through thriving expansion in markets in which they would like to establish a long-term interest' [36].

'The effects on the industrial countries would be the same in both cases' (the traditional creation of reserves in the form of gold or dollars on the one hand, and a link between SDR creation and development on the other); 'the effects on the developing countries would differ in that development projects may sooner or later help to increase the productivity of their people' [37].

Professor Johnson has rightly said that a transfer of real resources is 'entirely unnecessary from the standpoint of creating new international reserve assets' [38]. The remark of the Ossola Group that 'deliberately created new reserve assets *must, of their nature,* initially be distributed without the recipients' having to forego real resources in order to earn them' [39] is surely *not* correct. But if they are, they 'will thereafter com-

---

35 As Mr. Dell has remarked, even if total SDR creation linked to World Bank operations should amount to $ 5 billion in a single year, 'this would add less than one third of 1 percent to the demand for output in the O.E.C.D. countries, which amounted to about $ 1,700 billion in 1968' (*Hearing* before the Subcommittee *etc.* 1969, p. 10). A similar remark was made by Mr. Triffin (*ibid.*, p. 38). Mr. Horowitz has remarked that 'it hardly seems reasonable and realistic to assert that, say, $ 1 billion per annum for IDA, which amounts to one half per mille of the $ 2 trillion GNP of the developed world, would have an inflationary effect' (IMF/IBRD, Annual Meetings 1970, *Press Release* No. 52, p. 5).
36 Subcommittee, *etc., Hearing*, 1969, p. 72 (Harry G. Johnson).
37 F. Machlup, *Remarking the international monetary system*, p. 60. Similar remarks have been made by Triffin, Prebisch, Dell and many others.
38 Subcommittee *etc., Hearing*, 1969, p. 16.
39 *Ossola Report*, paragraph 120 (my italics).

mand real resources', as the Ossola Report immediately adds. After all, the money is created for the purpose of being used. The inflationary impact will only differ according to the time and place at which the newly created funds are spent.

On the subject of possible pressure for overlarge allocation of special drawing rights my conclusion is just the opposite of that reached by the Ossola Group. For the Group claimed in its report that 'it would be difficult to resist demands from developing countries, and the internal pressures in the industrialized countries to give aid in this form, which appears to avoid a cost in real resources' [40]. Now, the developing countries are not the fount of power in the Fund, where their voting power amounts to about one third of the total. Maxwell Stamp has said about the linking of reserve creation to IDA financing that not the least of the avantages thereof is 'that 'benefit' is quite largely divorced from 'control' of the note issue. If the major part of the profits go to the developing countries and the total of new credit or money to be issued is determined by those who are mainly industrial, there is less chance that an excessive amount will be issued' [41]. As for 'the internal pressures in the industrialized countries', surely an *inter*national team like the Ossola Group should not be concerned with the way in which domestic priorities are chosen.

In conclusion, it is not at-all clear whether the creation of special drawing rights exclusively in relation to development financing will be more or less inflationary[42] than allocation to individual countries. My own feeling is that it will be less so. But even if SDR creation proves to be inflationary, we can still choose between inflation plus the uncontrolled use of newly created purchasing power on the one hand, and inflation offset by the benefits of development finance on the other. However, one thing is certain: inflation can only be overcome by domestic measures in individual countries. The real question is how much priority the makers

40 *Ibid.,* paragraph 138.
41 'The reform of the international monetary system', *Moorgate and Wall Street,* Summer 1965, p. 15.
42 One final remark on this question. In judging the 'inflationary' impact of the 'link', the industrial nations always take into account the situation in their own countries, which represent a minor part of the world's area and population! I would rather quote Mr. Horowitz' comment on the 'link': 'The very fact that these SDRs are anyway being created invalidates the argument that this would be inflationary. In all modesty, it seems to me that the opposite is true, that the infusion of new money' (I would rather say: new economic activity) 'into countries with underutilized manpower and other factors of production would be less inflationary than its use in already overheated economies suffering from labor shortage' (IMF/IBRD Annual Meetings 1970, *Press Release,* No. 52, p. 5).

of economic policy wish to attach to domestic economic purposes on the one hand, and to international economic aims on the other.

III. WOULD THE 'LINK' BE MORE DEFLATIONARY THAN THE PRESENT ALLOCATION MECHANISM?

At first sight, the 'deflationary' argument against the 'link' seems to be stronger than the 'inflationary' one. It starts from the same assumption that deliberately created reserves must, 'of their nature', be freely distributed. According to this reasoning, if countries had to *earn* newly created reserves, they might have to introduce balance of payments restrictions and deflationary measures in order to ensure that they obtained the share of the reserves they felt they needed.

The first decision to create special drawing rights had to 'take into account, as special considerations, a collective judgment that there is a global need to supplement reserves, and the attainment of a better balance of payments equilibrium, as well as the likelihood of a better working of the adjustment process in the future' [43]. Not only was 'a better balance of payments equilibrium' considered a condition for reserve creation, but such a development would, according to the prevailing philosophy, necessitate reserve creation. The main imbalances concerned were the continuing deficits of the United States and the United Kingdom. Correcting these disequilibria would mean that other countries would have to consent to reserve losses or to smaller reserve gains than they might otherwise have had, to enable the reserve currency countries either to make reserve gains or to reduce their reserve losses [44]. This process would be impeded if other countries considered their own reserve holdings to be too low. Therefore, there would have to be deliberate reserve creation to forestall any reserve *shortage,* which would manifest itself by a more or less general tendency to introduce payments restrictions and deflationary measures. Now, it was argued implicitly, if the SDRs were *not* to be allocated to

---

43   *Fund Agreement,* Art. XXIV, Section 1 (b).
44   See for instance the Proposal by the Managing Director of the International Monetary Fund, *Allocation of special drawing rights for the first basic period,* 1969, p. 12/13: 'One assumption would imply maintenance of payments balance by the United States, no creation of reserves in the form of U.S. dollars, attainment of a substantial surplus by the United Kingdom, and net repayment over a five year period of some $ 5 billion of international credits (including Fund purchases) extended in recent years. On this assumption, reserves (. . .) might fall by $ 0.5 billion per annum'.

countries but linked to IDA operations so that reserve creation would not immediately result in 'reserve ease' for the major industrial countries, there might possibly be a reserve deficiency, and that would run counter to the very purpose of the SDR scheme.

It is not difficult to refute this argument for preferring allocation to in-individual countries over a link with development financing. First, the argument rests upon the assumption that there really is an imminent shortage of reserves, something that can hardly be proven. Second, SDRs will not be the only reserves to be created; traditional assets will most likely continue to be created, though perhaps in modest amounts. Third, total allocations of SDRs to countries will after all, only very slightly benefit those surplus countries which are supposed to be unwilling to lose reserves. Fourth, as the deficit countries also receive SDR allocations (in fact, the United States and the United Kingdom receive the biggest single allocations [45]) they will have less incentive to correct their deficits. Fifth, any spending by the developing countries in the developed world must necessarily result in reserve increases for the industrial countries, both in the deficit countries and in the surplus countries. If net reserve creation does occur, even with a 'link' there is no reason why the United Kingdom and the United States should not take steps to rectify their deficits without causing reserve losses on the part of 'unwilling' surplus countries.

There are in addition, certain points of principle to be noted. In the first place, the received view is a denial of the very notion of 'global reserve need'. The need that SDRs are to fulfill is supposed to be *'global'*; according to the 1966 report of the Group of Ten [46] SDR creation should be neither geared nor directed to the balance of payments needs of in-dividual countries (such as 'industrial surplus countries') but it should rather provide for the 'global needs of the system'. There must be a sufficient supply of new reserves, but this is not to say that countries should receive them free of charge instead of earning them. It was not the fact that reserves had had to be earned in the past that prompted international cooperation for reserve creation, but the likelihood that reserves would cease to be available in sufficient supply. This meant in particular the threat of a failure to produce a sufficient volume of new reserve assets with desirable qualities. There was never any complaint because gold had to be earned in exchange for real resources; what com-

45 On the basis of the new Fund quotas agreed in 1970 the United States will receive 23.2 percent and the United Kingdom 9.7 percent of any amount of newly created SDRs.
46 Paragraph 37.

plaints were voiced dwelt on the fact that not enough of it could be earned due to the limited physical supply of gold. The disadvantages of increasing the price of gold as a means of raising the monetary value of what gold was earned were thought to outweigh the advantages. 'The willingness to earn reserves through payments surpluses is a far more substantial demonstration of a perceived need' [47] than any declarations about reserve needs that may be uttered during deliberations about the magnitude of free allocations of SDRs. If the creation of SDRs is linked to IDA operations, the industrialized part of the world will be able to earn the reserves it needs from the developing world [48], and these earnings will be available, among other things, for financing payments between the industrialized countries themselves.

If some industrial non-reserve currency countries were nevertheless to lose reserves against their will, what objection would there be to *financing these individual reserve needs initially through drawings on the General Account of the Fund,* thus enabling the country concerned to restore its earning position? This would be a matter for political decision; provided the need existed, it is unlikely that any member would be denied access to the General Account of the Fund. On the contrary, the Fund Board would surely approve requests for drawings that were either the result of a 'better working of the adjustment process' or designed to promote its better working.

The correct criterion for deciding on the best form of SDR application is whether the system chosen will really serve to finance the difference between world balance of payments surpluses and world balance of payments deficits, thereby diminishing the total amount of deficits, needed to offset a given total of surpluses. This function can only be performed by a non-national currency, which SDRs are intended to be, just like gold. Special drawing rights would not lose this essential quality by being linked to development. They would create new liquidity in the same way as gold does on entering the monetary circuit; in the case of special drawing rights linked to IDA this would take the form of the currencies provided by the Special Drawing Account to IDA. (It should be noted that the designation of a country to provide currency for IDA projects in exchange for newly created SDRs does not change the level of that country's monetary reserves unless the currency is its own [49]). The coun-

47 See footnote 61 to chapter V.
48 If the deficit incurred by a deficit country is due to domestic inflation, in the interest of anti-inflation policy and international balance of payments equilibrium adjustment must take place regardless of whether the country receives SDRs or not.
49 To the extent that the Special Drawing Account provides currencies that will

tries that earn the new reserves enjoy surpluses that are not matched by balance of payments deficits in the developing countries that spend the new reserves. The purpose of reserve creation is thus achieved even better than if reserve creation takes place through circulating newly mined gold. The first beneficiaries of the new money are not the countries where gold mining happens to take place on an economic basis, but countries that are chosen by international economic policy.

afterwards be spent by the developing countries in the issuing countries (for instance, U.S. dollars which will be spent in the United States), no net international liquidity is created in the process, unless the currency has been provided by designation of the issuing country itself. This is equally true in the present system (where such a procedure would lead to reserve destruction, as SDRs are counted as reserves on allocation. To the extent, that the United States uses its allocations to obtain an equivalent amount of its own currency held by another participant, dollar reserves vanish – see chapter III, section 3); this is the consequence of the use of gross reserve concepts instead of net figures. Liquid liabilities in the hands of monetary authorities in foreign countries are counted as 'world reserves', even though on a net basis they would have to be subtracted from the monetary reserves of the issuing country. According to current statistical methods a decrease in the level of, say, sterling balances held by foreign monetary authorities represents destruction of international reserves. On the other hand, truly 'international' reserves like SDRs never vanish when spent within the monetary circuit. SDRs are everlasting (cf. chapter III, section 3). Therefore, one result of continuing SDR creation will be an eventual increase in total world reserves on a *net* basis. Only to the extent that the *Fund* takes in SDRs will the world reserve level decrease. If SDRs were allocated in connection with IDA projects, they would be *created only by designation,* and designation would take place only when the IDA actually needed currency. If country A provides its *own* currency in exchange for SDRs (according to the Fund's 'designation' rules) and that currency is spent in country A, reserve creation has occurred to the amount of the original designation. However, when the currency of country A eventually ends up in the hands of countries B or C, reserve creation amounts to 200 percent of the original creation of SDRs. Reserve creation amounts to 100 percent of the designation figure when country A provides the currency of country D, for instance its main reserve currency, U.S. dollars, and the dollars end up in the monetary reserves of countries B and C. Reserve creation amounts to zero percent if country A provides the currency of country D and this currency is afterwards spent in country D. If this happened to x percent of the total amount of SDRs created in any given year, and the procedure leading to creation of 200 percent of the original creation occurs to an amount of y percent, *net reserve creation through SDR designation* would equal to $(100 - x + y)$ percent of the amount of SDRs used by IDA in that year. The same result would be obtained with the present system using the official accounting methods; the net effects of the functioning of the SDR system on the total of world reserves amount to $100 - x + y$ percent of total SDR *allocations.* One case of zero creation of reserves is that of reserve currency countries purchasing their own currencies with SDRs that have been allocated to them. As more SDRs are created and replace reserve currency holdings, limiting these to working balances, the likelihood of countries providing their own currencies will increase. A country may, however, only provide its own currency when it has been declared acceptable as 'currency convertible in fact' by the Fund (See *Fund Agreement, Art.* XXV, Section 4 and Art. XXXII (b) and IMF *Annual Report* 1970, p. 31).

VII. Variations on the theme of linking international money creation to international development policy

I. THE 'ORGANIC' LINK (STAMP, TRIFFIN)

This chapter will review briefly a number of recent proposals regarding the link [1]. With the possible exception of Gerald M. Meier (see page 81) I have found no academic economists opposed to the idea of the link as such. Probably the greatest opposition to the idea is to be found among government economists in the industrial countries.

When the Subcommittee on International Exchange and Payments of the Joint Economic Committee of the Congress of the United States held its hearing on the subject on May 28, 1969, the only objections were put forward by Professor Harry G. Johnson, and, to a lesser extent, Professor Tibor Scitovsky [2]. Professor Johnson's main point was that 'the real transfer involved is entirely unnecessary from the standpoint of creating new international reserve assets' [3], so that this method of reserve creation might be unnecessarily inflationary. This is a typical short-term argument relating to the timing of the 'first spending round' of SDRs. It is entirely irrelevant to the second and subsequent rounds. Yet, SDRs are created for the long term, i.e. for any number of rounds after their creation. We have discussed the inflationary and the deflationary aspects that are allegedly inherent in the 'link' in the previous chapter.

---

1 No attempt at completeness has been made; plans are mentioned mainly for illustrative purposes.
2 Professor Scitovsky's view will be discussed below.
3 Subcommittee *etc., Hearing,* 1969, p. 16.

On the other hand, Johnson agreed that from the inflationary stand-point, there would be no difference between real aid to domestic poor and real transfers to foreign poor. If there were excess capacity in the developed countries, the link might indeed well be non-inflationary [4]. As said earlier, Johnson considers 'creation' and 'development' separate issues, but, according to his own words, 'that argument is subject to the counter-argument, which may have gained in force in recent years, that if governments are prepared or can be persuaded to accept a linkage of additional reserve creation to development assistance, and if by this means they will agree to create an adequate amount of additional reserves whereas otherwise they would not, both the world in general and the less developed countries in particular will benefit and no one will be harmed' [5]. So Johnson (the only one of the group of economists heard who offered resistance to the *idea* of the link as such) is not an absolute opponent but simply very critical and cautious in his approach. One of the requirements, Johnson rightly observes, is 'that aid-linked SDRs would virtually have to be and should be created as an integral part of the decision to create new international reserves, and that they would not constitute a net addition to the total of SDRs created, only a redistribution of a predetermined quantity of SDRs' [6]. What I have tried to defend on economic grounds in the previous chapters is an 'integrated' or 'organic' [7] link that meets this requirement, as opposed to proposals that leave the present allocation method virtually intact (see section 3).

Sir Maxwell Stamp [8] deserves the credit of being the first to advocate the 'organic' link *on monetary grounds*. Before the appearance of Professor

---

4 *Ibid.*, p. 78–80. Mr. Dell concluded: 'It does seem to me that by saying that you can reach a position of full employment without inflation, either by distributing goods and services to the domestic poor or by distributing goods and services to the foreign poor, Professor Johnson has in effect conceded (. . .) that a noninflationary link is possible (. . .). It is an alternative (. . .) to distributing a similar volume of goods and services to the domestic poor' (p. 79).
5 *Ibid.*, p. 19.
6 *Ibid.*, p. 17. I myself, in view of the scheme proposed in chapter V, would not use the phrase '*re*distribution' but rather 'a particular distribution'. See also the interesting reference in footnote 21 below.
7 Other expressions are 'functional', 'direct', 'compulsory'.
8 I learn from R. Triffin, *Gold and the dollar crisis*, p. 118, that Maxwell Stamp has been Advisor to the Governor of the Bank of England; British Alternate Executive Director of the Fund (1951–1953); and Director of the Fund's European Department for some time. The years mentioned in the footnotes below refer to the following articles: 1958: 'The Fund and the future' (*Lloyds Bank Review,* October 1958, pp. 1–20); 1961: 'Changes in the world's payments system' (*Moorgate and*

Triffin's *Gold and the dollar crisis* (1960) [9] and before the 'Myth of Backing' had been definitely scuttled [10], Stamp not only described the possibility of the Fund performing the banking function of credit creation, but also put forward a scheme whereby countries simply would 'agree to accept certificates of indebtedness from the Fund in settlement of international accounts, and *to treat these certificates in all respects as though they were gold'* [11]; the certificates would be to all intents and purposes like money irrespective of their 'backing'. As early as 1958 he suggested the creation by the IMF of credit 'to be put into circulation through the IBRD' – the latter having 'an effective mechanism for choosing projects which are likely to add to the wealth of the countries sponsoring them and which will in the long run be repayable out of that extra wealth' [12].

In 1961 Stamp published two schemes relating to liquidity, his Plans 'A' and 'B'. The essential features of Plan B were in fact adopted before the end of the year through the conclusion of the 'General Arrangements to Borrow' [13]. Plan A ran as follows:

'If the Indian Government were to discover a forgotten hoard of $ 5 billion of gold, the news would be widely welcomed. The Indians could import more to speed their development; other countries would export more and find their reserves rising. (. . .) The Indians will not discover such a gold hoard; but we could achieve the same happy result by the following scheme:
The Board of Governors of the Fund would authorise the issue of Fund Certificates' (we would now say SDRs) 'to a value of, say $ 3000 milions over the next twelve months. The value of these certificates would be expressed in gold, but they would not automatically be convertible into gold. Each member would agree to accept them when tendered by the Fund or a central bank and to provide its own national currency in exchange. Countries such as the United States which at present undertake to sell gold at a fixed price when their currency is tendered by a central bank could modify that obligation: henceforward, they would have the option of selling gold or tendering any Fund Certificates in their possession. The holder of a Fund Certificate would be able to exchange it at known rates into the currency of any country which is a member of the Fund' [14].

Wall Street, Spring 1961, pp. 3–22); 1962: 'The Stamp Plan – 1962 version' (*Ibid.*, Autumn 1962, pp. 5–17); 1965: 'The reform of the international monetary system' (*Ibid.*, Summer 1965, pp. 5–16).
9 A condensation has been reprinted in Herbert G. Grubel, *World monetary reform, plans and issues*, Stanford, 1963, p. 15–54. Stamp's 1962 article is also contained.
10 See footnote 1 to chapter V. 'The myth of backing is dead. It was buried in Rio de Janeiro on September 29, 1967' (Machlup, *Remaking the international monetary system*, p. 66).
11 1958, p. 13/14; my italics.
12 1958, p. 18.
13 See footnote 20 to chapter I.
14 1961, p. 10/11.

It would be interesting to know whether any other monetary expert described the special drawing rights scheme ahead of time with such precision [15]. It will be noticed that he mentioned the Board of Governors of the Fund as a decision-taking body; the expression of value in terms of gold; the character of SDRs as a 'final asset', not requiring convertibility into gold [16]; the transferability against currency at known rates [17]; the offering of SDRs instead of gold by the United States when foreign-held official dollars are presented for conversion [18], all of which are features of the Special Drawing Account. In fact, all the six 'main prerequisites' of the SDR scheme mentioned by Dr. Emminger, were included in the Stamp Plan, of which the author himself in 1961 said: 'It all looks too easy'. In his view SDRs should be used purely for international reserve purposes; they should not 'bear the mark of a particular country' and should not arise out of the balance of payments deficits of any one particular country; they should be a claim against the whole community of countries; they should be a final reserve asset, having a gold guarantee; they should be usable as a truly 'owned reserve', and the volume of reserve creation should be governed by deliberate decisions of the community of nations and be adjusted to the slowly growing collective need of the world economy for reserves [19].

Stamp continues:

'The Fund would then give the certificates to an aid coordinating agency which would allocate them to the underdeveloped countries under an agreed programme. The country receiving the certificates would use them to buy, say, machinery in Germany, the United States and the United Kingdom, by tendering them to the central bank and acquiring D-marks, dollars or sterling. If Germany were in overall surplus she would add the certificates to her reserves; if the United States were in

15 Even the suggested amount of reserves to be created, about $ 3 billion, turned out to be similar to the actual figure chosen for the first three years of the operation of the Special Drawing Account. In the 1962 version of the Stamp Plan, which was intended to remove a number of features that seemed unacceptable, the amount of $ 2 billion a year was mentioned.
16 As has been observed in chapter III, SDRs are used as a reserve means to be converted, whenever tendered to a participant, into 'currency convertible in fact', or as a means of payment to the General Account of the Fund instead of gold or convertible currency in specified cases (see *Fund Agreement*, Art. XXV, Section 7). *De facto*, however, a participant may, when 'designated' to provide currency, also present gold to the Fund, utilizing Art. V, Section 6 (a), the Fund then delivering the currency required by the participant that wants to 'cash' the SDRs.
17 SDRs must be accepted against a currency that is a currency 'convertible in fact', as approved by the Executive Board of the Fund. But this does of course imply that, as in the Stamp Plan, the currency of any country can be obtained indirectly.
18 See footnote 36 to chapter III.
19 Taken *verbatim* from O. Emminger, 'The Brave New World of SDRs', p. 6/7.

overall deficit she could, if she desired, use them to meet that deficit instead of losing gold. The certificates would end up with the countries which are in overall surplus – which, therefore, would have automatically lent part of that surplus to the rest of the world' [20].

In essence this is the scheme described in chapter V. The aim of the present study has only been to reexamine the issue in view of the actual coming into being of SDRs on January 1, 1970. The birth of the child is no longer a pious wish. It is already alive; the only thing still needed is a small surgical intervention. The point that now seems to require the most effort to bring about – the idea of linking the creation of SDRs to an international policy on their initial use – was regarded by Stamp as only natural and essential. Now that SDRs have been brought into existence, the whole Stamp mechanism, which at the time looked unrealistic and 'too easy', could now be completed by a simple amendment. The points that in 1962 seemed likely to present thorny problems have in fact all been adopted [21]. Almost all the topics discussed during the years when the SDR scheme was in preparation dealt with the rules for holding and use. The actual method of creating SDRs was adopted without much debate, and the principle of allocation to willing Fund members on the basis of their quota in the General Account was accepted without any extended discussion. The link with development financing is the only essential feature of the Stamp Plan not covered by the SDR scheme.

It is also remarkable that Stamp in 1962 further anticipated the qualities of the asset now offered to participants in the Special Drawing Account.

First he pointed out as a matter of course that physical certificates were not essential; 'credit entries in the Fund books could have the same effect' [22]. Second, he introduced a uniform acceptance limit in terms of Fund quotas [23]. Third, he formulated the essential principle of the balance-of-payments need as a requirement for the use of the asset; the new

20 1961, p. 11; 1962, p. 6.
21 For instance, all the objections against the Stamp Plan mentioned by Harry G. Johnson shortly after Stamp's 1962 article was written, are taken care of by the SDR agreement like it is now. Professor Johnson, at that time, did not concern himself with the link to development but with problems of the holding and use of the certificates envisaged by Stamp (see his article 'International liquidity – problems and plans' in: *World monetary reform, plans and issues,* ed. by Herbert G. Grubel, Stanford, 1963, p. 380/381.)
22 1962, p. 15.
23 The limit would be equal to the member's quota in the Fund (*ibid.,* p. 15). The principle of proportionality according to Fund quotas was thus also fully accepted by Stamp. The present acceptance limit is 200 percent of SDR allocations, these allocations themselves being proportional to Fund quotas (see footnote 29 to chapter III).

reserves should not be used for the mere purpose of a change in the composition of a country's reserves [24]. Thus, by implication he also provided for the principle of *harmonization of SDR holdings* by surplus countries (see chapter V, section 6).

An important feature of the Stamp scheme implied in the above mentioned transferability was the *uncoupling* of the financial backing (obligation to accept the new assets) from the real backing (supply of goods in exchange for reserves) for the scheme [25], in a way similar to that adopted by the authors of the SDR scheme. Irrespective of the amount of real resources supplied by a member country, it was 'obligated to receive its quota of Fund Certificates when presented by other central banks' [26].

A fourth feature that Stamp added to his plan in 1962 was that if a country could not find a participant to redeem its certificates, the Fund itself would do so [26]. This provision was a harbinger of two elements now built into the SDR system: the Fund's guarantee of the liquidity of the asset (Art. XXV, Section 5 of the Fund Agreement: 'The Fund shall ensure that a participant will be able to use its special drawing rights') and the possibility of the General Account itself holding SDRs (Art. XXV, Section 7). However, the two Articles are not interconnected.

---

24 'Member countries (...) would hold these certificates as reserves and would undertake to use them in payment only if under pressure and not for the purpose of adding to their gold or dollar reserves' (*ibid.*, p. 15).
25 *Ibid.*, p. 16. Stamp provided however for a direct opting out possibility for a country that might 'not wish the proceeds of the IDA loans to be spent within its economy', because of over-full employment. But he added that such a country could only insulate itself from the 'primary', not from the 'secondary' pressures to *accept certificates* (e.g., if they were to be tendered by the United States at a moment when it needed foreign exchange to support the dollar). Stamp observed further that 'it might be necessary to devise other special rules to protect countries which were suffering from temporary 'over-heating' from the consequences of the extra demand which would be created by the issue of the certificates' (*ibid.*, p. 16). It should be noted that in the Stamp Plan, in contrast to the scheme proposed in chapter V above, the purchases to be financed by the issue of certificates were to be made in the country accepting the certificates. This country had, however, only the 'primary' obligation to accept certificates; it could subsequently use them as normal reserve assets.
In my opinion, no special provisions as meant by Stamp need to be built into the scheme itself. What would a country gain if it succeeded in shielding itself from demand created by IDA but not from other foreign demands, or from internal inflationary pressures? Even if it notified IDA that it would temporarily not allow orders to be placed within its economy, it could not avert secondary demand pressures from other countries whose imports from the overheated country increased. On the analogy of the history of the Indian gold hoard, the overheated country should resort to over-all anti-inflationary measures, for instance a revaluation of its currency if total foreign demand were the main culprit.
26 *Ibid.*, p. 16.

Finally, the 1962 version of the Stamp Plan allowed an individual member of the Fund to refuse to join, 'if the safeguards failed to satisfy' it, although this certainly would be 'a less desirable alternative' [27]. There is a similar provision in the SDR scheme: no Fund member is obliged to become a participant [28] and a participant is not obliged to accept allocations of SDRs [29].

Maxwell Stamp thus appears to have been a precursor of the drafters of the SDR agreement in its final form. Except for certain features that were not needed in his scheme (such as the rules for reconstitution), he really produced a blueprint of the SDR system in its finished form; in his words, providing for 'the creation of money, and getting this money out into permanent circulation as an increase in the amount of 'owned reserves' [30]. However, the asset side of the Special Drawing Account (representing the SDR allocations) looks quite different from what Stamp envisaged. The Executive Directors of the Fund have no policy on that point, although as I tried to show in the previous chapter, perhaps more emphatically than Stamp, the asset side in many respects has a monetary impact on developments on the liability side of the balance sheet (representing the holdings of SDRs).

As for the question 'who gets the profit on the note issue', – the asset side of the operations of any reserve creating agency – Stamp made some adjustments in the 1962 version of his proposal. The proceeds of the 'note issue' could be *lent* instead of *given* to the poor countries; the lending could be done via the IDA, on its usual terms. And the certificates would be offered to the countries concerned not by the borrowing developing countries but by IDA. The IDA would pay the very modest interest it receives from its borrowers back to the Fund, which would in turn 'as far as practicable' credit it to the members holding the Fund Certificates, in proportion to their holdings [31]. The earning of interest by participants is another feature of the SDR scheme now in force. One step further that Stamp could have done, was to leave the *designation* of those who were to receive the certificates wholly to the Fund, so that IDA would get the convertible currency proceeds of the certificates (SDRs) *via* the Fund, as proposed in chapter V. The designation rules are indeed one of the most valuable elements of the SDR scheme in its present form.

27 *Ibid.*, p. 17.
28 *Fund Agreement,* Art. XXII, Section 1.
29 *Ibid.*, Art. XXIV, Section 2 (e).
30 1965, p. 15.
31 1962, p. 15.

'Is it possible', Stamp asked in his 1962 article, 'whilst retaining most of the advantages of the plan, to remove enough of the features to which the opponents object, to make the plan acceptable?' [32]. Then he suggested the further steps in the direction of the present SDR scheme that have been just discussed. In the meantime, all the difficulties he foresaw have been overcome by means of a remarkable effort of international cooperation. The monetary framework for the entry into force of the remaining element of the Stamp Plan is now complete.

The other monetary economist favoring the 'organic link' whom I would like to discuss briefly is Robert Triffin.

Triffin's first proposal for a link appeared in his book *Gold and the dollar crisis* (1960) [33]. His suggestions for the asset side of the Fund's activities went further than Stamp's, although those on the liability side were less far reaching since he retained, at least in part, the concept of backing. 'A primary consideration in determining the pattern of Fund investments would be the need to preserve the full liquidty of its members' deposits' [34]. But in the next sentence he added: 'It should be noted, however, that the Fund would be in a particular strong position in this respect as the total amount of its required deposits (. . .) could hardly decline in practice, but would on the contrary grow year by year with the increase of world reserves. Any withdrawals of deposits by members whose over-all reserves are declining would be more than matched by increases in the required deposits of members whose reserves are increasing'. Later he stressed Professor Machlup's point 'that the amounts, quality and composition and liquidity of a bank's assets are irrelevant for payments among customers of the same bank and become relevant only for payments to customers of other banks', so that an international reserve bank would have to retain sufficient liquidity 'only to finance payments to persons, banks or reserve banks on other planets' [35]. The implication of course is that the liquidity of the Fund's liabilites need not to be preserved by 'the pattern of Fund investments', and that it can be fully maintained if members agree to treat the deposits as money (since no 'withdrawals' are made). This point, recognized by Stamp as early as in his 1958 article, was included in the SDR scheme; the 'excess

---

32 *Ibid.*, p. 13.
33 See Subcommittee *etc., Hearing*, 1969, p. 39.
34 *Gold and the dollar crisis*, New Haven, 1961, (first published May 1960), p. 118 *(World monetary reform*, p. 49).
35 See, for instance, Subcommittee *etc.*, 1969, p. 39. See also footnote 82 to chapter V.

holdings' of SDRs (holdings of SDRs as a consequence of a country having been designated to accept them) are essentially 'compulsory deposits in the Special Drawing Account' whose money-like nature is based on an agreement backed by international treaty.

In Triffin's conception, the Fund would be a fully operative international reserve bank, the Stamp Plan and the present Fund being merely steps in that direction [36]. Making its deposits compulsory would only be a way of ensuring that the Fund had sufficient financial resources *until* 'members have grown fully familiar with the system and with the security, liquidity and earning power of this new form of reserve asset' [37]. The main difference between Triffin's proposals and any mechanism of SDR creation *exclusively* through the IDA is that Triffin has proposed that the Fund should have a wider field for its credit operations than development finance. 'The major safeguard against an inflationary level of Fund lending would lie in the over-all limitations placed on the net increase of the Fund's loans during any twelve-month period' [38]; *qualitatively,* however, the scope of the loans would be much broader. They 'should fall into two broad categories, similar in many respects of those of national central banks' credit operations: 1. Advances or rediscounts, undertaken at the initiative of the borrowing country; 2. Open-market operations, or investments, undertaken at the initiative of the Fund itself [38]. In such cases agreement with the monetary authorities of the countries concerned 'would be necessary in any case to attach to these investments the same guarantees against exchange and inconvertibility risks as those which protect the Fund's own deposit liabilities' [39]. A portion of the Fund's investments 'might even be channeled into relatively long-term investments for economic development through purchases of IBRD bonds or other securities of a similar character' [40].

Here the link to development finance appears for the first time. Because Triffin was slow to abandon the requirement of backing for Fund's liabilities by liquid assets, 'relatively' long-term investments might *'even'* be taken into account without however being a primary consideration.

This is not the place to discuss the appropriateness of a Fund with powers as broad as those suggested by Triffin. It seems to me that 'to

---

36 Stamp, in his 1965 article, rightly observed: 'If the Stamp Plan is expanded to make the Fund a lender of last resort if it ever be necessary, it is a workable and sensible scheme' (p. 16).
37 *Gold and the dollar crisis,* p. 105 (*World monetary reform,* p. 40).
38 *Ibid.,* p. 115 (*World monetary reform,* p. 46).
39 *Ibid.,* p. 117 (*World monetary reform,* p. 48).
40 *Ibid.,* p. 117/118 (*World monetary reform,* p. 49).

meet the need, as and when it arises, for a supplement to existing reserve assets' [41] the additional powers are not required. There is unlikely to be a need for a kind of 'super-central bank' similar to a national central bank until the countries of the world form a single monetary union, and this presupposes far-reaching changes in political institutions. Until then there will be separate national money systems, and international monetary policy will continue to depend on the cooperation of nations in matters of common interest.

In any case, the 'link' as such was proposed by Robert Triffin in 1960 [42]. He criticised the present mechanism for creation on numerous occasions, because 'the *automatic* allocation of SDRs is in blatant contradiction with the recurrent theme of previous Group of Ten reports that reserve creation should be linked with a strengthening of the adjustment process' [43].

The principle point Triffin has stressed is that the benefit of the 'note

41 *Outline of a facility based on special drawing rights in the Fund*, Introduction (IMF *Annual Report* 1968, p. 171).
42 Regarding his previous support for a 'link', Triffin himself stated before the Subcommittee on International Exchange and Payments of the U.S. Congress (*Hearing*, 1969, p. 37): 'The idea of linking reserve creation and development assistance goes back at least more than ten years. It was forcefully presented and defended by two illustrious officials and practical bankers: Mr. Maxwell Stamp in an article 'The Fund and the future', published by the *Lloyds Bank Review* of October 1958 (pp. 1–20) and by Sir Oliver Franks in his annual statement to the shareholders of the same bank. In 1959, I integrated their suggestions in the articles later assembled in my book on *Gold and the dollar crisis* (Yale University Press, New Haven, 1960, pp. 118–119). I came back repeatedly to the same point in all my subsequent writings, and particularly in my appearances before this very body (See, for instance, p. 2944 of the October 1959 *Hearings* of the Joint Economic Committee on 'Employment, growth and price levels' (Part 9 A), pp. 178–179 and 360–361 of the 1965 *Hearings* of the Subcommittee on International Exchange and Payments on 'Guidelines for international monetary reform', p. 139 of the same Subcommittee's 1966 *Hearings* on 'Contingency planning for U.S. international monetary policy', p. 137 of its 1967 *Hearings* on 'New plans for international monetary reform', and p. 145 of its 1968 *Hearings* on 'Next steps in international monetary reform.''
43 Subcommittee *etc.*, *Hearings* on 'Next steps in international monetary reform', 1968, p. 144. Triffin continues: 'It is, moreover, morally repugnant as it assigns the lion's share of such allocations to two of the richest and most capitalized countries of the world, irrespective of the wisdom or folly of the policies responsible for their deficits and of the acceptability of such policies to the prospective lenders called upon to underwrite their financing in advance by their SDR commitments. Thirdly, such a system of allocation is, for these very reasons, unviable politically and would merely lead, in the event of deep-seated policy disagreements, to a refusal to recognize an actual liquidity shortage and to activate SDRs. Finally, it would break the traditional link which has always existed in the past between fiduciary reserve creation – i.e. primarily dollar and sterling reserve accumulation – and the financing of overseas developments' (see also footnote 37 to chapter IV).

issue' must be used for internationally agreed objectives ('No taxation without representation' [44]). Thus he does justice to the nature of international cooperation which, using the terminology of chapter II, is qualified by the juridical norm of *international public interest*. Keeping this principle in mind, he suggests a number of purposes for which the lending power associated with SDR creation could be used; of these, development financing is only one. He further mentions 'recycling of speculative funds such as is contemplated in the 'General Arrangements to Borrow' of the IMF; supplementing 'the funds available to the IMF to finance its traditional monetary stabilization assistance to members'; providing 'some of the resources that might be needed to implement international efforts to stabilize the prices of primary products'; and finally 'a fifth purpose, now that the principle of 'non-reconstitution' has been accepted and embodied in the present (Draft) Agreement, could even be the support of United Nations peace-keeping and other agreed objectives' [44].

In principle all this would be fine from the point of view of the international public interest. But in the present circumstances, and in the light of the present organization of international monetary cooperation, especially through the IMF, I see no reason for pressing for more uses of SDRs than the financing of development operations under the lead of IDA.

There is a considerable advantage in concentrating on the merits of linking SDR creation to development financing, as has been done in the previous chapters. In particular, only a relatively simple amendment to the Articles of the Fund would be needed. *Economic* cooperation is at present one of the most promising fields for international agreement. Indeed, a most suitable institution – the General Account of the Fund – already exists for carrying out Triffin's first three objects [45]. The separation of the two activities of the Fund: *temporary* assistance to members (General Account) and global reserve creation (Special Drawing Account) seems to me very useful. In the General Account the Fund is actively engaged in a policy of asset distribution under agreed principles implemented through discretionary powers of the Executive Board. In the Special Drawing Account the emphasis should be on the creation and

---

44 Subcommittee *etc.*, *Hearing*, 1969, p. 41. See also Triffin's article in the FAO Review *Ceres,* Vol. III, No. 1, January/February 1970, pp. 26-28: 'The missing link in special drawing rights'.
45 As already mentioned in chapter IV, the Fund has dealt with the problem of stabilization of prices of primary products by deciding that 'it will be prepared to extend assistance to members in connection with the financing of international buffer stocks of primary products' (June 25, 1969).

management of new international 'owned' reserves, leaving asset distri--bution to a separate independent body. The amount of the new reserves should be determined by an agreed formula that is not directly linked to the particular needs of individual countries, and it should be reviewed before the start of each basic period of five years.

II. THE 'TIED' LINK (SCITOVSKY)

In 1966 [46] Professor Scitovsky made an interesting proposal for what could be called a 'tied' link – the word 'tied' having the same meaning as in the expression 'bilateral tied aid'. Newly created reserves would be made available primarily to deficit countries *directly* in exchange for goods and services to be granted to developing countries via IDA. Of course, besides 'tied' such a link would also be 'organic', but I call Professor Scitovsky's plan one for a 'tied' link, because this is its most characteristic feature.

The 'organic' link between 'the creation of international reserves and the granting of development aid, though often criticised, is', according to Scitovsky, 'a very natural one with plenty of precedents on the national level. Money in the modern world, whether central-bank money or commercial-bank deposits, has always been *earned* by the people holding it, and paid for in terms of resources' [47]. This is the same line of reasoning as has been followed in the present study.

Scitovsky wishes to *tie* the aid to be financed by reserve creation to exports of the particular country that wants its reserves to increase, for a reason that seems to contrast with the view quoted above. Although Scitovsky considers it natural that new money should be 'paid for in terms of resources' he believes that 'the only excuse for creating new reserves is the economic possibility of creating something out of nothing, and this is only possible when unemployed and re-employable resources are present' [48]. This statement is, in turn, a direct outcome of Scitovsky's fundamental point that the principle of functional finance, advocated by

46 Tibor Scitovsky, 'A new approach to international liquidity', *American Economic Review*, December 1966, pp. 1212–1220.
47 *Ibid.*, p. 1218/1219. Scitovsky's oral statement a few years later was however in the opposite sense: if the 'unconditional' ('untied') link 'were the only kind of link available, then I should fully agree and side with those who are arguing against the link on the ground that it is undesirable and improper to link two altogether separate issues, reserve creation and development assistance' (Subcommittee *etc.*, *Hearing*, 1969, p. 32).
48 'A new approach', p. 1219.

Professor Lerner a quarter century ago, meaning that 'public spending and taxation should be governed exclusively by the goals of full employment and price stability, without regard to whether the budget was balanced' [49], could be 'extended to the international sphere' [49]. However, as I have tried to point out, although national and international economics may be similar, there are also many differences, and these are often overlooked, especially in monetary matters. Governments and the national communities which they represent are economic subjects with quite different 'individuality structures' (characteristics) from private persons or other communities. Hence international economics, while governed by the same basic principles of economics, is concerned with applications of *typical* economic norms which are different from the economics of households, commerce, or the state. Explaining such states of affairs is the great contribution of Dooyeweerd to theoretical thinking.

If Scitovsky was correct, it would be impossible to meet the need for reserve creation if there were full employment throughout the world.

If the specific structure of international economic relations is ignored they can only be explained in terms of the economics of other societal individuality structures or in terms of other modal spheres (see chapter II). Scitovsky uses both these devices: he not only transfers a rule of national budget management to the problem of international balance-of-payments equilibrium; he also calls the principle of maintaining long-run equilibrium between balance-of-payments a *'moral* doctrine', a matter of 'ethics rather than economics' [50].

Balance-of-payments theory belongs to the theory of international relations as such; basically, there are economic problems involved, so that it primarily should be classified under the heading of economics. 'The functional approach to international finance is to forget about payments

49 *Ibid.,* p. 1212.
50 'Our moral conscience tells us that it is not *right* for anyone or any country to get something for nothing – although that, precisely, is what an indefinite balance of payments deficit implies. If the deficit is on the current account of the balance of payments, there is the further connotation that the country lives beyond its means and spends more than it earns, with all the moral disapprobation that this calls forth' (*ibid.,* p. 1212). Scitovsky's use of the word 'conscience' and of italics for the word 'right' could point to what Dooyeweerd has historically traced as the basic thinking motive of 'nature and freedom', the realm of freedom being that of 'conscience' and 'norms' (the word '*right*') and the realm of nature being that of natural laws and economic and other social sciences as conceived by positivistic theory. We shall return to the relation between economic science and ethical and other sciences and to *economic norms* in the next chapter. At this stage it may be remembered that the fact that there are moral aspects to balance-of-payments policy does not detract from its *economic* aspects (see foornote 7 to chapter II).

equilibrium in the long run as well as the short run and to ask instead whether it might not be possible to let each country have the kind of balance of payments that best serves its domestic goals' [51]. Furthermore, Scitovsky's theory appears to assume that an international problem can be approached as if the domestic problems of individual countries were not interrelated.

One of the main theoretical questions in examining changes in payments balances is whether these changes may be caused by or themselves cause inflation or deflation. Now, it is fairly generally agreed that global reserve growth is needed to forestall any deflationary trend that might be caused by a scramble for inadequate reserves. Professor Scitovsky himself says that he is 'proposing to increase the supply of international reserves in order to eliminate restrictive national policies when these lead, or threaten to lead, to unemployment' [52]. But what could be done if there were no significant excess capacity in large parts of the industrial world and there were still a demand for additional reserves? Under Scitovsky's scheme, no reserve creation would occur (apart from traditional sources) and surplus countries would try to export real resources, thus possibly increasing excess capacity in the deficit countries. When this had occurred, the deficit countries could call for reserves to be created through the 'tied link', but this indirect and 'sticky' adjustment could be avoided by adopting the *un*tied link, under which surplus countries would be able to export directly to developing countries.

The reason why Scitovsky prefers a 'tied' link to an 'unconditional' one is that it 'does not add to the inflationary pressures that reserve creation may put on surplus countries. On the contrary, it provides a safeguard against excessive inflationary pressures, by making the acquisition of SDRs by deficit countries subject to cost, which may be considered prohibitive, if these countries happen to be in an inflationary situation already' [53]. A further explanation was given orally by Professor Scitovsky during the 1969 hearing on the 'link' before the Subcommittee on International Eychange and Payments of the U.S. Congress: 'I am very much in favor of the (tied) link from the point of view of offering some kind of safeguard to those countries most likely to oppose the creation of SDRs and I am trying to look at it from the point of view of how we can increase the volume of SDRs that will be created'. But he added: 'I mention the inflationary danger not as something I believe in, but as something

51 *Ibid.*, p. 1213.
52 *Ibid.*, p. 1216.
53 Oral statement before the Subcommittee *etc.*, *Hearing,* 1969, p. 32.

many of the central banks, especially of surplus countries, are fearful of' [54].

One question is whether the tied link really would not have any inflationary effect. Another is whether it might not have an unfavorable impact on the balance-of-payments adjustment process; Scitovsky recognizes that 'payments adjustment must not and cannot always be avoided' [55]. On the second point he himself seems to provide an answer when he says that a 'permanent payments disequilibrium, and especially one due to misalignment of price levels, should be remedied by exchange-rate readjustment' rather than by applying 'the principle of functional finance' [56]. He argues, however, that the country concerned could weigh the 'opportunity cost of buying reserves with development aid' (no social cost being involved in the short run, at a time of under-employment) against alternatives like currency devaluation (involving a worsening of the terms of trade). 'There might well be situations in which the country would prefer to keep its currency overvalued indefinitely and finance the resulting payments deficit out of newly created reserves paid for by products'.

Again, this is putting international problems in national terms. A better way of absorbing the unused capacity and improving the reserve position would be devaluation – the situation being indeed the 'schoolbook case' for that. Deliberately to maintain a currency in an overvalued state causes undue distorsions in international production and unnecessary monetary problems in other countries. Scitovsky comments on the international effects of overvaluation as follows: 'Other developed countries would probably accept and even prefer it. For they usually regard a fellow developed country not so much as a market in which to buy as one in which to sell and as a competitor in third markets' [57]. This view seems rather questionable. Under the 'tied' link system, the country having an overvalued currency tries to protect itself from competition in the markets of the developing countries by superseding the competitive supply from other developed countries. It would probably have to acquire a large share of

---

54 *Ibid.*, p. 61; it may be remembered that the date of the hearing was May 28, 1969. Shortly thereafter the Group of Ten reached agreement on the creation of SDR 9.5 billion for the three-year period 1970–1972. This agreement became the basis of the subsequent proposal of the Manging Director of the IMF, adopted on October 3, 1969, by the Board of Governors of the Fund. It would hardly be possible to bring about the same amount of reserve creation by means of a 'tied link' mechanism probably involving budgetary processes (see footnote 58).
55 'A new approach', p. 1216.
56 *Ibid.*, p. 1217.
57 *Ibid.*, p. 1217/1218.

total exports to developing countries, in order to compensate for the reserve losses caused by its sustained over-all balance-of-payments deficit. Such a course may well end up with wholesale support for the country's export industries as well as protection for those producing for the home market.

All of this could be avoided through the adoption of the 'unconditional' link, which, in sharp contrast to the tied link, is 'fully consistent with the principle of multilateral trade and with the high degree of competitiveness that would prevail in world trade' [58]. Dr. I. G. Patel has rightly stated: 'The provision of larger contributions to multilateral aid agencies, whose aid is untied to any particular source of procurement and has, therefore, the most beneficial effect not only on development in the short run but also on the long-term promotion of world trade on the most efficient lines, represents an advance which is most in keeping with the objectives of the two Bretton Woods institutions – the IBRD and the IMF' [59]. Competing

58 See footnote 66 to chapter V. See also Mr. Dell's rejection of the tied link, Subcommittee *etc. Hearing,* 1969, p. 67; also Professor Johnson (*ibid.,* p. 72): 'I would think that there could be very substantial objection to a scheme under which a country could create markets for itself, financed by these international reserves, and enable itself to sell its goods at higher prices than its competitors could, using this scheme as the justification'. Professor Scitovsky of course recognizes this problem (see: Subcommittee *etc., Hearing,* 1969, p. 34): 'Since this kind of link involves the provision of tied aid, which is usually more expensive than untied aid, means would have to be found to make it acceptable to the developing countries. With this in view, I once proposed that development assistance linked to the creation of SDRs should take the form of grants, rather than loans, since the objections to tied loans do not apply to tied grants' (cf. 'A new approach', p. 1219). 'Another way of dealing with the same problem might be to link the acquisition of SDRs to the making of tied contributions to the IDA. The U.S. contribution of $ 160 million per annum now under discussion shows that tying is not an impossibility, although more tying would be desirable. Since the IDA can grant loans so soft as to be almost indistinguishable from grants (e.g. interest-free, with long grace periods), the tying of such loans would not be too objectionable. A third and perhaps the best solution might be to link the acquisition of SDRs to development assistance in the form of tied loans; but with the deficit country's government bearing the excess cost of tying. In other words, the value of the lowest bid would determine the value of the loan, the developing country's repayment obligations, and the amount of SDRs made available to a firm in the deficit country, with the government paying the difference between its bid and the lowest bid. Such an arrangement would render the acquisition of SDRs by a particular country the more expensive, the more that country's price level exceeded the world price level – this fact might well be considered an advantage too'.

The latter suggestion would seem to entail an export subsidy; a country might well be induced to extend subsidies to its whole export industry. These would present a substantial budgetary burden and might lead to international price distortions.
59 I. G. Patel, 'The link between the creation of international liquidity and the provision of development finance', Subcommittee *etc., Hearing,* 1969, p. 12–14; I quoted from page 13.

developed countries would be more likely to concentrate their export efforts on the markets of the developing countries than under Scitovsky's scheme. The argument for the tied link is one that serves the short-term domestic interest of deficit countries. But even for those countries it would be better to earn to desired reserves not through one item of the balance-of-payments, development aid, but through raising the general level of exports, or to tackle idle capacity through appropriate domestic measures.

The question whether a tied link would really avoid inflation may be answered in the following way. First, a tied link as suggested by Professor Scitovsky might well sustain domestic inflation in countries with large balance-of-payments deficits, and thus stimulate world inflation. When there is idle capacity in only one or two developed countries this probably means that they have allowed their currencies to become overvalued as the result of domestic inflation; otherwise international demand would spontaneously tend to absorb the unemployed productive resources. If there were idle capacity all over the world, Scitovsky would probably agree that the untied link would be the best approach. Second, any country – whether surplus or deficit – that merely wished to increase its reserves [60] could claim to have unused capacity and apply for new reserves as the counter part of supplying aid to the developing countries, thus enhancing inflation at home. Third, in a country with genuinely idle capacity, the production of aid goods might still lead to imports that could have an inflationary impact on the rest of the world.

Unused capacity is after all often caused by structural deficiencies within a national economy. For instance, a 4 percent unemployment figure is usually considered in the United States as the minimum required for avoiding domestic inflation.

The conclusion so far must be that the tied link, far from offering advantages additional to those offered by the untied link, actually has major disadvantages.

The argument that the only excuse for reserve creation is that it would give countries a chance to acquire reserves at no social cost (see footnote 48) is similar to that put forward by the Ossola Group to the effect that new reserves 'of their nature' must be freely distributed, and not involve possibly inflationary real transfers. The 'tied' link may cause no inflationary problems in the country concerned but when activated it is bound to raise the level of monetary reserves held by that country, and thus its

60 When a surplus country outside the sphere of international competition adds more to its surplus in this artificial way, payments imbalances would further increase, thus adding to the problems connected with reserve composition and confidence in general.

potential demand for foreign real resources; these in turn may perhaps not be produced without real costs for the other countries. While the social cost for the supplying country benefiting from the 'tied link' may be zero or small, the social cost for the international community may still be large.

An important objection to the tied link is the fact that this is not reliable as a mechanism of reserve creation. Without the occurrence of cyclical unemployment (a situation which is intended to be *prevented* through the help of reserve creation), no reserve creation would be possible.

However, my main objection to the tied link is related to the other aim of SDR creation, namely, to provide a mechanism for the creation of international reserves that would be independent of the domestic economic policies or situations of individual countries.

III. MIXED SYSTEMS

Many techniques that have been put forward in an attempt to overcome the main objections to the present mechanism of SDR creation in fact are half-hearted, and some of them might even be considered dangerous. These proposals are often inspired by the desire of developing countries to receive more financial means for their development, or by the wish of people in the richer countries to provide the means for satisfying this desire more easily than by the traditional means, which may not be politically feasible. Many of these proposals are therefore compromises and not the result of pure economic thought [61]. Nevertheless, the economist should take them into account and pass judgment in the light of their effectiveness in overcoming the main defects of the present SDR scheme. Some of them will be discussed very briefly, as they offer hardly any new economic insights. In any event, they are all combinations of the present system and certain forms of a 'link' and they thus leave the present mechanism for the creation of special drawing rights essentially or partially untouched.

First, there is the *'voluntary link':* under this scheme the industrial countries could agree to give or lend to IDA or the World Bank contributions financed out of their monetary reserves, the contributions to

---

61 Cf. the remark of Mr. Márquez ('Developing countries and the international monetary system', p. 134): 'It is probably because of the passion with which many of the negotiators of the Group of Ten rejected the idea of *directly* linking the creation of liquidity with the financing of economic development and the long-run transfer of real resources that the developing countries, even in UNCTAD, generally speaking took refuge in a non-functional indirect link'.

be made on the occasion of their receiving SDR allocations and to amount to an agreed uniform percentage thereof [62].

Each country is of course free to finance its international development contributions in the way it chooses. If some countries see no difficulty in investing or granting some of their reserves as aid, they are free to take an internal decision to do so. Naturally this would also be true if there were no special drawing rights, and a number of central banks hold already World Bank notes as part of their reserves. [63] One of the difficulties of a 'voluntary' link between SDR creation and development assistance, being a disadvantage unless the scheme is adhered to by all the rich countries together, has been pointed out by the CIAP experts [64]:

'Countries which did in fact increase their aid, or liberalize its use, would be likely to gain less from the creation and distribution of new reserve assets than would countries which did not increase their aid. This is because at least part of the extra *financial* aid which the former countries gave would be spent on the goods and services of the latter, with the result that a deterioration would be produced in the

62 For instance the proposal of the Italian Governor of the IMF, Emilio Colombo, in his statement to the Annual Meeting 1968: 'The new (SDR) facility, being the outcome of a very difficult compromise aimed at reaching a general consensus, is not perfect. The main deficiency, according to some, is the lack of a link between reserve creation and the provision of resources for development needs, a link which, on the contrary, exists in the present system. An improvement which could be carefully studied and eventually made, without modifying the text of the Articles of Agreement, could consist of a pledge by the main industrial countries to use the part of their reserves corresponding to a portion of their special drawing rights allocations for the replenishment of IDA or for subscription to World Bank bonds' (IMF, *Summary Proceedings, Annual Meeting 1968*, p. 81). A year later Mr. Colombo came back to the same point: 'We continue to believe that it is worthwhile to examine the possibility of implementing this proposal. One of its advantages is that, without the need to amend the Articles, some mitigation would be introduced of the rigidity of the parameter – the Fund quotas – which has been chosen as the basis for the allocation of SDRs. Balance-of-payments permitting, we do not exclude a unilateral implementation of this proposal' (*ibid.*, 1969, p. 71). Similarly Governor Ali bin Haji Ahmad from Malaysia: '... it bears repeating that we in the developing world have always been given a limited role in the decision-making process and that we shall also be given an unreasonably small portion of the special drawing rights to be created. We have always questioned the logic and even the morality of this because we consider that the magnitude of our needs for liquidity are not necessarily reflected by the size of our quotas in the International Monetary Fund. While we hope and expect this inequitable basis of allocating special drawing rights to be changed in the near future, we feel that the effects of this system should also be mitigated in the meantime. One approach that has considerable merit is for the major industrial countries to set aside for purposes of development aid the equivalent of a portion of what they will receive in special drawing rights (*ibid.*, 1969, p. 44/45).
63 Cf. footnote 83 to chapter V.
64 *International monetary reform and Latin America,* Report to CIAP by the Group of Experts, Washington, 1966, p. 33.

balance of payments of the former group and an improvement in those of the latter. Reserves would then tend to flow from countries which increased their aid to countries which did not, so that at least part of the increase in reserve assets which the former countries received in the initial (gratuitous) distribution would end up in the reserves of the latter. *From the reserve point of view,* therefore, countries which gave more aid would be penalized for their 'good' behavior [65]; preoccupation of many developed countries with the state of their international reserves, and a lack of mutual confidence in each's other's aid policies, might well produce a general reluctance in the developed world as a whole to increase the flow of aid.'

The advantage of the 'voluntary link' proposals is that they are easy to implement, and that no amendment of the Fund Agreement is required. Domestically, however, they may encounter considerable difficulties.

Most central banks probably could not invest liquid monetary reserves for comparatively long terms without guarantees on the part of their Treasuries, and this might introduce the practical obstacles to aid that the proponents of this form of link wish to avoid.

The main objection to a 'voluntary link' is the fact that it is indeed voluntary. It may of course be implemented by a large number of countries, but it is more likely that only a few, or perhaps just one, will support the scheme, and then only 'balance-of-payments permitting'. As a general system therefore, it is not likely to be very successful. Again, the direction and the moment of the first use of the new reserves, although created in the international public interest must be decided on by countries individually, and this is unnecessary. All the objections mentioned in section 2 of chapter IV remain unanswered. Even if industrial countries were to contribute the equivalent of 100 percent of their SDR allocations, all the other countries in the world could dispose of their new SDRs without regard to any agreed international policy.

The 'voluntary' link turns out to be in practice no more than a *partial* link. Only part of the total amount of SDRs to be created is linked to development finance. Whether such a partial link is voluntary, organic and unconditional, or organic and tied [66], its partial nature is a great

65 The following footnote was added here: 'Countries which neither increased the flow of financial aid to developing countries nor competed successfully for export orders financed by the increased flow of aid from other countries would see their reserves rise by as much as, but not by more than, the initial allocation of new reserve assets to them; and countries, which, although not increasing their financial aid, did compete successfully for the orders of the developing countries (and therefore would be giving aid in real terms by their trade surpluses with developing countries) could find their reserves rising by more than their initial allocation.'
66 A 'tied link' à la Scitovsky is of course also 'voluntary' as has been shown in the previous section; but in the present section the word 'voluntary' is used as the

disadvantage. If the SDR system is maintained in its present form, the partial link would be subject to all the objections listed in chapter IV and *the tendency to undue pressures for SDR creation would be strongly enhanced*. For just as the present reconstitution rule requiring use of no more than 70 percent (on average within a five-year period) of any SDRs allotted to individual countries is likely to induce them to press for about 40 percent more SDR creation [67], a collectively agreed partial link of, say, 50 percent of SDR allocations to the rich countries would cause a bias to 100 percent more SDR creation. Although the reasons for such demands might not be openly stated, and the precise effect of the bias could not be established, the *tendency* would certainly be present, in view of the individual aims of the countries concerned. Thus, unless it is completely unilateral, a partial link could be not only more inflationary than the integral link, but even more inflationary than the present SDR mechanism [68].

Advocates of 'flexibility' in SDR creation would probably favor a partial link if there is to be any link at all. The 'Ossola Report' does indeed state that 'the difficulties' (connected with the link) 'might not be insuperable if, (. . .) the amount of reserve creation associated with development finance were kept at a modest fraction of the total creation of reserves' [69]. The 'flexibility' argument, however, has been rejected in chapters V and VI.

A partial link was also suggested in the Report of the Group of Experts appointed by the United Nations Conference on Trade and Development: *International monetary issues and the developing countries* (1965) [70]. In this report the case for the link was very clearly set out. The version chosen can be characterized as a *partial, organic, untied link*. As has been agreed on monetary grounds in the preceding chapters, however, any link should be such that *all* SDR creation is directly connected with development.

opposite of 'organic': individual countries can unilaterally decide how great a proportion of existing SDRs will be 'linked' to development finance. It is thus a *post hoc* link.
67 43 percent of 70 percent equals 30 percent. 30 percent plus 70 percent equals the intended 100 percent. As suggested in chapter V, with an 'organic' link there is no reason at all for 'reconstitution'.
68 An argument may still be made in favor of the partial link on the grounds that it would increase international development activity. The present study, however, deals with the international monetary aspects of the link.
69 *Ossola Report*, paragraph 138.
70 U.N. Publication, Sales No. 66. II. D. 2. The Group was headed by Dr. Gamani Corea, Chairman, and Lord Kahn, Vice-Chairman. Among the members was also Professor Scitovsky.

Newly created reserves, according to the report, should both be linked to development finance, *and* be allocated to developing countries, because these countries 'need both additional liquidity and more development finance' [71]. However, such a proposal raises the objection put forward in chapters IV and V above, namely, that international money on its creation will be spent without any international policy. The liquidity needs of developing countries are mainly determined by their economic structure; the need for development finance and for payment means to meet balance-of-payment deficits are to a large extent inseparable. Cyclical liquidity needs ought, in my opinion, to be met by the General Account of the Fund. Some flexibility in this respect could, if necessary, be applied both by the Fund and by the IDA, which can choose the extent to which it wishes to finance *local currency* costs of development projects by providing *foreign exchange* [72].

It follows from the analysis in the preceding chapters, that any allocation of internationally agreed money to individual countries, even developing countries, would not be favorable. Thus, I would certainly not support any arrangement which doubled SDR allocations under the present system to them or allocated *all* SDRs to these countries; both courses of action were suggested at the 1970 Annual Meeting of the Bank and the Fund [73].

The link as proposed by the UNCTAD Group in 1965 was partial in the sense that only part ('a sizable part' [74]) of the new reserves allocated to the rich countries would be linked to development. In more general terms, the Group stated that 'the amount of any new reserve creation should be determined by the monetary requirements of the world economy and not by the need for development finance. But once the need for additional reserves has been demonstrated and the amount of the addition determined on the basis of monetary requirements, the introduction of a link with development finance is entirely proper and desirable' [75]. As I have suggested in the previous chapters, the monetary

---

71 *Ibid.*, paragraph 100.
72 'IDA only rarely finances local expenditure, but might do so, say, when the foreign exchange cost of a worthwile project is very low, and when there is a shortfall in domestic savings. IDA will also finance local expenditure when a local supplier wins a contract for a component of an IDA project. In these circumstances, IDA purchases local currency from the central bank of the country with foreign exchange' (International Development Association, *50 Questions and answers*, Washington, May 1970, p. 23).
73 See *Press Release* No. 6, p. 1 and No. 51, p. 3.
74 *UNCTAD Report*, 1965, paragraph 90.
75 *Ibid.*, paragraph 103.

requirements of the world economy are, by definition not precise and, if necessary, certainly do allow for some adjustment to development needs.

Probably the Group of Experts itself did believe in the need for a short-term tuning of the amount of reserve creation, though in rather a different form from that described earlier; it considered it an advantage that (paragraph 104 of the report:) 'in the general scheme outlined above, the tuning or distribution of the initial liquidity creation does not depend on disbursements by the (World) Bank. The fears sometimes expressed about the creation of liquidity being dependent on the uncertainty of the rate of disbursements would not be warranted if the link were of the type suggested here'. 'Unlike some of the earlier schemes envisaging such a link (e.g. Mr. Maxwell Stamp), the UNCTAD Group of Experts envisaged the creation and distribution of international liquidity first and channeling a part of the national currencies mobilized for this purpose towards development finance only as a next step, so that the original liquidity created would at no time be immobilized' [76]. The national currencies referred to were envisaged as the counterpart of the reserve units to be created, and were intended to serve as *backing* for those units. The Fund would distribute 'Fund units' to all members against currencies contributed by the members. These currencies would be made available to the World Bank and its affiliates [77]. Although such monetary backing of Fund units by national currencies is now considered completely unnecessary, it must be recognized that it would provide one interesting feature: new reserves could be put in the hands of national monetary authorities without the need for any corresponding simultaneous disbursement by the IDA. However, as the need for reserve creation is a matter of long-term trends, any delay due to the IDA decision-making process could not be serious; in any event, 'backing' is now a forgotten subject [78].

---

76 I. G. Patel in: Subcommittee *etc., Hearing*, 1969, p. 12/13. Dr. Patel was a member of the UNCTAD expert panel.
77 See the 1965 *UNCTAD Report*, paragraph 90–92.
78 A Second Group of Experts appointed by UNCTAD, also headed by Dr. Corea, issued a report in 1969, entitled *International monetary reform and cooperation for development* (U.N. Publication, Sales No. E. 70. II. D. 2). It restated the case for the link after completion of the SDR scheme. No specific proposals were made, but for illustrative purposes two possibilities were mentioned: both 'voluntary': 1) 'direct contribution of SDRs by the developed countries to IDA out of their allocations' (the wording suggests that the contributions might amount to less than 100 percent) and 2) 'contributions in national currencies by the developed countries to IDA in proportion to SDRs annually allocated to them' (paragraph 41). The second suggestion preserves the advantage offered by the counterpart currencies envisaged in the first report. The national budgetary problems might be greater,

Finally, two proposals for a partial link put forward for consideration by the Joint Economic Committee of the 91st Congress of the United States may be mentioned. The first one is the staff study by John Karlik, April 1969 [79]. It combines features of Scitovsky's tied link proposal, in that individual countries unilaterally may influence the amount of reserve creation through the 'link', with some from the untied link, since it provides a form of financial aid not bilaterally tied with real aid. Additional reserves would be created by permitting 'a multinational organization to sell, in return for convertible currencies, a reserve asset that is fully guaranteed and accepted by all IMF members as a means of international settlement. (. . .) The most expedient course (. . .) would apparently be to provide a special issue of SDRs that Fund members desiring international reserves could purchase at their own volition' [80].

The proposal rests on the assumption that with the present SDR mechanism allocations are likely to be made in inadequate amounts so that a worldwide deflationary trend would set in [81]. Hence the need for the creation of supplementary SDRs by the IMF [82] or some other multinational organization authorized by the IMF – where the link to development could come in [83].

As world deflation is assumed this kind of partial link would not involve inflationary dangers. The objections to it are, however, that it is both unilateral and partial. Now that the principle of deliberate reserve creation through collective decisions has been accepted – a principle that would still apply in a SDR system linked exclusively to development finance – the presupposition of a world scarcity of reserves, for that matter, is no longer relevant.

The second publication of the U.S. Congress also contained a proposal for a link that was only partly organic, but it did not propose any unilateral initiative. This was the Report of the Subcommittee on International Exchange and Payments (Chairman, Henry S. Reuss) issued in

however; the situation would resemble the present practice of budgetary contributions to IDA. In the scheme outlined by the first expert group the granting of currencies to IDA could simply be done by the IMF, which would be holding these currencies as a result of the working of the reserve creation mechanism (see paragraph 90 of the 1965 report).

79 *On linking reserve creation and development assistance,* a study for the use of the Subcommittee *etc.,* by John Karlik (see footnote 61 to chapter V).

80 *Ibid.,* p. 8/9.

81 *Ibid.,* p. 3, 7, 8.

82 If the IMF sold SDRs and itself held the currency proceeds, no net reserve creation would occur, if countries provided not their own currency but a reserve currency. See footnote 49 to chapter VI.

83 *Ibid.,* p. 12.

August 1969, after the hearing that it held on May, 28 of that year.

The report made the following proposal: '(a) Permitting the IMF to retain as 'treasury stock' 25 percent of the SDR allocations of the 18 wealthy members that have contributed to IDA. (. . .). (b) Allowing the retained SDRs to be cashed at IDA/IMF direction, irrespective of the balance-of-payments and reserve positions of the initial recipients' [84].

This is in principle the same as the proposal in chapter V above, except that the link would be only partial. One difference, however, is that the Special Drawing Account would apparently be managed in accordance with a joint IDA/IMF policy, ignoring the normal designation policy of the Fund. This kind of 'mixed' monetary policy is quite unnecessary. The IMF could itself lay down the rules for cashing the SDRs as it is entirely responsible for administering the Special Drawing Account in accordance with a jointly agreed policy on the holding and use of SDRs. It should be realized that if 25 percent of the SDRs are initially made available outside the normal designation policy, and that policy remains as it is under the present rules, the effect would be to neutralize any special designation procedure for special drawing rights linked to IDA.

It is interesting that after its hearing, the Subcommittee opted for the (partial) *organic* link. It is also interesting that the Committee proposed to apply the reconstitution provisions only to that part of the SDR allocations that is not retained under the Subcommittee's proposal for allowing the IMF to reserve 25 percent for use by IDA. The reconstitution obligation of the 18 wealthy countries would then fall from 30 percent of 100 percent of SDR allocations to 30 percent of 75 percent, 75 percent being the amount of the actual allocations made to the countries concerned. For the purposes of the management of the Special Drawing Account the 18 countries would be deemed to have accepted the whole of their 'normal' allocations, so that the reconstitution obligations would amount to 22.5 percent of that figure, 'not a very serious reduction when one considers that the original 30 percent figure was largely picked out of the blue' [84].

A formal element of *direct* financial aid by the rich countries was, however, retained, as the acceptance and cancellation provisions of the present SDR agreement would 'apply to the wealthy Fund members just as if they had obtained 100 percent of their allocations' [84], just as would

---

84 *A proposal to link reserve creation and development assistance,* report of the Subcommittee on International Exchange and Payments of the Joint Economic Committee, Congress of the United States, August 1969, p. 6.

have occurred with a 'voluntary' link. This means that after creation of a certain amount of special drawing rights and subsequent total cancellation of that figure, the wealthy countries would have to pay to the IMF 133 1/3 percent of the cumulative allocations they had actually received if 25 percent of the nominal figure is retained for financing IDA operations. In view of the argument put forward in chapter V, section 6, there is no necessity for such a provision from a strictly monetary standpoint; IDA itself could settle the balance due to IMF by making appropriate financial arrangements in such an unlikely situation.

VIII. Some further methodological remarks

I. ECONOMICS, ETHICS OR POLITICS?

Most current literature draws a contrast between the 'economic' point of view and the 'ethical' or 'humanitarian' point of view, and between 'economics' and 'politics'. Those who oppose the 'link' on 'economic' grounds, for instance, occasionally admit that a strong case can be made for it from the 'ethical', 'political' or 'practical' standpoint. Such views not only cause great theoretical problems, but also practical difficulties. For while our scientific approaches may differ, there is only one choice to be made in any given real situation. Current writings suggest that it is possible to find oneself in a particular situation in which, for instance, an economic approach may lead to a conclusion that would be rejected on the basis of, say, an ethical approach. To add to the confusion, it is also in vogue to talk of the *political 'aspect'* when the *subjective aims* of a particular state are concerned. In this way confusion arises between law-spheres and individuality structures of reality [1], between *economics* and *economic subjects* like the body politic. These confusions are so widespread and common in economic literature that I can refrain from giving examples. However, by way of illustration, a sentence of Professor Boulding may be quoted: 'Welfare economics tries to set up standards of judgment by which events and policies can be judged as 'economically' desirable, even though on other grounds (political, national,

1 See chapter II, sections 2 and 3.

ethical) they might be judged to be undesirable' [2]. Here things are compared ('national' versus 'ethical' grounds) which are not comparable. A *nation* is an individuality structure (entity) that *functions* in the economic and ethical and other *modal* aspects of reality [3]. National economic life is an aspect of national life; one cannot contrast the 'economic aspect' of the national economy with the national 'aspects' of it.

Whenever it is suggested that there may be a difference between 'economics' and 'politics' in the above sense, an antithesis of particular *interests* is likely to be involved: for instance between international interest and national interest. If a formalized concept of economics is used, there is bound to be a conflict of views. Thus the fact that some of the major economic problems of our days are called 'social' problems is the result of the *individualistic* approach to economics that has prevailed in the past. Zijlstra has made the remark that the problems encountered by *employers* (costs, income, profits, losses) are often called 'economic' problems while the problems of workers (wages, social security) are called '*social*' problems. When the debate is conducted in these terms, it is sometimes said that something is 'socially desirable' but, unfortunately, 'economically impossible', and at that point discussions are broken off, just when they were beginning to become significant [4]. There are many examples of a particular economic group claiming its own economic behavior or norms to be in accordance with 'objective' economic principles. Every economic system, i.e. every set of particular attitudes to and materializations of economic norms, has an impact on the interests of all parties concerned. *Harmonization* of these economic interests means a deepening of economic life, or, in more specific Dooyeweerdian terms, an opening of the juridical *anticipatory* moment in the structure of the modal economic aspect (see chapter II, section 2). References to the 'requirements' of economic systems, often made by 'conservatives' (i.e. those whose interests are served primarily or sufficiently by the prevailing system), must, therefore, always be judged with a critical eye. This is why an attempt was made in chapter II to debunk the concept of the international monetary system. Economic science as such cannot deliver absolute standards of judgment; it has to analyze

---

2 Taken from P. Hennipman, 'Doeleinden en criteria der economische politiek', *Theorie van de economische politiek*, p. 31, who cites K. E. Boulding, 'Welfare economics', *A survey of contemporary economics*, Part II, Homewood 1952, p. 3.
3 See chapter II, section 2.
4 J. Zijlstra, *Economische orde en economische politiek*, Leyden, 1956, p. 97, 105.

the economic aspect of human life in the various structures of society. The coherence between the various aspects of reality means that any conflict between the points of view of representatives of various disciplines must be the result of the use of formalized models of thought rather than attributable to reality itself.

While theoretical thought cannot fully describe reality itself, it has to take reality into account, and that it cannot do on the basis of *a priori* formalizations. Only a careful analysis of the relationship between the various aspects of reality can prevent theoretical antinomies or false conclusions from being reached.

The 'economic principle', it is always stated, implies that a certain productive end be reached at the least cost, or that, given a certain amount of means, certain needs be met in the most effective way. The economic principle defined in this way would therefore be narrowed down if it were viewed from the standpoint of a single person or a single firm. The possible use of credit implies that economic means for a single economic subject are not absolutely fixed; even the needs are, for that matter, influenced by social factors. As was pointed out in chapter II, the economic aspect of reality is founded in the social aspect. It is not conceivable apart from its social substratum; the same applies to the 'economic principle', which is what Dooyeweerd calls the 'law-side' of the economic aspect.

Any undue restriction or formalization of the subject matter of economics is likely to lead to distinctions such as those between the 'theoretical' and the 'practical' side of a particular problem, or between its 'economic' and 'social' aspects, or between 'economics' and 'ethics' or 'politics', or even between 'monetary' and 'economic' problems.

When an economic problem is called a political problem, no contradiction can be involved, since reference is only being made to the type of economic subject whose economic problem is investigated. 'Politics' is the field of action of states, and thus concerns all those economic affairs in which governments do play a role. If the economist is not competent in these matters [5], who else can be consulted by the politician if he wants an economic advise? The 'politicalization' of monetary policy, as it is sometimes called, cannot be considered as putting it beyond the scope of economics. Monetary policy 'necessarily meshes with governmental policy generally' [6]; this is only natural, except perhaps in the

5 Cf. the first sentence quoted in footnote 1 to chapter VI.
6 J. Dewey Daane, 'Perspective on monetary policy', *Monthly Review,* Federal Reserve Bank of Richmond, March 1970, p. 3.

eyes of those who consider monetary policy to be 'neutral' [7].

The economic aspect of reality is very often restricted in a formalized way by those who deny its normative character. These people see economics as a 'positive' science, trying to explain only relationships that necessarily exist. As everyone knows that in economic life choices are in fact made on the basis of particular rules and policies this, 'normative' side of 'practical' issues is consigned to the field of 'ethics'. The foregoing chapters may have shown, that economic analysis can quite well lead to practical conclusions. Ethics may come into the picture [8] of course, but ethical support is not necessary in order to form a normative economic point of view as such [9]. As far as our own particular subject is concerned, we may endorse Professor Cohen's statement that 'There is no need to fall back on considerations of charity and humanitarianism, or even of convenience. A sufficient case for a link between reserve creation and development assistance can be made on strictly *economic* grounds' [10].

These remarks are, of course, much too brief to be even an introductory discussion of the principles of economic science. They are only intended to indicate certain views on matters that are essential for an understanding of the direction of economic thought, including international monetary economics.

II. THE NORMATIVE CHARACTER OF ECONOMIC SCIENCE

'A 'norm' is always a *rational* standard, founded in the logical manner of distinction' [11]. As economic science studies human behavior according to economic norms, economics is *per definitionem* a normative science, in contrast with the study of the 'laws of nature'.

A normative point of view is, therefore, indispensable in trying to establish 'economic facts' and their relationships. Norms are always involved in economic analysis; they may be the norms of the economic subject whose behavior is studied, past or present normative methods in economic theory, or economic norms as seen by ourselves, which may

---

7 Cf. the end of chapter V, section 2.
8 Cf. chapter IV, section 2, 'Third objection'.
9 The opposite view is held by T. P. van der Kooy, *Over economie en humaniteit*, Wageningen 1954, p. 29.
10 Subcommittee *etc.*, *Hearing*, 1969, p. 111 (Letter from Professor Benjamin J. Cohen).
11 H. Dooyeweerd, *A new critique of theoretical thought*, Vol. II, p. 156.

differ from those of the subjects under study or those assumed in current economic theory. Although the economic principle is not man-made but is a precondition for economic life, the particular historical shapes it takes are the result of human actions. In Dooyeweerdian terminology, 'positivations' of the normative principle are subject to the human formative will [12]. Our normative insight performs the function of recognizing the facts or relationships that we consider relevant for our analysis, which is of course closely bound up with our synthesis. I would endorse the following sentence of Gunnar Myrdal, were it not that he also bases himself on the distinction between 'fact' and 'value' that has given rise to the numerous confusing discussions on the difference between 'normative' economics and 'empirical' economics, which Dooyeweerd in his profound analysis of Neo-Kantian philosophy has shown to be unsound. 'Valuations', says Myrdal, 'enter into social analysis, not only when conclusions concerning policy are drawn, but already in the theoretical endeavour to establish what is objectively true – in the choice of a field of enquiry, the selection of assumptions, even the decision as to what is a fact and what is a value' [13].

To give an example: how do we establish the 'fact' that the balance of payments of a country shows a 'deficit'? The determination of a balance of payments imbalance 'has the clearly normative aspect of providing a guide for economic policy. To bring this normative aspect into the open we may define a surplus or deficit in terms of the need for action' [14]. Thus, a mere description of economic facts and the economic implications of facts presupposes an answer to the methodological question countered in current literature, which he does in a section entitled 'The relevance of our descriptions and analysis depends on the methodology on which they are based.

Professor Hennipman, in the essay on economic policy he wrote in 1962, lists four types of thought on economic policy that he has encountered in current literature which he does in a section entitled 'The specific character of the theory on economic policy'. Calling thought on economic policy *specific* is generally related to the opinion that it is the 'normative' point of view which is 'specific'; therefore, I will briefly comment on each of the current conceptions.

---

12 *Ibid.*, p. 238/239. Above I used the word 'materialization' instead of 'positivation'.
13 G. Myrdal, ' 'Value-loaded' concepts', in *Money, growth and methodology*, ed. by Hugo Hegeland, Lund, 1961, p. 274.
14 P. Høst-Madsen, 'A deficit in the balance of payments', *Finance and development*, September 1966, p. 172.

First, thought on economic policy is sometimes described as *applied pure theory* [15]. I touched on this in chapter II [16]; if economic science deals with economic reality, which can only take shape as a result of human economic policy, there can be nothing 'impure' in thought on economic policy.

Second, thought on economic policy is seen as being of a 'teleological' character, studying 'reversed causalities'; i.e., it does not seek to answer the question: what are the consequences of given actions, but how are given objectives to be reached? Hennipman rightly observes that thus the same relations are studied as generally in current economic analysis; only they are considered from the other end. No specific method is involved [17]. The relationship between end and means, very often considered to be the specific subject matter of economic theory, is not a specifically economic problem at all. I consider confining the economic principle to that of efficiency one of those formalizations of the economic aspect that inevitably lead to theoretical confusions. Van der Kooy, for instance, has written a chapter about the relation between ethics and economics under the title: 'The conflict between love for one's fellowmen and efficiency' [18]. Such conflicts, if any, are the result of a methodology, and cannot stand up to logical criticism. For not only *economic* behavior, but also social, legal, and ethical behavior itself can be judged by standards of suitability; efficiency is not something that can be applied to economic action alone. A lawyer too has to know everything about how to reach his ends.

Third, economic policy is seen from the standpoint of a fixed criterion, implying that economic life as such is characterized by a precise general aim. The particular example is welfare theory [19], which examines economic behavior against the yardstick of an assumed objective of economic life. It is in danger to forget the fundamental right and responsibility of every man to *choose* his own aims. If 'science' (that means a particular scientist or group of scientists) were to be able to do this for us, we would lose our responsibility and freedom. Moreover, this view runs into great theoretical problems. A particular goal of

15 P. Hennipman, 'Doeleinden en criteria der economische politiek', *Theorie van de economische politiek*, ed. by J. E. Andriessen and M. A. G. van Meerhaeghe, Leyden, 1962, p. 27.
16 See footnote 28 to that chapter.
17 Hennipman, 'Doeleinden', p. 27/28.
18 *Over economie en humaniteit*, p. 34–51 ('De spanning tussen naastenliefde en doelmatigheid').
19 Hennipman, 'Doeleinden', p. 30/31 (about the 'criteriological point of view').

human action has not only an economic aspect but all the other modal aspects of reality as well. Hence this method, like the previous one, precludes any useful delimitation of a field of *economic* inquiry.

Fourth, there is the idea, also endorsed by Van der Kooy [20], that *economic* theory *as such* needs to apply *ethical* standards. This is the conception for which most often the term 'normative' economics is used [21]. In my view, this argument tries to compensate for a lack of *intensity* in the economic method itself by an *extensive* idea of the economist's task brought on by a fundamental deficiency in the concept of the economic aspect.

All these various conceptions differ from the idea of normative economics as I take it from the writings of Professor Dooyeweerd. Economic science must be empirical in the full sense of the word. As the normative economic aspect is ineluctably interwoven with the modal structure of human life, empirical economic action does always correspond to certain economic norms. Not only the theory of the economic policy of the state, but also the theory of the economic process with which it is concerned deals with the implications of particular forms of normative economic behavior.

It is the very separation that is made between both kinds of theory which is confusing. The actual economic process is the result of the combined actions of all economic subjects *including* the state. The study of the typical economic behavior of the state is not based on another general methodological viewpoint than the investigation of the economic life of other economic subjects; the theory on the economic actions of the state is only a particular part of economic science. For the material subdivisions of economic theory must be drawn in accordance with the different *typical* economic norm-complexes of the various individuality structures of society [22].

These particular contents of economic norms depend on the character of the communities, or inter-individual and inter-communal relationships involved. Economic analysis has to study not only the economic actions of particular individual economic subjects, but also the relationships between the economic behavior of different economic subjects, either with the same character (for instance two competing firms) or with a different character (for instance, a firm and the state). The economist

---

20 *Over economie en humaniteit*, p. 29.
21 Hennipman, 'Doeleinden', p. 31.
22 Cf. H. Dooyeweerd, *Inleiding tot de encyclopaedie der rechtswetenschap*, Amsterdam, n.d. p. 100.

has in particular to ask whether the subjective aims which the economic subjects have chosen according to their own typical structures are *consistent* with one another; in other words, whether the economic opportunities in a particular field would not be damaged by the pursuit of certain economic policies in another field.

Historical development is tending increasingly toward integration of international economic relationships. This is understandable as the economic aspect of life has its foundations in the sphere of human intercourse. Social contacts have expanded rapidly in recent years, not least because of the extension of international economic relations itself. The historical process of differentiation of social structures and integration of functional relationships 'tends to increase the interweaving of individual interests' [23]. This integrating tendency reveals itself especially in typical economically qualified inter-individual and inter-national relationships [24]. The ultimate alternative to harmonious integration can only be warfare, stemming from inner weakness of the economically strong countries.

The great merit of the proposals to establish an organic link between creation of special drawing rights and international development policy is that such a link is in accordance with the historical process of differentiation and integration, notably the differentiation between the 'aid' policies of individual 'donor' countries and an emerging international development policy. 'Aid' is more an ethical notion than an economic concept. International development financing techniques rather than national 'aid' favor the shaping of the world *economy*. The 'link' will benefit the 'international monetary system' and probably also the 'international development system'; in both systems it will be a major historical improvement.

---

23 H. Dooyeweerd, *A new critique*, Vol. III, p. 595/596.
24 See *ibid.*, p. 593.

IX. Summary and conclusion

Chapter I is a short introduction. It is noted that monetary economics, in the broad sense, concerns the whole economic process. The introduction of the special drawing rights system is called an important event, but one which has so far remained strictly within the domain of monetary affairs in the narrow sense. It has reflected the desire to create a new form of world reserves, but it has not been directly linked with other matters of international economic policy.

As to the need for additional reserves, reference is made to the structural differences between developed and developing countries. Liquidity needs of individual countries are directly related to their capacity to adjust their external payments position. Developed countries need only the political will to correct payments imbalances; they are able to adjust their economies without being hampered by the problems implicit in a lack of development. Adjustment of balance of payments deficits of developing countries, however, often causes great setbacks to the development process. The present method of creating SDRs does not pay due regard to this state of affairs.

Those involved with preparing the SDR agreement – the amendment of July 28, 1969 to the Articles of Agreement of the International Monetary Fund originally drawn up at Bretton Woods in 1944 – and especially the representatives of the 'Group of Ten' countries frequently referred to the aim of improving the 'smooth functioning' of the international monetary 'system'. Chapter II is an attempt to do away with the myth that this concept of an international monetary 'system' often seems to imply, namely, that it has its own particular rules and independent principles. The international monetary system can be nothing but the result of cooperation between nations to handle the difficulties arising from the fact that they have different currencies and currency systems. This international cooperation should not be viewed in isolation from the whole field of international cooperation; otherwise inconsistencies may occur. To study international economic relations and deliberate actions, it is essential to have an implicit view both of the economic aspect of life, and of what international cooperation is about. To acquire such a view would require extensive methodological investigations; chapter II contains no more than a brief summary.

The economic aspect of human life manifests itself as the saving or frugal way or modus of life. The economic aspect or law-sphere is a normative one because it is based on the normative logical sphere. Economic life and the positive norms applied in it are subject to human formative power. International cooperation, including cooperation in matters of the economic relations between nations, leads to institutions that are qualified by the principle of international public interest and based on the same cultural power. No useful abstraction of economic problems can be made without taking into account the character of the institutions whose typical economic aspect is being investigated. Neither can economic theory lead to successful results if it starts from formalized theoretical models; one of the mistakes of the past has been to ignore the social dimension of economics. Chapter VIII contains a few additional methodological remarks.

Chapter III pays some attention to the difference between international money and national money, the concept of an 'international money standard', and a number of the essential features of SDRs. In particular, special drawing rigths are compared to 'reserve positions in the Fund', i.e. unconditional drawing rights in the General Account of the IMF.

The main issue is one that has been completely neglected by the negotiators on the SDR scheme, perhaps because it has raised a new problem for the international community. This is how to distribute the newly created SDRs. The primary concern of those who worked on the establishment of the SDR facility was the world level of SDRs, not their initial distribution. Of course, there had to be a distribution and the quota pattern in the Fund was used as the yardstick. Chapter IV, therefore, tells something about the origin and purposes of quotas in the Fund. It is argued that, even if the quota structure is adequate for its traditional purposes, it is unsuitable as a basis for distributing unconditional financial resources such as SDRs.

Seven major disadvantages of the present system are mentioned, most of which are especially damaging to the process of adjusting international payments imbalances. There is a built-in tendency to create excessive amounts of SDRs. Although the reason for all liquidity creation is precisely to minimize adjustment costs, *no* regard at all is paid to the fact that the adjustment costs of developing countries are always substantial, and those of developed countries generally small. The international distribution of wealth is also ignored. Furthermore, the quota structure is the result of past developments which do not necessarily provide a basis for future policies. In addition, the purchasing power associated with newly created SDRs, being a claim on the real resources of the international community as such, is given away to national policy makers that may spend it for purely national purposes. Another objection is that the process for determining the periodical increases of Fund quotas becomes a distorted one in that striving after a large quota increase becomes profitable for the country concerned in terms of real reserve assets; until 1970 quota increases did not earn such a premium – members acquired only conditional drawing rights. Finally, the surveillance function of the General Account is weakened to the extent that members can postpone or avoid requests for conditional drawings by using the special drawing rights allocated to them.

Chapter V outlines an easy way to overcome all these deficiences in the Special Drawing Account. The bulk of SDR allocations in the present system accrues to the developed countries, mainly the countries of the 'Group of Ten'. This is in accordance with earlier views (now abandoned) that newly created reserves should accrue exclusively or mainly to major industrial nations, which alone could provide the 'backing' for the new reserves. The whole 'backing' philosophy has rightly been rejected, however, and with it the main reason for both formal and *de facto* 'limited group' approaches to the initial distribution of new reserve assets. The money-like characteristics of the new assets remain unquestioned, regardless of the first use by which they effectively enter into the monetary circuit, and of the first user.

As the new money can command real resources, it is in the international interest to have a policy regarding the purposes for which it is firstly spent, its direction of flow and the timing of the first spending.

Therefore, spending should be brought under international control and made to serve an internationally agreed activity. The International Development Association is the institution most eligible to benefit from the lending power associated with the creation of SDRs.

At present there is an inconsistency between the international development target as well as the export aims of the industrial countries on the one hand, and the international monetary and financial system on the other. This will be eliminated when it becomes possible to finance the required flow of real resources to the developing countries; for this the use of newly created reserves can be of great help.

The monetary advantages of devoting any special drawing rights that may be created to long-term credits to IDA are substantial. The present biases toward creating unduly large amounts of special drawing rights would be removed. Those who decide whether or not to create special drawing rights will not be the direct beneficiaries. Developed countries with a need for reserves will acquire additions to their holdings only when they are prepared to adjust their economies in order to restore their earning capacity. Countries that are not prepared to do so will receive no share of the new reserves, and surplus countries will receive only what they earn as a result of their competitive position. The increase in international trade on a competitive basis would certainly be less inflationary than the present system of giving more reserve ease to every country regardless of its adjustment policies.

The quality of the SDR as a financial instrument would be enhanced by the possibility of raising the interest rate on holdings of special drawing rights: payments could be financed out of the profits on loans by the World Bank, which might be a secondary beneficiary of SDR financing. In addition, there would be no further need for 'reconstitution'. Cancellation of SDRs, for instance in the event of withdrawals from participation in the system, would be made through the financial machinery of the IDA and the World Bank. Communist countries might become more interested in holding SDRs. A useful further step would be taken in the direction of a more comprehensive international financial and monetary policy.

Chapter VI shows the logical deficiencies in the main arguments so far put forward against the idea of linking reserve creation with development financing. Far from being incompatible, *both* require a steady flow of new money. The view that SDR creation must be 'flexibly' managed cannot mean that it would not be possible or desirable to decide on a fixed amount of special drawing rights for each basic period. Even on the national plane doubts arise as to the benefits of 'flexible' management of the money supply; it is surely more difficult to see such benefits with respect to additions to world reserves. The General Account of the Fund provides adequate scope for a flexible response to liquidity demands within any basic period; that is, indeed, the particular purpose of the General Account. The change from one basic period to the next gives a proper opportunity for taking a 'flexible' decision. The 'need for reserves' is discussed both in chapter V, section 5, and in chapter VI, section 1.

The argument that the link between reserve creation and development finance would be unduly inflationary is rejected as being unprovable. The link offers the oppertunity to *economize* the supply of new SDRs, which can hardly be called an inflationary bias. Payments imbalances, which are caused by inflation and themselves induce inflation elsewhere, are not fed by allocations of SDRs. Price movements will be checked to a certain extent because of the enhanced international trade competition. For that matter, in the present system, spending financed by IDA and the World Bank may also cause inflation; whether in the existing system or one based on the use of SDRs by IDA, inflation can only be stopped by proper national cyclical policies, and by managing total domestic and foreign effective demand instead of the way in which single items of it are originally financed. International development spending financed through SDRs is, in any event, unlikely to exceed 1 per mil of the total output of the developed world, which has already exceeded the $ 2 trillion mark.

Finally, it is demonstrated that the argument that the 'link' would cause deflation in a group of industrial countries, which now benefit by free allocations of special drawing rights, comes into conflict with the very notion of '*global* reserve need' that is the basis of the whole SDR undertaking. It is the world supply of SDRs that matters, not the specific need of individual industrial countries, which are mostly in a position to finance their adjustment processes through the General Account of the Fund if they run into liquidity shortages.

In chapter VII several recent and less recent proposals for the link are briefly discussed. Full justice is done to the 'father' of the 'link' idea, Sir Maxwell Stamp. It is remarkable how closely his proposals foreshadowed the present SDR system – apart from the 'link'. The Stamp Plan, particularly in the 1962 version, was not primarily a device for creating additional development financing, but a full-grown monetary scheme.

The earlier writings of Triffin, and his present penetrating critique of the fact that there is no link between the SDR system and an internationally agreed objective to be financed through it, are next examined. After a review of a specific proposal by Professor Scitovsky for a so-called 'tied link' (reserve creation takes place on the initiative of individual countries and the proceeds are to be spent on aid goods within that country), attention is paid to a number of proposals which have been made in recent years on the official side, notably by UNCTAD and the Subcommittee on International Exchange and Payments of the U.S. Congress.

The conclusion of the preceding chapters must inevitably be that no proposal for a link that retains partly the present system of SDR allocation can be satisfactory; such schemes even may encourage the tendency to create unduly large amounts of SDRs, as individual countries will still try to obtain the largest possible allocations. A mixed system may well become particularly inflationary.

The only cure for the deficiencies of the present system is a full 'organic' link, i.e. any newly created SDRs must be allocated to international institutions, preferably to the International Development Association, or through it to other institutions. The particular advantages of such a procedure judged on its own merits give it a double strong case. I have tried to state this case on the basis of monetary arguments relevant to the international community whose interests are at stake, or, in current terms, on the basis of arguments pertaining to the 'good functioning of the international monetary system'.

Bibliography *

Akademie der Wissenschaften der UdSSR, *Politische Oekonomie, Lehrbuch*, Berlin, 1964.
Altman, Oscar L., 'Quotas in the International Monetary Fund', *Staff Papers*, August 1956, pp. 129–150.

Bank of England, 'The International Monetary Fund: use and supply of resources', *Quarterly Bulletin*, 1968, pp. 37–51.
Barrett, Martin, 'Activation of the special drawing rights facility in the IMF', *Monthly Review*, Federal Reserve Bank of New York, February 1970, pp. 40–46.
Benham, Frederic, *Economics, a general introduction*, 5th ed., London, 1955.
Beyen, J. W., *Money in a maelstrom*, New York, 1949.
Bos, P. C., *Money in development*, Rotterdam, 1969.

Cohen, Benjamin J., *Adjustment costs and the distribution of new reserves*, Princeton, 1966 (Princeton Studies in International Finance No. 18).
Congress of the United States, 'Next steps in international monetary reform', *Hearing* before the Subcommittee on International Exchange and Payments of the Joint Economic Committee, September 9, 1968.
Congress of the United States, *On linking reserve creation and development assistance*, a staff study, prepared (by John R. Karlik) for use of the Subcommittee on International Exchange and Payments of the Joint Economic Committee, April 1969.
Congress of the United States, 'Linking reserve creation and development assistance', *Hearing* before the Subcommittee on International Exchange and Payments of the Joint Economic Committee, May 28, 1969.
Congress of the United States, *A proposal to link reserve creation and development*

* Sources quoted or mentioned.

assistance, Report of the Subcommittee on International Exchange and Payments of the Joint Economic Committee, August 1969.

Day, A. C. L., *Outline of monetary economics,* Oxford, 1957.
Daane, J. Dewey, 'Perspective on monetary policy', *Monthly Review,* Federal Reserve Bank of Richmond, March 1970, pp. 2–8.
Dooyeweerd, Herman, *Inleiding tot de encyclopaedie der rechtswetenschap,* Amsterdam, n.d.
Dooyeweerd, Herman, 'Het wetsbegrip in de economie', *Mededelingen van de Vereniging voor Calvinistische Wijsbegeerte,* August 1946, pp. 2–3.
Dooyeweerd, Herman, 'De sociologische verhouding tussen recht en economie en het probleem van het zgn. 'economisch recht' ', *Opstellen op het gebied van recht, staat en maatschappij, aangeboden aan Prof. Dr. A. Anema en Prof. Dr. P. A. Diepenhorst,* Amsterdam, 1949, pp. 221–265.
Dooyeweerd, Herman, 'De modale structuur van het juridisch oorzakelijkheidsverband', *Mededelingen der Koninklijke Nederlandse Akademie van Wetenschappen, Afd. Letterkunde,* Nieuwe Reeks, Deel 13, No. 5, Amsterdam, 1950, pp. 93–141.
Dooyeweerd, Herman, *A new critique of theoretical thought,* four volumes, Amsterdam, Philadelphia, 1953–1957.
Dooyeweerd, Herman, 'De analogische grondbegrippen der vakwetenschappen en hun betrekking tot de structuur van den menselijken ervaringshorizon', *Mededelingen der Koninklijke Nederlandse Akademie van Wetenschappen, Afd. Letterkunde,* Nieuwe Reeks, Deel 17, No. 6, Amsterdam, 1954, pp. 171–192.
Dooyeweerd, Herman, *In the twilight of Western thought,* Philadelphia, 1960.
Dooyeweerd, Herman, *Verkenningen in de wijsbegeerte, de sociologie en de rechtsgeschiedenis,* Amsterdam, 1962.

Emminger, Otmar, 'The Brave New World of SDRs', *International Currency Review,* 1969, reprint, pp. 3–12.
Emminger, Otmar, 'The situation of the key currencies', remarks at the International Financial Conference on the Financial Outlook, Geneva, May 19, 1970 (Deutsche Bundesbank, *Auszüge aus Presseartikeln,* June 5, 1970).
Eucken, Walter, *Die Grundlagen der Nationalökonomie,* 7th ed., Berlin, Göttingen, Heidelberg, 1959.

Federal Reserve System, *Federal Reserve Bulletin* (issued monthly).
Fleming, J. Marcus, *The International Monetary Fund, its form and functions,* Washington D.C., 1964 (IMF Pamphlet Series, No. 2).

Gold, Joseph, *The reform of the Fund,* Washington D.C., 1969 (IMF Pamphlet Series, No. 12).
Gold, Joseph, *Special drawing rights,* Washington D.C., 1969 (IMF Pamphlet Series, No. 13).
Goudriaan, J., 'De goudwissel-grondstoffenstandaard', *De Economist,* November/ December, 1966, pp. 760–825.
Group of Ten, *Ministerial statement and Annex prepared by Deputies,* 1964.
Group of Ten, *Report of the study group on the creation of reserve assets, report to the Deputies of the Group of Ten,* 1965 (*'Ossola Report'*).
Group of Ten, *Communiqué of Ministers and Governors and Report of Deputies* 'on improvements needed in the international monetary system, including arrangements for the future creation of reserve assets, as and when needed', 1966.

Financial Times, September 17, 1970, 'The counter-revolution of monetary theory', (Milton Friedman), p. 12.

Haan, R. L., 'Monetaire methodologie; aantekeningen bij een studie over geldwaarde en geldgebruik', *Maandschrift Economie*, March 1970, pp. 318–330.
Heimann, Eduard, *History of economic doctrines*, 8th printing, London, New York, Toronto, 1959.
Hennipman, P., *Economisch motief en economisch principe*, Amsterdam, 1945.
Hennipman, P., 'Doeleinden en criteria der economische politiek', *Theorie van de economische politiek*, ed. by J. E. Andriessen and M. A. G. van Meerhaeghe, Leyden, 1962.
Holtrop, M. W., 'Monetary policy in an open economy: its objectives, instruments, limitations and dilemmas', *Internationale monetaire vraagstukken*, introduced by F. de Roos, Amsterdam, Brussels, 1967.
Hooft-Welvaars, M. J. 't, 'De grondstoffenproblematiek met betrekking tot de ontwikkelingslanden', *De Economist*, July/August, 1965, pp. 509–526.
Horsefield, J. Keith, 'Fund quotas', *Finance and Development*, September 1970, pp. 7–12.
Høst-Madsen, P., 'A deficit in the balance of payments', *Finance and Development*, September, 1966, pp. 171–178.
Houthakker, Hendrik S., *The public interest in the balance of payments*, remarks at the Fall Conference of the Financial Analysts Federation, Baltimore, Maryland, October 1969 (press release by the Executive Office of the President of the United States).

Inter-American Committee on the Alliance for Progress, *International monetary reform and Latin America*, report to CIAP by the Group of Experts, Washington D.C., 1966.
International Bank for Reconstruction and Development/International Development Association, *Annual Report, 1970*.
International Development Association, *50 Questions and answers*, May 1970.
International Financial News Survey, January 16, 1970, 'Arrangements for South African gold sales to the Fund', p. 13–14.
International monetary arrangements: the problem of choice, Report on the deliberations of an international study group of 32 economists, Princeton, 1964.
International Monetary Fund, *Annual Reports*, 1962–1970.
International Monetary Fund, *Articles of Agreement of the –*
International Monetary Fund, *International Financial Statistics* (issued monthly).
International Monetary Fund, 'The adequacy of monetary reserves', *Staff Papers*, Vol. III (1953), pp. 181–227; a report for the Economic and Social Council of the United Nations.
International Monetary Fund, *Compensatory financing of export fluctuations*, a report, 1963.
International Monetary Fund, 'Introduction to the Fund', Washington D.C., 1st ed. 1964 (IMF Pamphlet Series, No. 1).
International Monetary Fund, *Summary Proceedings*, Annual Meetings 1965, 1968, 1969; *Press Releases*, Annual Meeting, 1970.
International Monetary Fund, *Compensatory financing of export fluctuations – Developments in the Fund's facility*, a second report, 1966.
International Monetary Fund, *Allocation of special drawing rights for the first basic period (Proposal by the Managing Director)*, 1969.
International Monetary Fund, *By-Laws, Rules and Regulations*, 28th issue, 1969.
International Monetary Fund, *The problem of stabilisation of prices of primary*

products, report of the Executive Directors: Scope for action by the Fund (Part II of a Staff study), 1969.

International Monetary Fund, *Selected decisions of the Executive Directors and selected documents*, 4th issue, 1970.

International Monetary Fund, *The role of exchange rates in the adjustment of international payments*, a report by the Executive Directors, 1970.

Johnson, Harry G., 'International liquidity – problems and plans', *World monetary reform, plans and issues*, ed. by Herbert G. Grubel, Stanford, 1963, pp. 369-391.

Kalsbeek, L., *De Wijsbegeerte der Wetsidee*, Amsterdam, 1970.

Kessler, G. A., *Monetair evenwicht en betalingsbalansevenwicht*, Leyden, 1958.

Kolb, Gerhard, 'Vorzüge und Gefahren der IWF-Sonderziehungsrechte', *Zeitschrift für das gesamte Kreditwesen*, August 1, 1970, pp. 709-714.

Kooy, T. P. van der, *Over economie en humaniteit*, Wageningen, 1954.

Korteweg, C. J. S., and Keesing, F. A. C., *Het moderne geldwezen*, 8th ed., Amsterdam, 1961.

Kroc, Rudolf, *The financial structure of the Fund*, Washington D.C., 1965 (IMF Pamphlet Series, No. 5).

Machlup, Fritz, *International monetary economics*, London, 1964.

Machlup, Fritz, 'The cloakroom rule of international reserves: reserve creation and resources transfer', *Quarterly Journal of Economics*, Vol. LXXIX, August 1965, pp. 337-355.

Machlup, Fritz, *Remaking the international monetary system – The Rio Agreement and beyond*, Baltimore, 1968.

McNamara, Robert S., President, World Bank Group, *Address to the Board of Governors*, Washington D.C., 1968, 1970.

Márquez, Javier, 'Developing countries and the international monetary system', *The future of the international monetary system*, ed. by Hans W. J. Bosman and Frans A. M. Alting von Geusau, Leyden/Lexington, 1970.

Meier, Gerald M., *The international economics of development*, London, Tokyo, 1968.

Mendès-France, Pierre, 'Opbouw van een stabiel monetair systeem', *Nieuwe Rotterdamse Courant*, September 30, 1969.

Myrdal, G., ' 'Value-loaded' concepts', *Money, growth and methodology*, ed. by H. Hegeland, Lund, 1961, pp. 273-288.

Organisation for Economic Cooperation and Development, *The balance of payments adjustment process*, a report by Working Party No. 3 of the Economic Policy Committee, 1966.

'Pearson Report' (*Partners in Development*, report of the Commission on International Development; Chairman: Lester B. Pearson), New York, Washington, London, 1969.

Polak, J. J., 'Money – national and international', *Essays in honour of Thorkil Kristensen*, Paris, 1970, pp. 171-185.

Robbins, Lionel, *An essay on the nature and significance of economic science*, London, 1952 (reprint).

Roos, F. de, *De algemene banken in Nederland*, 3rd ed., Utrecht, 1958.

Rostow, W. W., *The stages of economic growth*, Cambridge, 1960.

Scitovsky, Tibor, 'A new approach to international liquidity', *American Economic Review*, December 1966, pp. 1212–1225.

Scheffer, C. F., and Smeets, M. J. H., *Geld en overheid*, Utrecht, Antwerpen, 1961.

Schweitzer, Pierre-Paul, 'New arrangements to supplement world reserves and their implications for the developing countries', Arthur K. Salomon Lecture, reprinted in *International Financial News Survey*, December 15, 1967.

Smith, John S. and Bouter, Arie C., 'The treatment of reserves and of reserve creation in the balance of payments accounts', *Staff Papers*, July 1969, pp. 202–224.

Stamp, Maxwell, 'The Fund and the future', *Lloyds Bank Review*, October 1958, pp. 1–20.

Stamp, Maxwell, 'Changes in the world's payments system', *Moorgate and Wall Street*, Spring 1961, pp. 3–22.

Stamp, Maxwell, 'The Stamp Plan – 1962 version', *Moorgate and Wall Street*, Autumn 1962, pp. 5–17.

Stamp, Maxwell, 'The reform of the international monetary system', *Moorgate and Wall Street*, Summer 1965, pp. 5–16.

Statuut voor het Koninkrijk der Nederlanden (Statute for the Kingdom of the Netherlands).

Stokvis, H. J., *Bretton Woods en het internationaal monetair bestel*, Leyden, 1948.

Tinbergen, Jan, *Shaping the world economy, suggestions for an international economic policy*, New York, 1962.

Triffin, Robert, *Gold and the dollar crisis*, New Haven, 1961 (first published 1960).

Triffin, Robert, *The world money maze*, New Haven, 1966.

Triffin, Robert, *Our international monetary system, yesterday, today, and tomorrow*, New York, 1968.

Triffin, Robert, *The fate of the pound*, Paris, 1969.

Triffin, Robert, 'The missing link in special drawing rights', FAO Review *Ceres*, Vol. III, No. 1, January/Februari 1970, pp. 26–28.

Tweede Kamer der Staten-Generaal, zitting 1970/1971, 10935 (R 750) (Second Chamber of the States General of the Netherlands, session 1970/71, document No. 10935 (R 750)).

United Nations, Charter of the –.

United Nations Conference on Trade and Development, *International monetary issues and the developing countries*, report of the Group of Experts, New York, 1965.

United Nations Conference on Trade and Development, *International monetary reform and cooperation for development*, report of the Expert Group on International Monetary Issues, New York, 1969.

Wemelsfelder, J., 'De kansen ten aanzien van een Calvinistische wijsgerige fundering van de economische methodologie', *Philosophia Reformata*, 1949, pp. 171–187.

Williams, David, 'The fifth general review of quotas', *Finance and Development*, September 1970, pp. 13–18.

Zijlstra, J., *Economische orde en economische politiek*, Leyden, 1956.

Index

References to Articles of Agreement of the International Monetary Fund

Appendix: Fund quotas and allocations of SDRs to participants [1]

(Millions of U.S. dollars)	maximum quotas under Resolution No. 25-3 [2]	percentages of total [3]	effective quotas as of Dec. 31, 1970, if different from (1)	SDR allocations on Jan. 1, 1970 [4]	SDR allocations on Jan. 1, 1971 [5]
	(1)	(2)	(3)	(4)	(5)
United States	6,700	23.16		866.9	716.9
United Kingdom	2,800	9.68		409.9	299.6
Germany, Fed. Rep. of	1,600	5.53		201.6	171.2
France	1,500	5.19		165.5	160.5
Japan	1,200	4.15		121.8	128.4
Canada	1,100	3.80		124.3	117.7
Italy	1,000	3.46		105.0	107.0
India	940	3.25		126.0	100.6
Netherlands	700	2.42		87.4	74.9
Australia	665	2.30		84.0	71.2
Belgium	650	2.25		70.9	69.6
China (Taiwan)	550	1.90		6	6
Argentina	440	1.52		58.8	47.1
Brazil	440	1.52		58.8	47.1
Spain	395	1.37		42.0	42.3
Mexico	370	1.28		45.4	39.6
Venezuela	330	1.14		42.0	35.3
Sweden	325	1.12		37.8	34.8
South Africa	320	1.11	200	33.6	21.4
Austria	270	0.93	175	29.4	18.7
Denmark	260	0.90		27.4	27.8
Indonesia	260	0.90		34.8	27.8
Norway	240	0.83		25.2	25.7
Pakistan	235	0.81		31.6	25.1
Yugoslavia	207	0.72		25.2	22.1
New Zealand	202	0.70		26.4	21.6
Iran	192	0.66		21.0	20.5
Finland	190	0.66		21.0	20.3
United Arab Rep.	188	0.65		25.2	20.1
Malaysia	186	0.64		21.0	19.9

(Millions of U.S. dollars)	maximum quotas under Resolution No. 25-3 [2]	percentages of total [3]	effective quotas as of Dec. 31, 1970, if different from (1)	SDR allocations on Jan. 1, 1970 [4]	SDR allocations on Jan. 1, 1971 [5]
	(1)	(2)	(3)	(4)	(5)
Chile	158	0.55		21.0	16.9
Colombia	157	0.54		21.0	16.8
Philippines	155	0.54		18.5	16.6
Turkey	151	0.52		18.1	16.2
Greece	138	0.48		16.8	14.8
Nigeria	135	0.47		16.8	14.4
Saudi Arabia	134	0.46	90	[7]	[8]
Thailand	134	0.46		[7]	14.3
Israel	130	0.45		15.1	13.9
Algeria	130	0.45		12.6	13.9
Peru	123	0.45		14.3	13.2
Ireland	121	0.42		13.4	12.9
Portugal	117	0.40	75	[7]	[8]
Congo, Dem. Rep. of	113	0.39		15.1	12.1
Morocco	113	0.39		15.1	12.1
Iraq	109	0.38		[7]	11.7
Ceylon	98	0.34		13.1	10.5
Ghana	87	0.30		11.6	9.3
Korea	80	0.28	50	8.4	5.3
Zambia	76	0.26		8.4	8.1
Sudan	72	0.25		9.6	7.7
Uruguay	69	0.25		9.2	7.4
Kuwait	65 [9]	(0.22) [9]		[7]	[8]
Trinidad and Tobago	63	0.22		7.4	6.7
Singapore	62	0.21	30	[7]	[8]
Viet-Nam	62	0.21		6.6	6.6
Burma	60	0.21		8.1	6.4
Lebanon	56	0.19	9	[7]	[8]
Jamaica	53	0.18		6.4	5.7
Ivory Coast	52	0.18		3.2	5.6
Syrian Arab Rep.	50	0.17		6.4	5.3
Kenya	48	0.17		5.4	5.1
Tunisia	48	0.17	35	5.9	3.7
Dominican Rep.	43	0.15		5.4	4.6
Tanzania	42	0.15		5.4	4.5
Uganda	40	0.14		5.4	4.3
Afghanistan	37	0.13		4.9	4.0
Bolivia	37	0.13		4.9	4.0
Guatemala	36	0.12		4.2	3.9
Panama	36	0.12		4.7	3.9

(Millions of U.S. dollars)	maximum quotas under Resolution No. 25-3 [2]	percen- tages of total [3]	effective quotas as of Dec. 31, 1970, if different from (1)	SDR alloca- tions on Jan. 1, 1970 [4]	SDR alloca- tions on Jan. 1, 1971 [5]
	(1)	(2)	(3)	(4)	(5)
Cameroon	35	0.12		3.0	3.7
El Salvador	35	0.12		4.2	3.7
Senegal	34	0.12		4.2	3.6
Ecuador	33	0.11		4.2	3.5
Costa Rica	32	0.11		4.2	3.4
Southern Yemen	29	0.10		3.7	3.1
Liberia	29	0.10		3.4	3.1
Ethiopia	27	0.09		7	8
Nicaragua	27	0.09		3.2	2.9
Malagasy Rep.	26	0.09		3.2	2.8
Cyprus	26	0.09		3.4	2.8
Cambodia	25 10	(0.09) 10		3.2	2.7
Honduras	25	0.09		3.2	2.7
Sierra Leone	25	0.09		2.5	2.7
Libyan Arab Rep.	24 11	(0.08) 11		7	8
Luxembourg	24	0.08	19	3.2	2.0
Guinea	24	0.08		3.2	2.6
Iceland	23	0.08		2.5	2.5
Jordan	23	0.08		2.7	2.5
Mali	22	0.08		2.9	2.4
Mauritius	22	0.08		2.7	2.4
Guyana	20	0.07		2.5	2.1
Burundi	19	0.07		2.5	2.0
Haiti	19	0.07		2.5	2.0
Paraguay	19	0.07		2.5	2.0
Rwanda	19	0.07		2.5	2.0
Somalia	19	0.07		2.5	2.0
Malta	16	0.06		1.7	1.7
Gabon	15	0.06		1.6	1.6
Malawi	15	0.05		1.9	1.6
Togo	15	0.05		1.9	1.6
Nepal	14	0.05	10	7	1.0
Barbados	13 10	(0.04) 10		–	1.4
Central African Rep.	13	0.04		1.6	1.4
Chad	13	0.04		1.7	1.4
Congo, People's Rep. of	13	0.04		1.7	1.4
Dahomey	13	0.04		1.7	1.4
Laos	13	0.04		1.7	1.4
Mauritania	13	0.04		1.7	1.4
Niger	13	0.04		1.7	1.4

(Millions of U.S. dollars)	maximum quotas under Resolution No. 25-3 [2]	percen- tages of total [3]	effective quotas as of Dec. 31, 1970, if different from (1)	SDR alloca- tions on Jan. 1, 1970 [4]	SDR alloca- tions on Jan. 1, 1971 [5]
	(1)	(2)	(3)	(4)	(5)
Upper Volta	13	0.04		1.7	1.4
Yemen Arab Rep.	10 [10]	(0.03) [10]		–	1.0
Equatorial Guinea	8	0.03		1.0	0.9
Swaziland	8	0.03		1.0	0.9
Gambia, The	7	0.02		0.8	0.7
Botswana	5	0.02		0.5	0.5
Lesotho	5	0.02		0.5	0.5
Total of allocations of SDRs				3,414.0	2,949.2

Source: Documents of International Monetary Fund

1 Allocations on January 1, 1972 will be practically the same as on January 1, 1971 (see footnote 20 on page 47).
2 Board of Governors Resolution No. 25-3, adopted February 9, 1970. Resolution No. 25-4 added Cambodia to the list. Cambodia became a member of the Fund on December 31, 1969. The Yemen Arab Republic and Barbados joined the Fund in the course of 1970.
3 Total of quotas as proposed under Resolution No. 25-3 ($ 28,928). These quotas are the same as the amounts listed in column (1) with the following differences. Quotas for Cambodia, Barbados and the Yemen Arab Republic have here been added (see footnote 2). The maximum quotas proposed by the Resolution for Kuwait and the Libyan Arab Republic were different from the quotas that were actually accepted by these countries and are mentioned in column (1) for that reason.
4 Allocations were based on 16.8 percent of participants' quotas as of December 31, 1969.
5 Allocations were based on 10.7 percent of participant's quotas of December 31, 1970.
6 The Republic of China is a participant in the Special Drawing Account; pursuant to Art. XXIV, Section 2 (e) (ii) of the Fund Agreement it notified the Fund that it did not wish special drawing rights to be allocated to it under the decision of the Fund on the allocation of special drawing rights for the first basic period (1970-1972).
7 Not a participant on January 1, 1970.
8 Not a participant on January 1, 1971.
9 Resolution No. 25-3 proposed a maximum quota of $ 114 million for Kuwait (See footnote 3).
10 See footnotes 2 and 3.
11 Resolution No. 25-3 proposed a maximum quota of $ 67 million for the Libyan Arab Republic (See footnote 3).

The New York Times of January 2, 1971 wrote: 'Developing countries as well as the World Bank and other organizations associated with development assistance are pressing governments of rich countries to use the world's newest reserve asset as a means of increasing aid. The central bankers of the rich countries are opposed, in a debate that promises to become one of the hottest on the international agenda in the new year'.

The present study is devoted to this problem of linking special drawing rights with development: It is the author's view that a sound case can be presented for establishing a **full and organic link** between SDR creation and the financing of institutions of multilateral development assistance. Putting SDRs into circulation through the International Development Association would in fact do more to improve the functioning of the world's monetary system than simply donating them to individual countries as is done at present.

To prepare the ground for such a further development of the SDR system, a short period with no creation at all may be appropriate; this would not seem inconsistent with present conditions of international liquidity.

The author spent some five years (1966-1971) in the International Monetary Affairs Division of the Netherlands Ministry of Finance. From April 1968 until July 1969 he acted as assistant to the Executive Director of the International Monetary Fund representing the Netherlands, Yugoslavia, Israel and Cyprus. At present he is working in the Faculty of Economics of the 'Free University' of Amsterdam.